STANDARD LEVEL

P9-CAL-976

essentials

PEARSON BACCALAUREATE

Environmental Systems and Societies

ANDREW DAVIS • GARRETT NAGLE

SERIES EDIOR: CHRISTIAN BRYAN

Supporting every learner across the IB continuum

Published by Pearson Education Limited, Edinburgh Gate, Harlow, Essex, CM20 2JE.

www.pearsonglobalschools.com

Text © Pearson Education Limited 2013
Project managed, edited and typeset by Cambridge Publishing Management Ltd
Original illustrations © Pearson Education 2013
Indexed by Marie Lorimer

The rights of Andrew Davis and Garrett Nagle to be identified as authors of this work have been asserted by them in accordance with the Copyright, Designs and Patents Act 1988.

First published 2013

18 17 16 15 14 13

IMP 10 9 8 7 6 5 4 3 2 1

British Library Cataloguing in Publication Data

A catalogue record for this book is available from the British Library

ISBN 978 1 447 95034 9
ISBN eBook only 978 1 447 95035 6

Printed in Italy by Lego S.p.a.

Acknowledgements
The authors and publishers would like to thank Ellen Vriniotis of ACS Athens, Rizma Rizwan of City and Islington College, Ellen Dittmar of Western Academy of Beijing, Susanna Joachim of Nymphenburger Schulen, Kania Grazyna of 33 Liceum IMM Kopernika, Sami Sorvali of Kannas School, Diane Howlett of Szczecin International School, Brian Hull of AIS Kuwait, Jacques Weber of British International School of Jeddah, and Michael Ashleman of Wellington, for their invaluable help in the development of this series by piloting the concept material.

With thanks to our EAL reviewers, Baljit Nijjar and Alison Walford, and the subject specialist Alistair Robertson, for their helpful and constructive advice that greatly improved the clarity and accuracy of the text. Thanks also to Sarah MacBean, for her expert coordination and support throughout this project.

Andrew Davis and Garrett Nagle

The publisher would like to thank the following for their kind permission to reproduce their photographs:
(Key: b-bottom; c-centre; l-left; r-right; t-top)

Andrew J Davis: 17b, 31t, 31b, 142c, 162t, 195b, 215c; **Corbis:** Hulton-Deutsch Collection 131b, Stephanie Maze 73t; **Digital Vision:** 129t; **Garrett Nagle:** 32c, 33b, 39t, 71b, 91t, 94b, 95c, 97c, 105b, 112c, 114b, 124b, 126c, 128c, 166c, 167t, 170b, 177b, 180b, 183c, 184b; **Patrick Nagle:** 130t; **Science Photo Library Ltd:** Jeff Lepore 29t; **US Geological Servey:** 78t, 78b, 79t

All other images © Pearson Education

Every effort has been made to trace the copyright holders and we apologise in advance for any unintentional omissions. We would be pleased to insert the appropriate acknowledgement in any subsequent edition of this publication.

Websites
Pearson Education Limited is not responsible for the content of any external internet sites. It is essential for tutors to preview each website before using it in class so as to ensure that the URL is still accurate, relevant and appropriate. We suggest that tutors bookmark useful websites and consider enabling students to access them through the school/college intranet.

Dedications
For my mother, Mary Davis, and in memory of my father, Brian Davis, who is remembered here.
– *Andrew Davis*

To Angela, Rosie, Patrick and Bethany – for their continued support, patience and good humour – and for making life fun. – *Garrett Nagle*

Contents

Introduction

Welcome to your Essential Guide to Environmental Systems and Societies. This book has been designed to solve the key problems of many Diploma students:

- relating material you have been taught to the syllabus goals and outcomes
- remembering it from one lesson to the next
- recalling it months later in an exam situation
- demonstrating your understanding of it in an exam situation within a strict time limit.

Who should use Essential Guides?

Essential Guides have been carefully designed with all IB (International Baccalaureate) students in mind as they serve as highly effective summaries and revision guides.

However, they have also been created with the particular interests in mind of IB **students whose first language is not English**, and who would like further support. As a result, the content in all Essential Guides has been edited by an EAL (English as an additional language) expert to make sure that the language used is clear and accessible, key terms are explained, and essential vocabulary is defined and reinforced.

Key features of an Essential Guide

Reduced content: Essentials guides are not intended to be comprehensive textbooks – they contain the essential information you need to understand and respond to each Learning Outcome (LO) published in the IB subject guide. This allows you to understand, review, and revise material quickly and still be confident you are meeting the essential aims of the syllabus. The content is precise and to the point. We have reduced the number of words as much as possible to ensure everything you read has clear meaning, is clearly related to the LO, and will help you in an exam.

Format and approach: The content of the book is organized according to the Learning Outcomes (LOs). Each LO is looked at separately so that you can study each one without having read or understood previous LOs. This allows you to use the book as a first-text, or a revision guide, or as a way to help you understand material you have been given from other sources. The content is explained as clearly as possible, and you can be sure the information relates directly to the LO at the top of each page.

Sub-headings: The pages are organized using logical sub-headings to help you understand the most important points of the LO. This organization also provides you with a guide on what an effective exam answer would look like. The subheadings can be used to help you during revision, as a planning model before you start writing your answer, or for the actual answer to help you focus the examiner on how you are addressing the question.

Opening sentences: These are suggestions on how to refer to the LO at the very start of your answer in the exam. They are intended either to be memorized or to give you suggestions about how your writing should look when you first begin writing in an exam. For example:

> ## Opening sentence:
> In this answer I will discuss why tropical rainforests are **perceived** to be **vulnerable**. I will also discuss their value in contributing to **global** biodiversity when compared to other biomes.

Model sentences: These are intended to summarize key material in a way that you can use in an exam. We have done the phrasing for you so that you can focus on planning what content to include. For example:

> Model sentence: **Flows are movement from one place to another in the system and are shown by arrows.**

Vocabulary and synonym boxes: These are included to help identify and support your understanding of subject-specific and difficult words. These useful words and phrases are colour-coded in the margins. We have avoided using a highly academic tone which is often found in many textbooks in order to make the text more accessible to students whose first language is not English. However, at the same time we have ensured that the complexity of the content is at the level required by successful Diploma students, and so the key subject-specific vocabulary needed is highlighted in a separate box.

Glossary
to perceive/perceived to think of something in a particular way
vulnerable something that can easily be harmed
logging removal of trees from forests for commercial purpose

Internal Assessment section: This is intended to help you design and write your own investigations. It gives examples of research questions that you could investigate, and shows you what is required to achieve the top marks. Each investigation is organized around criteria from the IB markscheme, and includes key words and phrases.

Extended Essay section: This section contains example model sentences to illustrate how the different IB markscheme criteria can be applied in real essays. It is not intended to be used as a template, but should be used as a guide to help you prepare your own essays. We have also included a list of suggested extended essay titles.

eBook and audio: In the accompanying eBook you will find a complete digital version of the book with interactive audio glossary, along with links to spoken audio files of opening sentences, model sentences, and hints for success to help with comprehension and pronunciation.

In addition, all the vocabulary lists are located together as downloadable files.

Above all, we hope this book helps you to understand, consolidate, and revise your course content more easily than ever, helping you to achieve the highest possible result in your exams.

How to use your enhanced eBook

Jump to any page

Switch from single- to double-page view

Highlight parts of the text

Create notes

Search the whole book

Zoom

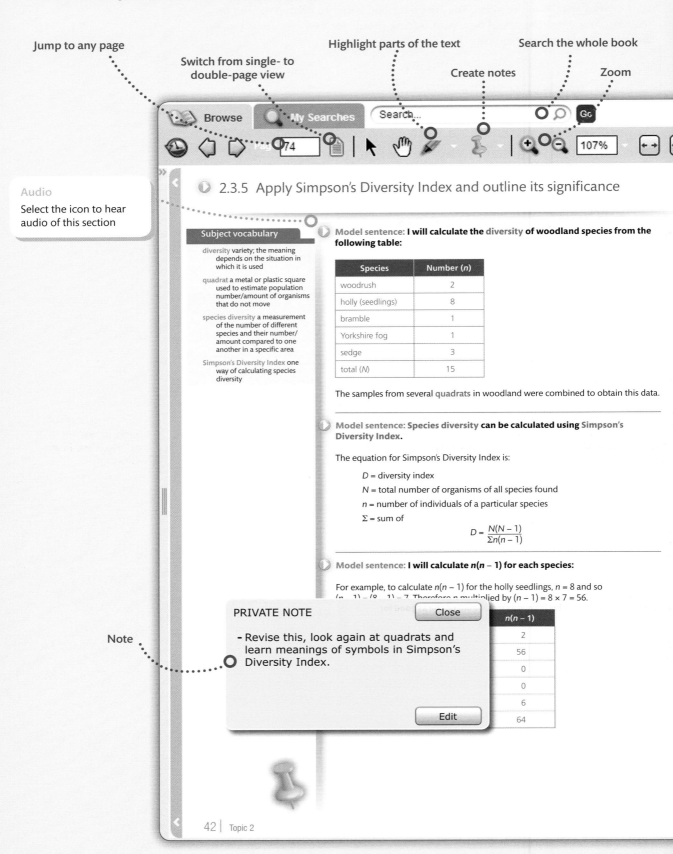

Audio

Select the icon to hear audio of this section

2.3.5 Apply Simpson's Diversity Index and outline its significance

Subject vocabulary

diversity variety; the meaning depends on the situation in which it is used

quadrat a metal or plastic square used to estimate population number/amount of organisms that do not move

species diversity a measurement of the number of different species and their number/ amount compared to one another in a specific area

Simpson's Diversity Index one way of calculating species diversity

Model sentence: **I will calculate the diversity of woodland species from the following table:**

Species	Number (n)
woodrush	2
holly (seedlings)	8
bramble	1
Yorkshire fog	1
sedge	3
total (N)	15

The samples from several quadrats in woodland were combined to obtain this data.

Model sentence: **Species diversity can be calculated using Simpson's Diversity Index.**

The equation for Simpson's Diversity Index is:

D = diversity index
N = total number of organisms of all species found
n = number of individuals of a particular species
Σ = sum of

$$D = \frac{N(N-1)}{\Sigma n(n-1)}$$

Model sentence: **I will calculate $n(n-1)$ for each species:**

For example, to calculate $n(n-1)$ for the holly seedlings, $n = 8$ and so $(n-1) = (8-1) = 7$. Therefore n multiplied by $(n-1) = 8 \times 7 = 56$.

PRIVATE NOTE   Close

- Revise this, look again at quadrats and learn meanings of symbols in Simpson's Diversity Index.

Edit

Note

$n(n-1)$
2
56
0
0
6
64

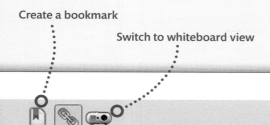

Create a bookmark

Switch to whiteboard view

Model sentence: **I will put the figures into the formula for Simpson's Diversity Index:**

$$N = 15$$
$$N - 1 = 14$$
$$N(N - 1) = 210$$
$$\Sigma n(n - 1) = 64$$
$$D = \frac{210}{64} = 3.28$$

Model sentence: **The Simpson's Diversity Index for a second woodland ecosystem was calculated at $D = 1.48$. I will comment on possible differences between the two woodland ecosystems.**

Communities with individuals evenly distributed between different species are said to have high 'evenness' and have high diversity as calculated by the Simpson's Diversity Index. This is because many species can coexist in the many available niches within a complex ecosystem. Communities with one dominant species have low diversity, which indicates a poorer ecosystem not able to support as many types of organism.

Model sentence: **A high value of D suggests a stable and ancient site, and a low value of D suggests pollution or agricultural management.**

The woodland with $D = 3.28$ could be an undisturbed ecosystem and the woodland with $D = 1.48$ could be a disturbed ecosystem. The higher value suggests a more complex ecosystem where many species can coexist. The lower value suggests a simpler ecosystem where fewer species can coexist.

Model sentence: **The woodland with the higher Simpson's Diversity Index is an area that would be better for conservation. The woodland with the lower Simpson's Diversity Index is an area that would not be as good for conservation.**

Hints for success: You are not required to memorize the Simpson's Diversity Index formula, but you must know the meaning of the symbols. You also need to know how the Index is significant for ecological studies: you might use it in a practical investigation, for example.

Subject vocabulary

ecosystem a community of organisms that depend on each other and the environment they live in

community a group of different species living together in a common habitat

niche where and how a species lives

Glossary

coexist live together

ancient very old

agricultural relating to farming

management actively looking after

conservation the preservation and protection of nature

Synonyms

stable................... unchanging

significant............. important

W

PDF

Glossary with audio

Click on highlighted terms to see the definition and hear the audio.

Vocabulary lists

Select the icons at the back of the book to see complete vocabulary lists

What is a system?

A **system** is made up of separate parts which are linked together and influence each other.

What are the characteristics of a system?

All systems have **inputs** and **outputs**. According to the system, these can be inputs and outputs of energy, **matter**, or information. All systems also have **storages**, **flows**, **processes**, and **feedback mechanisms**. The **systems method** allows different subjects, such as ESS, Economics, and Sociology, to be looked at in the same way and for connections to be made between them.

Systems can be shown as diagrams. Figure 1.1 shows a **systems diagram** containing:

● a box that shows storages – in this **example**, tree **biomass**

● arrows that show flows – the tree's inputs and outputs

● processes can be shown on the arrows to indicate which **transfers** and **transformations** are taking place.

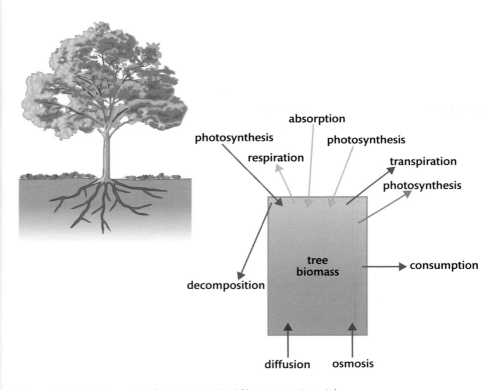

Figure 1.1 *A tree drawn using the systems method (diagram on the right).*

All systems diagrams are shown in the same way, with boxes representing storages, arrows representing flows, and processes indicated on the arrows.

Comparing different systems

Different subjects will contain different systems, but there are similarities between all systems. Examples of different subjects are ecology, economics, sociology, and philosophy. This table shows how the systems concept can be applied to different systems:

	Ecosystem	Economic system	Social system	Value system
Flows	Energy and matter	Production, income, and spending	Information, ideas, and people	Culture and society, decisions and actions
Storages	Biomass, the atmosphere, and soil	Banks, goods, and services	Ideas, beliefs, and customs	Personal value systems

Systems can be looked at in two **contrasting** ways. A **reductionist approach** looks at the individual parts of a system. This approach is usually used in traditional scientific investigations. A **holistic** approach looks at how the parts of a system work together as a whole. This approach is usually used in modern ecological investigations.

What are the advantages of using the systems method?

The advantage of using the systems method is that diagrams can be used to show how the **components** within the whole system **relate** to one another. Because the same method is used in all subjects, comparisons and links can be made between different academic subjects, as shown in the table above.

> **Hints for success:** Use the box and arrow method shown in Figure 1.1 to draw a systems diagram. Do not draw pictures: for example, do not draw a tree.

Subject vocabulary

systems concept the idea that something can be looked at as a collection of parts that interact and are interdependent on each other

reductionist dividing a system into parts, each of which can be studied separately

holistic looking at a system as a whole, rather than as individual parts

Glossary

contrasting where there are differences between two or more things

component one or several parts which together make up a whole system

Synonyms

approach.............. method
relate................... connect

1.1.2 Apply the systems concept on a range of scales

Glossary

concept an idea of how something is

example explains a particular problem or issue

scale a range of things from the smallest to the largest

global including the whole of the planet

bromeliad tropical American plants of the family Bromeliaceae; they have long stiff leaves and colourful flowers

climatic relating to rainfall, sunshine, humidity, wind, and temperature

daisy a flower, usually with white petals and a yellow centre

cycle a series of events that are regularly repeated in the same order

Subject vocabulary

ecosystem a community of organisms that depend on each other and the environment they live in

system a collection of parts and the relationships between them, which together make a whole

biome a collection of ecosystems sharing similar climatic conditions

Gaia hypothesis compares the Earth to a living organism in which feedback mechanisms maintain equilibrium

model a simplified description designed to show the structure of a system and how it works

equilibrium a state of balance among the parts of a system

negative feedback feedback that counteracts any change away from equilibrium. This form of feedback contributes to stability

Synonyms

range............. a variety of things

absorb........... take in

reflect............ send back

Model sentence: Ecosystems provide a good example of how systems can be applied to a range of scales.

Ecosystems can be any size, from small-scale to **global**. A forest contains many small-scale ecosystems, such as the species that live in **bromeliads** that are found towards the tops of the trees in tropical rainforests. The forest itself can also be seen as an ecosystem. The same type of forest ecosystem may be found in many different countries with the same **climatic** conditions. When an ecosystem is looked at on a global scale it is called a **biome**.

The following table shows a range of scales for different systems:

Scale	Ecosystem	Economic system	Social system	Political system
Small	Local ecosystem	Home economy	Community	Band
	Biome	Market economy	Nationhood	Tribe, chiefdom
Global	The Earth	Global economy	Global society	Nation state

Model sentence: At the largest scale, the Earth and its atmosphere can be viewed as an ecosystem. This idea is central to the Gaia hypothesis.

A **model** can be made that shows how the Gaia hypothesis works:

Daisyworld

Daisyworld is a model for the Gaia hypothesis. Daisyworld shows how the Gaia hypothesis could control life on Earth. The only plants on Daisyworld are black and white **daisies**; the rest of the surface is bare. The temperature of Daisyworld is controlled by how much sunlight is **absorbed** and how much sunlight is **reflected** by the daisies. If the temperature of Daisyworld increases, then white daisies survive and reproduce because they can keep cool by reflecting the Sun's energy. Daisyworld cools down following the growth of white daisies. As it cools the black daisies now have an advantage as they absorb more heat. There will now be large numbers of black daisies which will absorb the Sun's energy and warm the planet. The **cycle** then repeats itself. Over time, the temperature of the planet reaches **equilibrium**. In this way, the temperature of the planet controls itself through **negative feedback**.

1.1.3 Define the terms *open system, closed system* and *isolated system*

Model sentence: An open system can be defined as a system that exchanges **both matter and energy with its surroundings.**

An example of an open system is an ecosystem, such as a lake.

Model sentence: A closed system can be defined as a system that exchanges **energy, but not matter, with its surroundings.**

An example of a closed system is the Earth.

Model sentence: An isolated system can be defined as a system that does not **exchange matter or energy with its surroundings.**

An example of an isolated system is the Universe.

Model sentence: The following figure summarizes the differences between open, closed, and isolated systems:

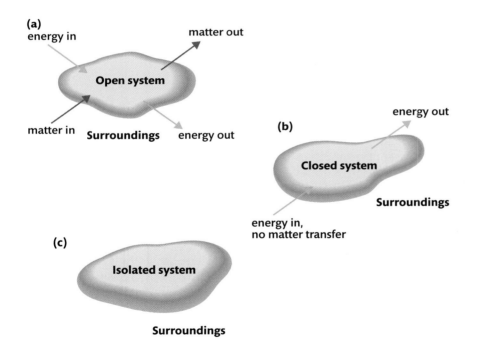

Figure 1.2 *The exchange of matter and energy across the boundary of different systems.*
(a) Open systems exchange both energy and matter; (b) closed systems exchange only energy; and (c) isolated systems exchange neither.

1.1.4 Describe how the first and second laws of thermodynamics are relevant to environmental systems

The behaviour of energy in **systems** is directly influenced by the laws of **thermodynamics**.

The first law of thermodynamics

The **first law of thermodynamics** states that energy cannot be created or destroyed: it can only be changed from one form into another. The first law of thermodynamics is known as the law of **conservation** of energy. This means that the total energy in any system is **constant** and all that can happen is that energy can change form.

The second law of thermodynamics

The **second law of thermodynamics** states that the **transfer** of energy through a system is inefficient and that energy is **transformed** into heat. This is shown in the following figure:

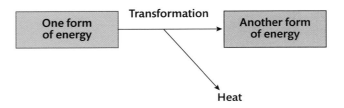

Figure 1.3 *The second law of thermodynamics states that some energy is converted into heat when energy is transformed from one form to another.*

The second law of thermodynamics explains that, in systems, energy goes from a **concentrated** form into a **dispersed** form. This means that less energy is available to do work and the system becomes increasingly disordered. In an isolated system, **entropy** increases **spontaneously**.

How are the first and second laws of thermodynamics relevant to environmental systems?

Energy is needed in **ecosystems** to create order, such as to hold complex molecules together. Natural systems cannot be **isolated** because there must always be an **input** of energy for work to replace energy that is **dissipated**. Because of this energy loss, the maintenance of order in living systems needs a constant input of energy to replace the energy lost as heat through the inefficient transfer of energy.

One way energy enters an ecosystem is as sunlight energy. This sunlight energy is then changed into **biomass** by **photosynthesis**. That is, photosynthesis captures sunlight energy and transforms it into chemical energy. Chemical energy in producers may be passed along **food chains** as biomass, or given off as heat during respiration.

Available energy is used to do work such as growth, movement, and making **complex molecules**. The transformation and transfer of useable energy is not 100 per cent efficient; whenever energy is **converted** there is less usable energy at the end of the process than at the beginning. This means that there is a dissipation of energy which is then not available for work. The total amount of energy in a system does not change but the amount of available energy for work does change.

All energy eventually leaves the ecosystem as heat. No new energy has been created, it has simply been transformed and passed from one form to another. Heat is released because of the inefficient transfer of energy. This is true of all systems. Although **matter** can be recycled, energy cannot, and once it has been lost from a system in the form of heat energy, it cannot be made available again. Because the transfer and transformation of energy is inefficient, food chains tend to be short.

Model sentence: **The following diagram summarizes the energy and matter transfers and transformations in environmental systems:**

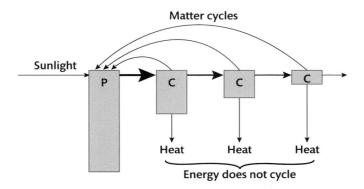

Figure 1.4 *Energy flow through a food chain; P = producers, C = consumers. The boxes show energy available to do work at each feeding level. Energy decreases through the food chain as some energy is converted to heat.*

Hints for success: You need to know the differences between the first and second laws of thermodynamics. The first law explains how energy entering a system must equal the energy remaining in the system plus the energy leaving the system. The second law of thermodynamics explains how energy transfers and transforms in living systems, which then leads to loss of energy from the system as heat. The order in living systems is only maintained by continuing input of new energy from the Sun.

Glossary

conserved kept and not lost

concentrated a lot of a substance in one place

dispersed when a substance is spread thinly and widely

spontaneously happening without an obvious external cause

isolated separated from others

dissipated lost/caused to disappear

complex molecule a molecule that contains many atoms, and is made from two or more molecular elements

converted changed into

Synonyms

constant......... kept the same

matter .... substance/material

1.1.5 Explain the nature of equilibria

Subject vocabulary

equilibrium (plural – equilibria) a state (states) of balance among the components of a system

system a collection of parts and the relationships between them, which together make a whole

succession the orderly process of change over time in a community

steady-state equilibrium the condition of an open system in which there are no changes over the longer term, but in which there may be fluctuations in the very short term; there is overall stability in the system even though there are constant inputs and outputs of energy and matter

input the movement into something

output the movement out from something

static equilibrium equilibrium where there are no inputs or outputs of matter or energy, and no change in the system over time

Glossary

component one of several parts which together make up a whole system

fluctuation small increases and decreases

disturbance a change in the normal situation

integrity the state of being whole with all parts functioning normally

stability the state of not changing

deviation movement away from

example explanation of a particular problem

Synonyms

inanimate....... not living

Equilibrium can be defined as a state of balance among the **components** of a **system**.

This means that although there may be slight **fluctuations** in the system, these are within closely defined limits. Equilibrium allows systems to return to an original state after there has been **disturbance**. There may be long-term changes to the equilibrium of some systems while at the same time they retain **integrity**; for example, ecological **succession**.

Steady-state equilibrium

Most open systems in nature are in **steady-state equilibrium**. This means that even though there are constant **inputs** and **outputs** of energy and matter, there is overall **stability** within the system. Although there is overall stability there are usually changes, or fluctuations, in the system. These changes follow a fixed path and when there are **deviations** away from this path then there is always a return to equilibrium. The stability of this form of equilibrium means that the system can return to the steady-state after there has been disturbance. For **example**, when a tall tree that forms part of the roof of a tropical rainforest dies, the space it leaves behind is filled up again through the process of succession.

Static equilibrium

In **static equilibrium** there are no inputs or outputs of matter or energy and no change in the system over time. **Inanimate** objects such as a chair or table are in static equilibrium. No natural systems are in static equilibrium because all natural systems have inputs and outputs of energy and matter.

The following figures show the differences between steady-state and static equilibrium:

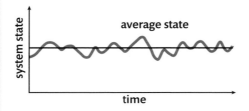

Figure 1.5a *Steady-state equilibrium*

Figure 1.5b *Static equilibrium*

Model sentence: Some natural systems, such as ecosystems, may return to their original equilibrium, whereas other systems may not.

Systems can experience disturbance. **Stable equilibrium** is when a system returns to the original equilibrium after a disturbance. **Unstable equilibrium** is when a system does not return to the original equilibrium after disturbance, but forms a new equilibrium.

The following figures show the differences between stable and unstable equilibrium:

Subject vocabulary

stable equilibrium equilibrium where a system returns to the original equilibrium after a disturbance

unstable equilibrium equilibrium where a system does not return to the original equilibrium after disturbance but forms a new equilibrium

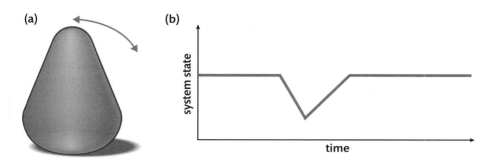

Figure 1.6a and b *Stable equilibrium. Disturbance to a system results in it returning to its original equilibrium.*

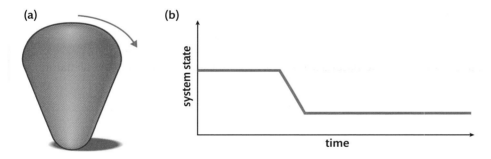

Figure 1.7a and b *Unstable equilibrium. Disturbance to a system results in it forming a new equilibrium very different from the first. Scientists believe that the Earth's climate may reach a new equilibrium following the effects of global warming and that conditions on Earth will be very different to what they are now.*

1.1.6 Define and explain the principles of *positive feedback* and *negative feedback*

What is feedback?

Feedback occurs when part of the **output** from a **system** returns as **input**, in order to influence later outputs.

The following figure shows a feedback **loop**:

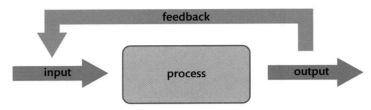

Figure 1.8 *Changes to the processes in a system lead to changes in the level of output. This feeds back to influence the level of input.*

Natural systems are able to control themselves by reaching **equilibrium** through feedback **mechanisms**.

Feedback involves **time-lags**, where it takes time for the feedback to have an effect.

Model sentence: There are two different types of feedback – positive feedback and negative feedback.

Positive feedback

Positive feedback can be defined as feedback that leads to increasing change away from equilibrium and contributes to instability.

An **example** of positive feedback is shown in the following figure:

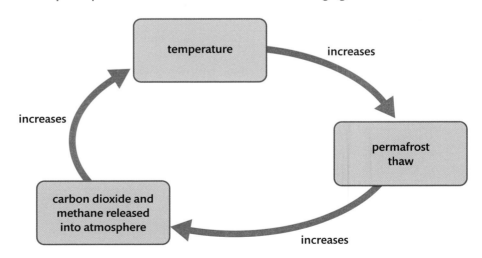

Figure 1.9 *How positive feedback can influence climate change.*

Negative feedback

Negative feedback can be defined as feedback that **counteracts** any change away from equilibrium. This form of feedback contributes to **stability**.

Negative feedback is a method of control that regulates itself. Through negative feedback, the system is able to maintain steady-state equilibrium.

See Figure 1.10 below for an example of negative feedback:

Glossary

counteract work against

stability the state of not changing

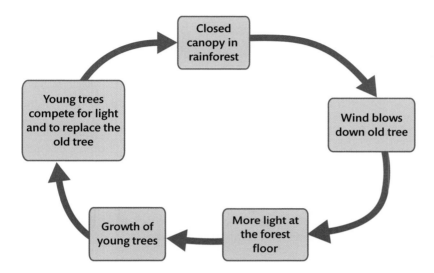

Figure 1.10 *How negative feedback can lead to steady-state equilibrium in a rainforest. Gaps in the forest canopy are closed when young trees compete for light and to replace the old tree.*

Hints for success: You need to know the differences between positive and negative feedback. Positive feedback speeds up deviation away from the equilibrium, for example the exponential growth of populations. Negative feedback counteracts deviation in a system and returns it to equilibrium, for example predator–prey relationships. Both positive and negative feedback involve time-lags.

Definitions of positive and negative feedback:

Positive feedback: feedback that leads to increasing change away from equilibrium and contributes to instability.

Negative feedback: feedback that counteracts any change away from equilibrium and contributes to stability.

Subject vocabulary

input the movement into something

output the movement out from something

system a collection of parts and the relationships between them, which together make a whole

transfer a process involving a change in location within the system but no change in state

organic matter biological material in the process of decaying or decomposing

diffusion the movement of particles from a higher to a lower concentration

nutrients substances that provide nourishment essential for growth and the maintenance of life

consumption when one organism eats another organism

biomass living matter, made from biological molecules

transformation a process that leads to the formation of new products or involves a change in state

decomposition breakdown of organic matter by decomposers

photosynthesis a process that captures sunlight energy and transforms it into the chemical bonds of glucose molecules; carbon dioxide, water, and light are transformed into glucose and oxygen

respiration a chemical process occurring in all cells that transforms the energy in glucose molecules into ATP, releasing energy in the process; glucose is transformed in the presence of oxygen into carbon dioxide and water

Glossary

state form that matter takes: solid, liquid, or gas

Inputs and outputs from systems can be either transfer or transformation processes.

What are transfer processes?

A transfer is a process where there is a change in location within the system, but there is no change in state. An example of a transfer is water falling from clouds to the ground as rain. Dead organic matter entering a lake is another example of a transfer process.

In Figure 1.1 (page 2) transfer processes would include:

- Diffusion: allows the movement of nutrients and water into the tree.

- Consumption: transfers biomass from one level of a food chain to another.

What are transformation processes?

A transformation is a process that leads to the formation of new products. It can also involve a change in state. An example of a transformation is water in clouds changing from water vapour to liquid water. The decomposition of dead organic matter is another example of a transformation process.

In Figure 1.1 (page 2) transformation processes would include:

- Photosynthesis: converts sunlight energy, carbon dioxide and water into glucose and oxygen.

- Respiration: changes biomass into carbon dioxide and water, and releasing some heat.

Transfers are processes that lead to a change in location but not a change in state;

Transformations are processes that lead to the formation of new products or a change in state.

1.1.8 Distinguish between flows and storages in relation to systems

System diagrams contain storages and flows.

Model sentence: Flows are movement from one place to another in the system and are shown by arrows.

Flows are either inputs or outputs. Inputs are movements into a storage and outputs are movements out of a storage.

Model sentence: Storages are where something is kept in a system and are shown by boxes.

The following diagram shows flows and storages in a social system:

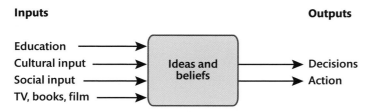

Figure 1.11 *A social system, showing flows and storage. Flows are inputs and outputs, and storage is the ideas and beliefs of the society.*

Flows are movements from one place to another in a system;

Storages are when something is kept in a system.

Subject vocabulary

system a collection of parts and the relationships between them, which together make a whole

storage where something is kept

flow movement from one place to another

input the movement into something

output the movement out from something

social system the people in a society viewed as a system and organized by a characteristic pattern of relationships

1.1.9 Construct and analyse quantitative models involving flows and storages in a system

Subject vocabulary

model a simplified description designed to show the structure and workings of a system

system a collection of parts and the relationships between them, which together make a whole

flow movement from one place to another

storage where something is kept

ecosystem a community of organisms that depend on each other and the environment they live in

Synonyms

structure .... organization/arrangement

workings .... how something is organized

linkage........... connection

complexity...... containing many parts which are difficult to understand

Glossary

excrete get rid of waste, produced by chemical reactions in cells, from the body

understory plants plants that grow underneath the leaf cover of other plants. For example, shrubs growing under a tree are understory plants

root the part of a plant which grows under the ground

leach into pass into

quantitative relating to the amount of something

relative compared to one another

in proportion (to) the correct relationship according to size, shape, or position

tissue decay the breakdown of biomass to form litter

mineralization the conversion of organic molecules into inorganic molecules by soil organisms

humification the process of the formation of humus from plant and animal remains

A **model** is a simplified description designed to show the **structure** and **workings** of a **system**. Models can be used to show the **flows**, **storages**, and **linkages** within **ecosystems**. While they are unable to show much of the **complexity** of the real system, they still help us to understand ecosystem function better. The following figure shows a model for an ecosystem:

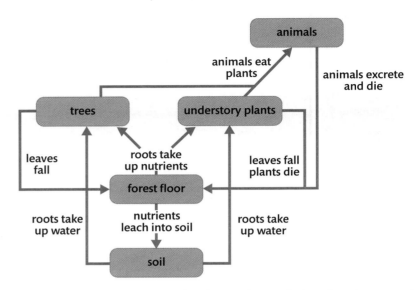

Figure 1.12 *Models are simplified versions of reality. They can show much about the main processes in the ecosystem and show key linkages. This is a model of an ecosystem.*

Model sentence: Quantitative models show the relative sizes of flows and storages.

The width of arrows can vary in size; wider arrows are used to show larger flows. This means that the size of flows can be drawn **in proportion to** other flows. The size of boxes can also vary; larger boxes are used to show larger storages. Quantitative models can be used to analyse and compare different models.

Model sentence: The following models compare and contrast two different systems:

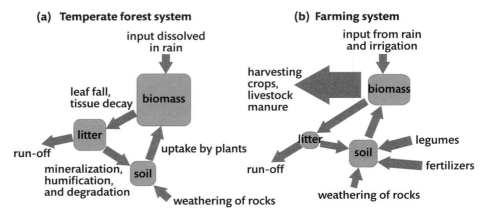

Figure 1.13 *Quantitative models showing nutrient cycles for two different systems. In each case the width of the arrow indicates the relative size of the flow. Similarly the size of the box indicates the relative size of the storage.*

Model sentence: The quantitative models shown in the figure can be analysed by comparing the relative size of flows and storages.

The models in Figure 1.13 show quantitative information about the different systems as the nutrient flows and storages have been drawn in proportion to one another. The biomass storage is larger in the woodland. The litter storage is larger in the forest. There is a large output flow in the farming system because of the harvested crops and livestock. The diagrams also show that legumes and fertilizers are additional inputs in the farming system. Other flows are the same in both systems, such as the input from dissolved rain. Models that include quantitative descriptions of the system provide more meaningful information.

Hints for success: When you draw a systems diagram make sure you write the processes on the input and output arrows. By labelling inputs and outputs in this way you can show which transfers and transformations are taking place.

Glossary

degradation wearing down and disintegrating

weather/weathering change through the long-term action of sun, rain, and wind

Subject vocabulary

nutrients substances that provide nourishment essential for growth and the maintenance of life

biomass living matter, made from biological molecules

Glossary

litter dead leaves and plants

harvest collect crops from the field

crop plants such as wheat or rice which are grown by farmers and used as food

livestock farm animals

legume pea or bean plant

fertilizer organic matter or chemicals used to increase the fertility of a soil

dissolve mix and form part of a liquid

Subject vocabulary

model a simplified description which aims to show the structure or workings of a system

system a collection of parts and the relationships between them, which together make a whole

Glossary

simplify/simplification make something easier or less complicated to understand

aquarium a glass container for fish and other water animals and plants

concept an idea of how something is

oversimplify/oversimplification describe something in a way that is too simple

Synonyms

structure .... organization/ arrangement

workings .... show how something is organised

complex .... complicated/ difficult to understand

limitation .... weakness/ disadvantage

What is a model?

A **model** can be defined as a **simplified** description, which aims to show the **structure** or **workings** of a **system**.

Some models are **complex**, such as models that predict the effect of climate change. Other models are simple, such as a model of an **aquarium** ecosystem. Even simple ecosystems like the aquarium ecosystem can show many ecological **concepts**.

Evaluation of models

Strengths of models

- Models allow scientists to predict and simplify complex systems.

- They allow inputs to be changed and outcomes examined without having to wait a long time, as we would have to if studying real events.

- Models allow results to be shown to other scientists and to the public, and are easier to understand than detailed information about the whole system.

Limitations of models

- Different models may show different effects using the same data. For example, models that predict the effect of climate change may give very different results.

- Systems may be very complex and when models of them are **oversimplified** they may become less accurate. For example, there are many complex factors involved in atmospheric systems.

- Because many assumptions have to be made about these complex factors, climate models may not be accurate.

- The complexity and oversimplification of climate models has led some people to criticise the **limitations** of these models.

- Any model is only as good as the data that are used in them. In addition, the data put into the model may not be reliable.

- Models rely on the expertise of the people making them and this can lead to inaccuracies.

- Different people may interpret models in different ways and so come to different conclusions. People who would gain from the results of the models may use them to their advantage.

> **Hints for success:** You need to be able to evaluate the use of models. The advantage of models is that they clearly show links between parts of a system and give a clear summary of complex interrelationships. The disadvantage of models is that they require scientists to simplify complex systems and include assumptions. These simplifications and assumptions can lead to loss of information and inaccuracies.

2.1.1 Distinguish between biotic and abiotic components of an ecosystem

Model sentence: **An ecosystem can be defined as a community of organisms that depend on each other and the environment they live in.**

Model sentence: **Ecosystems have parts that are living and parts that are non-living.**

The living parts are called biotic components and the non-living parts are called abiotic components.

Differences between biotic and abiotic components

	Biotic components	Abiotic components
Important differences	Living	Non-living
Examples	Animals Plants Algae Fungi Bacteria	Sunlight Air Water Temperature pH Soil Climate
Synonyms	Community	Non-living components

Figure 2.1 *An ecosystem is made from living parts, which are called biotic components, and non-living parts, which are called abiotic components.*

2.1.2; 2.1.3 Define the term trophic level; identify and explain trophic levels in food chains and food webs selected from the local environment

Subject vocabulary

trophic level the position that an organism, or group of organisms, occupies in a food chain

organism living thing

food chain a simple diagram that shows feeding relationships in an ecosystem

producer an organism that makes its own food; for example, a green plant that can photosynthesize

photosynthesis a process that captures sunlight energy and transforms it into the chemical bonds of glucose molecules; carbon dioxide, water, and light are transformed into glucose and oxygen

autotroph another name for a producer

consumer an organism that eats other organisms to get its food

herbivore an animal that only eats plants

carnivore an organism that eats other animals

omnivore an animal that eats both animals and plants

ecosystem a community of organisms that depend on each other and the environment they live in

flow movement from one place to another

food web a diagram that shows food chains linked together in an ecosystem

ecosystem a community of organisms that depend on each other and the environment they live in

Glossary

primary first level

secondary second level

tertiary third level

interconnected linked together

Model sentence: Trophic level can be defined as the position that an organism, or group of organisms, occupies in a food chain.

Trophic levels are feeding levels. The first trophic level contains **producers**: these organisms produce their own food by **photosynthesis**. An organism that makes its own food is also known as an **autotroph** (auto – 'by itself', troph – 'food'). All other trophic levels contain **consumers**: these are animals that eat other organisms to obtain their food. The second trophic level contains **primary** consumers: these organisms eat plants and are also known as **herbivores**. The third trophic level contains **secondary** consumers: these organisms eat other animals and are also known as **carnivores**. Some secondary consumers may eat both animals and plants and are known as **omnivores**. The fourth level contains **tertiary** consumers.

What is a food chain?

A food chain can be defined as a simple diagram that shows feeding relationships in an **ecosystem**. Arrows from one organism to the next represent energy **flow**.

Example of a food chain

The following figure shows a food chain from a local environment with its different trophic levels:

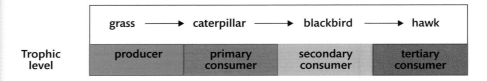

Figure 2.2 *A food chain showing its trophic levels.*

What is a food web?

A **food web** can be defined as a diagram that shows **interconnected** food chains in an **ecosystem**. The following figure shows a food web from a local environment with its different trophic levels:

Example of a food web

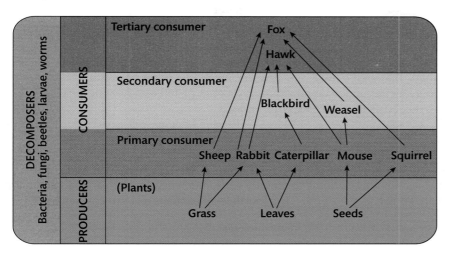

Figure 2.3 *A food web showing its trophic levels.*

The food web contains the food chain shown in Figure 2.2, as well as other food chains. One species may occupy several different trophic levels depending on which food chain it is present in. In the figure above, foxes and hawks are both secondary and tertiary consumers depending on which food chain they are in. **Decomposers** feed on dead organisms at each trophic level.

Subject vocabulary

decomposer an organism that feeds on dead organisms

A food chain is linear, showing energy flow through an ecosystem.

A food web shows the complex interactions between different food chains.

One species may occupy several different trophic levels in a food web depending on which food chain it is present in.

2.1.4 Explain the principles of pyramids of numbers, pyramids of biomass, and pyramids of productivity, and construct such pyramids from given data

Glossary

principles ideas/theories

quantitative relating to the amount/number of something

coexisting living together

symmetrically identical/the same either side of a central point or line

axis a line on a graph used for showing measurements

estimate obtain an approximate value

inverted upside down

Synonyms

graphical .... picture/diagram

typical .... normal/usual

Subject vocabulary

trophic level the position that an organism, or group of organisms, occupies in a food chain

ecosystem a community of organisms that depend on each other and the environment they live in

organisms living things

pyramids of numbers show the number of producers and consumers living together in an ecosystem

producer an organism that makes its own food; for example, a green plant that can photosynthesize

consumer an organism that eats other organisms to get its food

herbivore animal that only eats plants

pyramids of biomass show the amount of living matter present at each trophic level at a certain point in time

What are pyramid diagrams?

Pyramids are **graphical** models of the **quantitative** differences (i.e. differences in numbers) that exist between the **trophic levels** of a single **ecosystem**. These models provide a better understanding of the workings of an ecosystem by showing the numbers of **organisms** at each trophic level.

Pyramids of numbers

Pyramids of numbers show the number of **producers** and **consumers coexisting** in a particular ecosystem. A pyramid of numbers is produced by counting the numbers of organisms in an ecosystem and showing this quantitative data for each trophic level. Quantitative data is shown by drawing horizontal bars to scale. The horizontal bars are drawn **symmetrically** around a central **axis**. Numbers of organisms can be **estimated** by counting the number of individuals in a specific area (e.g. square metre) and multiplying this up to the total area of the ecosystem studied (e.g. a length of rocky shore).

Pyramids of numbers are not always pyramid shaped. For example, in a woodland ecosystem there will be more insect **herbivores** than the trees they are feeding on. This means the pyramid is **inverted**. This happens because the size of each producer (tree) is large and therefore there are few in number. Pyramids of numbers have limitations in showing useful feeding relationships because they can be inverted in this way. The following figure shows a **typical** pyramid of numbers and one that is inverted:

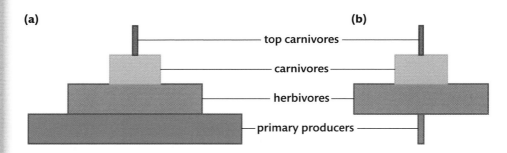

(a) **(b)**

top carnivores

carnivores

herbivores

primary producers

Figure 2.4 (a) *A typical pyramid where the number of producers is high, e.g. many seed-producing plants supporting many insects, which in turn support a few insect-eating birds, which support very few bird-eating birds (such as a falcon); **(b)** A limitation of number pyramids is that they are inverted when the number of producers is fewer than the number of herbivores.*

Pyramids of biomass

A **pyramid of biomass** shows the amount of biomass at each trophic level at a certain point in time. A pyramid of biomass represents the storage of each trophic level. The biomass at each trophic level is measured in grams of biomass per metre squared (g m^{-2}).

The **second law of thermodynamics** states that the amount of energy decreases along a food chain; as energy decreases, biomass also decreases. Because biomass decreases along a food chain, pyramids of biomass become **narrower** towards the top.

Although pyramids of biomass are usually pyramid shaped, they can sometimes be inverted. When they are inverted they show more biomass at higher trophic levels than lower trophic levels. They can be inverted because they show biomass present at a certain moment in time. The amount of biomass present at a certain moment in time is called the **standing crop biomass**. The standing crop biomass does not show the amount of **productivity** in the trophic level over time. For example, a field may have a lower standing crop biomass of grass than the herbivores that feed on it. Over time, as the grass grows and gets longer, the productivity of the grass will be higher than the productivity of the herbivores that feed on it (see pyramids of productivity, page 22). This results in an inverted pyramid of biomass. Inverted pyramids may also be the result of **seasonal variations** in biomass.

Both pyramids of numbers and pyramids of biomass represent **storages**.

Both pyramids of numbers and pyramids of biomass can be inverted, where the number or mass of producers is lower than the number or mass of herbivores.

Pyramids of numbers and biomass can be inverted because measurements are taken during one moment in time, when producers may be at a lower number or biomass than the primary consumers.

Subject vocabulary

second law of thermodynamics law that states that the transfer of energy through systems is inefficient as some of the energy is transformed into heat

standing crop biomass the amount of living matter present at a certain moment in time

productivity the amount of living matter generated by photosynthesis in a certain amount of time

storage where something is kept

Synonyms

narrower .... thinner

Glossary

seasonal variations differences that exist depending on the time of year, e.g. summer

Subject vocabulary

pyramids of productivity show the amount of living matter generated at each trophic level over a certain period of time

pyramids of numbers show the number of producers and consumers living together in an ecosystem

pyramids of biomass show the amount of living matter present at each trophic level at a certain point in time

storage where something is kept

flow movement from one place to another

trophic level the position that an organism, or group of organisms, occupies in a food chain

second law of thermodynamics law that states that the transfer of energy through systems is inefficient as some of the energy is transformed into heat

Synonyms

generated .... produced

Glossary

inverted upside down

plot put information on a chart/diagram

Pyramids of productivity

A **pyramid of productivity** shows the amount of productivity at each trophic level over a certain period of time, whereas **pyramids of numbers** and **pyramids of biomass** show the **storage** in the food chain at a certain time. Pyramids of productivity show the rate at which those storages are being **generated** (made, at each level). Productivity is defined as the amount of new biomass generated per unit area per unit time. Productivity is measured in mass or energy per metre squared per year ($g\ m^{-2}\ yr^{-1}$ or $J\ m^{-2}\ yr^{-1}$).

Pyramids of productivity represent the **flow** of energy through a food chain from one **trophic level** to the next trophic level. The **second law of thermodynamics** states that the amount of energy decreases along a food chain. Because energy decreases along a food chain, pyramids of productivity always become narrower towards the top. There are no **inverted** pyramids of productivity.

How are pyramids constructed?

Given data:

Species	Number of individuals
Leaves	40
Caterpillar	20
Blackbird	14
Hawk	6

Two axes are drawn on graph paper. The horizontal axis is drawn along the bottom of the graph paper and the vertical axis is drawn in the centre of the graph paper. Data from the table is **plotted** symmetrically around the vertical axis. As there are 40 leaves, the producer trophic level is drawn with 20 units to the left and 20 to the right of the vertical axis. The height of the bars is kept the same for each trophic level. Each trophic level is labelled with the appropriate organism.

Pyramids of productivity can never be inverted. Measurements are taken over one year: this takes into account any increase and decrease in numbers or biomass. Pyramids there demonstrate energy loss in food chains, where there is a reduction in energy from producers through to consumers.

Here is a graph of the given data:

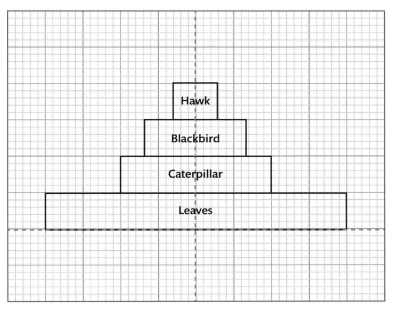

Figure 2.5 *Pyramid of numbers for given data.*

Pyramids of biomass and pyramids of productivity are constructed in the same way.

> **Hints for success:** When you are defining pyramids of biomass or pyramids of productivity do not forget to include units. The units for a pyramid of biomass are 'grams per metre squared' ($g\ m^{-2}$). The units for a pyramid of productivity are 'mass per metre squared per year' or 'energy per metre squared per year' ($g\ m^{-2}\ yr^{-1}$ or $J\ m^{-2}\ yr^{-1}$).

> **Hints for success:** Pyramids of productivity are always pyramid shaped because energy is always lost through the food chain. Pyramids of numbers or biomass may be inverted because they represent only the stock at a given moment in time.

Pyramids are symmetrical around a vertical axis: this needs to be taken into account when plotting data.

2.1.5 Discuss how the pyramid structure affects the functioning of an ecosystem

Model sentence: The pyramid structure of an ecosystem – numbers of organisms functioning at each trophic level – can be changed by human activities.

Organisms in higher trophic levels tend to be fewer in number than organisms in lower trophic levels. This is because energy is lost through food chains leading to fewer organisms in higher trophic levels. If there is a **reduction** in **producers** or **primary** and **secondary consumers**, this will lead to fewer top **carnivores**. For example, snow leopards are a top carnivore found in the mountains of Central Asia. Snow leopards feed on wild sheep and goats. **Overgrazing** of mountain grasses by farmed animals has left less food for wild sheep and goats. Because there are fewer wild sheep and goats, there is less food and therefore fewer snow leopards.

Two examples of how a pyramid structure affects the functioning of an ecosystem

Example 1: How deforestation affects pyramids of biomass structure

Deforestation will reduce the producer bar on pyramids of biomass leading to lower biomass of secondary and **tertiary** consumers. As a result, all bars on the pyramid will be smaller.

Example 2: How pesticide use affects pyramid structure

Top carnivores can be affected by harmful chemicals in their environment. Harmful chemicals include **pesticides** such as DDT. Farmers use pesticides to kill insects that would otherwise eat their crop (such insects are called **pests**). This improves the amount of **crop** the farmer produces, i.e. the **yield**. DDT is put on crops to kill insect pests. Harmful chemicals are called **toxins**. The toxin does not break down over a long time period and is not eliminated through waste, and so **accumulates** in the body fat of consumers.

The toxin becomes more **concentrated** within the biomass from primary consumers through to top carnivores. Organisms higher up the food chain are at greater risk as they have a lifetime eating organisms with higher concentrations of the toxin. Top carnivores are at risk from poisoning from the toxin and may be affected (e.g. reproductive capacity may be severely affected; if build-up of toxin is severe enough, animals may be killed). A reduction in the number of top carnivores affects the rest of the food chain. Because there are fewer predators, the number of consumers in lower trophic levels may increase. In this way, humans can influence pyramid structure.

2.1.6 Define the terms *species, population, habitat, niche, community* and *ecosystem* with reference to local examples

Model sentence: Species can be defined as a group of organisms that interbreed and produce fertile offspring.

An example of a species is the lion, *Panthera leo*.

Model sentence: Population can be defined as a group of organisms of the same species living in the same area at the same time.

An example of a population is the number of lions in a defined area.

Model sentence: Habitat can be defined as the place where a species lives.

An example of a habitat is the savannahs of Africa where the lion lives.

Model sentence: Niche can be defined as where and how a species lives.

No two different species can have the same niche because the niche completely defines a species.

An example of a niche is the ecology and behaviour of the lion. In this case, the niche would include the following: habitat, mating behaviour, grooming and other social behaviour, alertness, feeding behaviour, when it is active, and so on.

Model sentence: Community can be defined as a group of different species living together in a common habitat.

An example of a community are all the animals and plants of the African savannah, such as grasses, trees, lions, zebras, wildebeest, hyenas, giraffes, and elephants.

Model sentence: Ecosystem can be defined as a community of organisms that depend on each other and the environment they live in.

An example of an ecosystem is the savannah grasslands of Africa.

Hints for success: You must be able to define the terms species, population, habitat, niche, community, and ecosystem, and apply them to examples from your local area.

2.1.7 Describe and explain population interactions using examples of named species

Subject vocabulary

Subject vocabulary

population a group of organisms of the same species living in the same area at the same time

competition the demand by two or more species for limited environmental resources

parasitism interaction where one organism gets its food at the expense of another organism

mutualism interaction in which both species gain benefit

predation interaction where one animal hunts and eats another animal

herbivory interaction where an animal feeds on a plant

carrying capacity the maximum number of a species that can be maintained by an environment

intraspecific competition competition within a species

interspecific competition competition between different species

niche where and how a species lives

Glossary

interactions a process where two or more things affect each other

dynamics how a system works

overlap appear in the same place

Synonyms

influences............. effects

Model sentence: A population is a group of organisms of the same species living in the same area at the same time.

Model sentence: I will describe and explain the following population interactions: competition, parasitism, mutualism, predation, and herbivory.

Model sentence: I will explain interactions in terms of the influences each species has on the population dynamics of others. I will also explain interactions in terms of the effects of one population on the carrying capacity of the others' environment. I will give a named example for each type of population interaction.

Interaction 1: Competition

The named species for competition are *Paramecium aurelia* and *Paramecium caudatum*.

When resources are limited, individuals must compete in order to survive. This competition can be either within a species or between individuals of different species. When competition is within a species it is called **intraspecific competition**. When competition is between different species it is called **interspecific competition**. No two species can occupy the same **niche** (i.e. they cannot be identical in all ways) and so interspecific competition occurs when the niches of different species **overlap**. In this interaction, the stronger competitor (i.e. the one better able to survive) will reduce the carrying capacity of the other's environment.

The following figure shows the difference between intraspecific competition and interspecific competition:

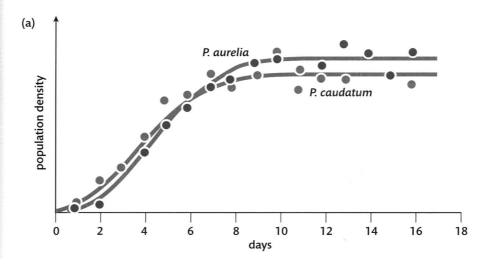

(a)

P. aurelia

P. caudatum

population density

days

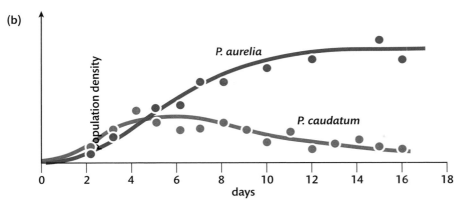

(b)

Figure 2.6 Paramecium *are single-celled animals that are easy to keep in a laboratory. These graphs show the interaction between two species:* Paramecium aurelia *and* Paramecium caudatum.
(a) *If these two species with very similar niches are grown separately, then both can survive and flourish. As they are grown separately there is no interspecific competition. Numbers of individuals – the population density in that area – level off for both species because of intraspecific competition for resources; each species reaches its carrying capacity.*
(b) *If the two species are grown in a mixed culture (i.e. together) then the stronger competitor,* P. aurelia, *being better able to gain food and reproduce in these conditions than* P. caudatum, *will reduce the carrying capacity of* P. caudatum *and so that species' numbers decrease.*

Interaction 2: Parasitism

The named species for parasitism is *Rafflesia*.

In this interaction, one organism gets its food from another organism that does not benefit from the relationship. The organism that benefits from the relationship is called the **parasite**. The organism from which the parasite gets its food is called the **host**. The parasite benefits from the interaction, but the host is harmed by the interaction. The carrying capacity of the host may be reduced because of the harm caused by the parasite.

An example of a parasite is *Rafflesia*. Rafflesias are plants that have giant flowers and no leaves. Because they have no leaves they cannot carry out **photosynthesis** and so cannot make sugar. Rafflesias get the sugars they need from a **vine** on which they live (i.e. they parasitize the vine).

Interaction 3: Mutualism

The named species for mutualism are polyps and single-celled algae called zooxanthellae.

Mutualism is an interaction in which both species **benefit**. An example of a **mutualistic** interaction is **coral**. In a coral, an animal **polyp** makes a hard structure from calcium carbonate. Single-celled **algae** live inside the polyp. These algae are called zooxanthellae. The zooxanthellae photosynthesize and make sugar for the polyp, and in return the polyp creates a hard structure that protects the zooxanthellae.

parasite the organism that benefits from a parasitic relationship

host the organism that is fed on and harmed by a parasite

photosynthesis a process that captures sunlight energy and transforms it into the chemical bonds of glucose molecules; carbon dioxide, water and light are transformed into glucose and oxygen

mutualistic relationship between two different species where each gains benefits from the other

coral a hard stony substance secreted by polyp animals as an external skeleton, typically forming large reefs in warm shallow seas

polyp a small animal with a cylindrical body and a mouth at the top surrounded by tentacles

algae often single-celled organisms, found in water, that can photosynthesize

vine a climbing or trailing woody-stemmed plant

benefit an advantage gained from something

Glossary

fluctuations increases and decreases

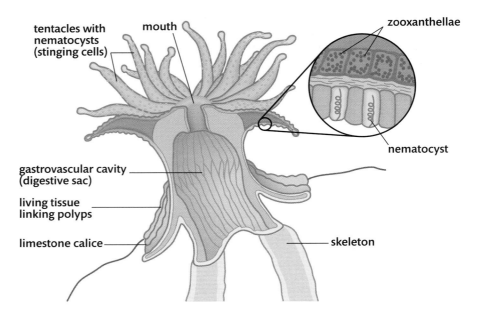

Figure 2.7 *The zooxanthellae living within the polyp animal photosynthesize to produce food for themselves and the coral polyp. The coral polyp produces a hard skeleton that protects both the polyp and the zooxanthellae.*

Interaction 4: Predation

The named species for predation are snowshoe hares and lynxes.

Predation is an interaction where one animal hunts and eats another animal. The predator is the animal that hunts and kills the other animal. The animal that is hunted and killed is called the prey. The **carrying capacity** of the prey is affected by the predator because the number of prey is reduced by the predator. The carrying capacity of the predator is affected by the prey because the number of predators is reduced when prey become fewer. These **predator-prey interactions** are controlled by **negative feedback** mechanisms. The following figure shows a predator-prey interaction:

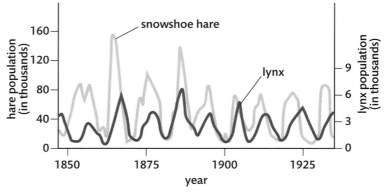

Figure 2.8 *Predator-prey interactions between the snowshoe hare and lynx.*

The lynx is a cat that lives in the forests of Canada and feeds on the snowshoe hare. The lynx is the predator and the snowshoe hare the prey. The graph shows **fluctuations** in numbers of both species over time. An increase in numbers of hare occurs when predator numbers are low. When hare numbers are high, there is more food for the lynx and so its numbers increase. Over-hunting of the hare by the lynx leads to a reduction in hare numbers. Reduction in hare numbers leads to a drop in predator numbers. The cycle then repeats. There is a **time-lag** in the feedback links; this is true of all **feedback mechanisms**, as it takes time for the system to respond to change.

Figure 2.9 *A lynx with a recently caught snowshoe hare.*

Interaction 5: Herbivory

The named species for herbivory are caterpillars and leaves.

Herbivory is an interaction where an animal feeds on a plant. The animal that eats the plant is called a **herbivore**. An example of herbivory is a caterpillar eating a leaf.

The carrying capacity of herbivores is affected by the quantity of the plant they feed on. An area with more abundant plant resources will have a higher carrying capacity than an area that has less plant material available as food for a consumer.

Population interactions include:

Competition: the demand by two or more species for limited environmental resources;

Parasitism: where one organism gets its food from another organism that does not benefit from the relationship;

Mutualism: an interaction where both species benefit;

Predation: where one animal hunts and eats another animal;

Herbivory: where an animal feeds on a plant.

2.2.1 List the significant abiotic components of an ecosystem

Subject vocabulary

abiotic component non-living part in an ecosystem

marine relating to the sea

freshwater water with no salt in it

terrestrial relating to land

biotic component living, biological part in an ecosystem

Glossary

estuary where a river joins the sea

salt marshes area of low/wet/soft ground with salt water under it

mangrove tropical trees that grow in/near water

wetland area of land that is partly covered in water/mostly wet

salinity amount of salt

dissolved oxygen the concentration of oxygen in water

turbidity cloudiness caused by suspended materials in water – soil particles, plankton, and so on

flow movement of water in a stream or river

slope a surface where one end is higher than the other

drainage process where water/waste liquid flows away

Synonyms

component........... parts

velocity............... speed

intensity.............. strength

Model sentence: Abiotic components are the non-living factors in an ecosystem.

Model sentence: Ecosystems can be divided into three types: marine, freshwater, and terrestrial.

Marine ecosystems include the sea, estuaries, salt marshes, and mangroves. Marine ecosystems all have a high concentration of salt in the water. Estuaries are included in the same group as marine ecosystems because they have a high salt content compared to freshwater. Freshwater ecosystems include rivers, lakes, and wetlands. Terrestrial ecosystems include all land-based ecosystems.

Each type of ecosystem has its own specific abiotic components. Each ecosystem also has abiotic factors that they share with other types of ecosystems.

Model sentence: Abiotic components of a marine ecosystem include: salinity, pH, temperature, dissolved oxygen, and wave action.

Model sentence: Abiotic components of a freshwater ecosystem include: turbidity, temperature, flow velocity, dissolved oxygen, and pH.

Model sentence: Abiotic components of a terrestrial ecosystem include: temperature, light intensity, wind speed, soil particle size, amount and angle of slope, soil moisture, drainage, and mineral content.

Hints for success: You must know methods for measuring each of the abiotic components and how they vary with depth, time, or distance.

Hints for success: Abiotic components are measured along with biotic components. Measuring both abiotic and biotic components allows species distribution data to be linked to the environment in which they are found. It also allows an explanation of the patterns to be proposed.

Figure 2.10 *Malham Tarn in Yorkshire, UK, is an example of a freshwater ecosystem.*

Figure 2.11 *Tropical rainforest in Borneo is an example of a terrestrial ecosystem.*

Different ecosystems have different abiotic components. Marine ecosystems have a large concentration of salt in the water; freshwater ecosystems include rivers, lakes and wetlands; terrestrial ecosystems include all land-based ecosystems.

2.2.2 Describe and evaluate methods for measuring at least three abiotic (physical) factors within an ecosystem

Method 1: Wind speed

How measured? Using an anemometer.

Technique: The anemometer is hand-held and pointed into the wind. The anemometer is held at the same height for each measurement.

Evaluation: Gusty conditions may lead to large **variations** in data. Care must be taken not to block the wind.

Figure 2.12 *An anemometer.*

Method 2: Temperature

How measured? Using a **digital** thermometer.

Technique: The digital thermometer can be used to measure temperature in air, water, and at different depths of soil. The digital thermometer is held at the same depth or height for each measurement.

Evaluation: Data will vary if temperature is not taken at the same depth each time. Temperature is measured for a short period of time. **Data-loggers** can be used to measure temperature over long periods of time.

Method 3: Light intensity

How measured? Using a light-meter.

Technique: The light-meter is hand-held and pointed towards the Sun. The light-meter is held at the same height above the ground. The reading is taken when there is no **fluctuation** in the reading.

Evaluation: Cloud cover will affect the light **intensity**. Shading from plants or the person operating the light-meter will also affect the light intensity. Care must therefore be taken when taking readings using a light-meter.

Method 4: Flow velocity

How measured? Using a **flow**-meter.

Technique: The impeller is put into water just below the surface. The impeller is pointed into the direction of the flow. A number of readings are taken to ensure accuracy.

Evaluation: **Velocity** varies with distance from the surface so readings must be taken at the same depth. Results can be **misleading** if only one part of a stream is measured. Water flows can vary over time because of rainfall or because of ice melting events.

Figure 2.13 *A flow-meter.*

Method 5: Wave action

How measured? Using a dynamometer.

Technique: The dynamometer is pointed into the waves. The dynamometer measures the force of the waves.

Evaluation: Results will be affected by changes in wave strength during a day and over a monthly period.

Method 6: Turbidity

How measured? Using a Secchi disc.

Technique: A Secchi disc is mounted on a pole or line and is lowered into water until it is just out of sight. The depth is measured using the scale of the line or pole. The disc is raised until it is just visible again and a second reading is taken. The average depth calculated is known as the Secchi depth.

Evaluation: Reflections off water will reduce visibility and make it difficult to take **turbidity** measurements. Measurements are **subjective** and depend, to some extent, on the technique used by the person taking the measurements.

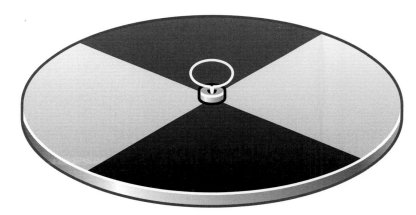

Figure 2.14 *A Secchi disc.*

Method 7: Dissolved oxygen

How measured? Using oxygen-sensitive **electrodes** attached to an oxygen-meter.

Technique: Oxygen-sensitive electrodes are connected to a meter that can be used to measure **dissolved oxygen**.

Evaluation: Readings may be affected by oxygen in the air when using an oxygen-meter.

Method 8: Soil moisture

How measured? Using an oven to heat the soil so the water **evaporates**.

Technique: Heat the soil until there is no further loss in weight. Loss of weight can be calculated as a percentage of the starting weight. Soil moisture probes can also be used.

Evaluation: If the oven is too hot when evaporating the water, **organic** content can also burn off.

Method 9: Slope

How measured? Using a protractor as shown in the following diagram.

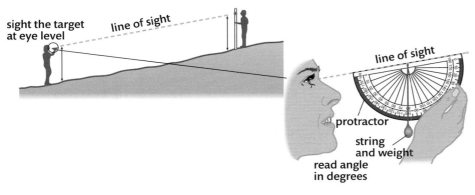

Figure 2.15 *The slope angle is taken by lining-up the protractor along the slope and reading the degree shown by the string.*

Technique: Surface **run-off** is measured by **slope**, which can be calculated using a clinometer (which measures slope angle).

Evaluation: The slope may vary in angle over its distance.

Evaluation of methods

Sampling must be carried out carefully so that an accurate **representation** of the study area can be obtained. An inaccurate representation of a study area may be obtained if errors are made in sampling.

Short-term and limited field sampling (i.e. small sample sizes taken over short periods of time) reduces how effective sampling methods are because **abiotic components** may vary from day to day and from season to season. Most abiotic components can be measured using **data-logging** devices. The advantage of data-loggers is that they can provide continuous data over a long period of time; this makes results more **representative** of the area. Results can be made more reliable by taking many samples.

Hints for success: You must be prepared to describe and evaluate at least three different methods from the range of techniques described here.

Glossary

evaporate turn from liquid into gas

organic made from living matter

slope a surface where one end is higher than the other

sampling examining a small part/ amount to learn about the whole

data-logger electronic device that records data over time

Subject vocabulary

run-off water flowing over the surface of the ground

abiotic component a non-living part in an ecosystem

Synonyms

representation .... picture/ description

representative .... typical

dichotomous key a guide where there are two options based on different characteristics at each step. The outcome of each choice leads to another pair of questions. This is done until the organism is identified.

Model sentence: I will use a dichotomous key to identify the items:

1	**a**	Organism is living	go to 4
	b	Organism is non-living	go to 2
2	**a**	Object is metallic	go to 3
	b	Object is non-metallic	pebble
3	**a**	Object has wheels	car
	b	Object does not have wheels	spoon
4	**a**	Organism is microscopic	amoeba
	b	Organism is macroscopic	go to 5
5	**a**	Organism is a plant	go to 6
	b	Organism is an animal	go to 8
6	**a**	Plant has a woody stem	go to 7
	b	Plant has a herbaceous stem	buttercup
7	**a**	Tree has leaves with small surface area	pine tree
	b	Tree has leaves with large surface area	sycamore tree
8	**a**	Organism is terrestrial	go to 9
	b	Organism is aquatic	shark
9	**a**	Organism has fewer than six legs	go to 10
	b	Organism has six legs	beetle
10	**a**	Organism has fur	go to 11
	b	Organism has feathers	eagle
11	**a**	Organism has hooves	horse
	b	Organism has no hooves	rat

Model sentence: I will show my dichotomous key as a diagram:

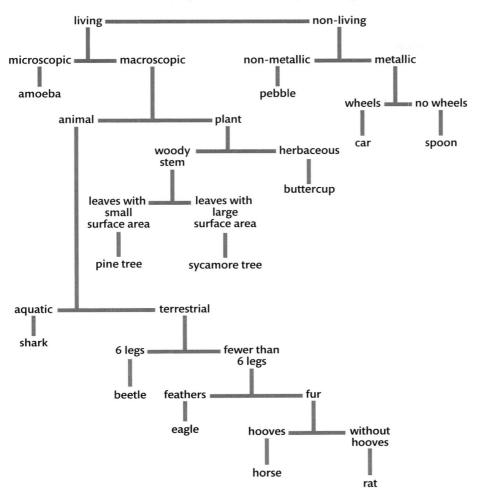

Figure 2.16 *A dichotomous key for a random selection of living and non-living objects.*

Hints for success: In an ecological study it is important to correctly identify the organisms being studied. You need to be able to use published keys to identify organisms. There are examples in past ESS exams for you to try. You can also practise using keys to identify plants and animals in your local environment.

2.3.2 Describe and evaluate methods for estimating abundance of organisms

Method 1: The Lincoln Index

Model sentence: The Lincoln Index is used to estimate the abundance of an animal that is mobile.

The Lincoln Index is also known as the capture-mark-release-recapture method. Animals are **captured**, **marked**, and then **released**. After a specific amount of time the animal population is resampled. Some of the animals initially marked will be caught again, or **recaptured**. The total population size of the animal is estimated using this equation:

$$N = \frac{n1 \times n2}{m}$$

N = total population size of animals in the study site

$n1$ = number of animals captured in the first sample and marked

$n2$ = number of animals captured in the second sample

m = number of animals captured in the second sample that are marked.

Evaluation of the Lincoln Index

Animals may move in and out of the sample area, making the capture-mark-release-recapture method less trustworthy and the data invalid. The density of the population in different habitats might vary: there may be many in one area, few in another. The assumption that they are equally spread all over may not be true. Some individuals may be hidden by vegetation and therefore difficult to find, hence not included in the sample. There may be seasonal variations in animals that affect population size, for example they may migrate in or out of the study area.

Model sentence: I will estimate a population size using given data.

The Lincoln Index can be used to calculate population size. The formula of the Lincoln Index is:

$$N = \frac{n1 \times n2}{m}$$

A snail population was sampled. Snails were marked using paint on their shell.

Data from the snail population sampled using the capture-mark-release-recapture method:

Number of snails captured in first sample and marked, $n1$ = 21

Number of snails captured in second sample, $n2$ = 13

Number of snails captured in second sample that are marked, m = 5.

Total population size of snails in the study site, $N = (21 \times 13)/5 = 55$.

The population size is rounded up to the nearest whole number.

Method 2: Quadrats

Model sentence: I will describe and evaluate methods for estimating the abundance of organisms using quadrats.

Subject vocabulary

quadrat a metal or plastic square used to estimate population number/amount of organisms that do not move

percentage cover the percentage of the area within the quadrat covered by one particular species; percentage cover is worked out for each species present

population density the number of individuals of each species in a specific area; it is calculated by dividing the number of organisms by the total area of the quadrats

percentage frequency the percentage of quadrats in an area in which at least one individual of the species is found

Figure 2.17 A quadrat. Dividing the quadrat into 100 squares helps to estimate percentage cover (see below) as each square is 1 per cent of the total area covered.

Glossary

tufts a small collection of fine leaves held together at their base

colony group of organisms growing together

Hints for success: The Lincoln Index is not given to you in exams. You need to learn the Lincoln Index formula and how it works.

To sample the abundance of a plant species, a grid is established over the area. The grid could be, for example, 10 m by 10 m, with 1 m between each part of the grid. A random number generator would be used to select quadrat locations within the grid. For example, if the grid is 10 m by 10 m, random numbers would be generated between 0 and 1000. The random number 596 would represent a point 5 m, 96 cm along one tape measure. The next random number would be the coordinate for the second tape. The point where the coordinates cross would be the location for the quadrat.

Percentage cover of plants in the total sample area is calculated by estimating the percentage cover of plants in each quadrat and multiplying by the total area.

Population density is calculated by estimating the number of individuals of each species in a specific area and then dividing the number of organisms sampled by the total area covered by the quadrats.

Percentage frequency is calculated by working out the percentage of quadrats in the sample area where at least one individual of the species was found.

Evaluation of quadrats

The quadrat method is difficult to use for very large or very small plants. It is difficult to count plants that grow in **tufts** or **colonies**. It is possible that plants that appear separate are joined by roots: this will affect calculation of population density. It is also difficult to measure the abundance of plants outside their main growing season when plants are largely invisible.

2.3.3 Describe and evaluate methods for estimating the biomass of trophic levels in a community

Subject vocabulary

biomass living matter, made from biological molecules

trophic level the position that an organism, or group of organisms, occupies in a food chain

dry weight biomass mass of an organism minus water content

primary producer an organism that can make its own food and is the base of all food chains

quadrat a metal or plastic square used to estimate population number/amount of organisms that do not move

Glossary

extrapolated estimated by extending or projecting known information

estimate obtain an approximate value

Model sentence: Biomass is calculated to show the amount of biological material – hence, energy – within a trophic level.

Biological molecules are held together by captured sunlight energy and so the greater the biomass, the greater the amount of energy present.

Biomass is taken as the mass of an organism minus water content: this is called the dry weight biomass. Water is not included in biomass measurements because the amount varies from organism to organism and, also, water contains no energy.

Method for estimating biomass

The sample is weighed in a container of known mass. The sample is put in a hot oven at around 80°C and left for a specific length of time. The sample is reweighed and replaced in the oven. This is repeated until the same mass is obtained on two subsequent weighings; no further loss in mass is recorded, as no further water is present.

Biomass is recorded per unit area, such as per metre squared. This is done so that trophic levels can be compared. Not all organisms in an area need to be sampled. Dry biomass measurements of sample areas can be extrapolated to estimate total biomass over the whole area being considered by the study. This means that the mass of one organism, or the average mass of several organisms, is taken. This mass is multiplied by the total number of organisms to estimate total biomass.

Evaluation of method

One criticism of the method is that it involves killing living organisms. It is also difficult to measure the biomass of very large plants, such as trees. There are also problems measuring the biomass of roots and underground biomass, as these are difficult to remove from the soil.

Hints for success: To estimate the biomass of a primary producer within a study area all the vegetation is collected within a series of quadrats. The vegetation will include roots, stems, and leaves. The dry-weight method is carried out and average biomass can then be calculated.

2.3.4 Define the term *diversity*

Model sentence: Diversity can be defined as variety, but the meaning depends on the context in which it is used.

There are different types of diversity: species diversity, habitat diversity, and genetic diversity.

When the term 'diversity' is used in a sentence it is usually referring to species diversity.

Model sentence: Species diversity is a function of two components: the number of different species and their relative abundance.

Species diversity is different from species richness because the relative abundance of each species is also taken into account in species diversity.

Species richness is the number of species in an area, whereas species diversity also includes the relative abundance of each species.

An increase in habitat diversity will lead to an increase in species diversity. This is because different habitats will have different species, and so more habitats will have a greater variety of species.

An increase in species diversity will lead to an increase in genetic diversity. This is because different species tend to have different genes, and so more species will have a greater variety of genes.

diversity variety; the meaning depends on the situation in which it is used

species diversity a measurement of the number of different species and their number/ amount compared to one another in a specific area

habitat diversity the range of different habitats in an ecosystem

genetic diversity the range of genetic material present in a species

species richness the number of species in a sample or area

Glossary

context situation in which something exists

relative compared to one another

Synonyms

components.......... parts

abundance .... number/ amount

2.3.5 Apply Simpson's Diversity Index and outline its significance

Model sentence: I will calculate the diversity of woodland species from the following table:

Species	Number (*n*)
woodrush	2
holly (seedlings)	8
bramble	1
Yorkshire fog	1
sedge	3
total (*N*)	15

The samples from several **quadrats** in woodland were combined to obtain this data.

Model sentence: Species diversity can be calculated using Simpson's Diversity Index.

The equation for Simpson's Diversity Index is:

D = diversity index

N = total number of organisms of all species found

n = number of individuals of a particular species

Σ = sum of

$$D = \frac{N(N-1)}{\Sigma n(n-1)}$$

Model sentence: I will calculate *n(n − 1)* for each species:

For example, to calculate $n(n-1)$ for the holly seedlings, $n = 8$ and so $(n-1) = (8-1) = 7$. Therefore n multiplied by $(n-1) = 8 \times 7 = 56$.

Species	Number (*n*)	*n(n − 1)*
woodrush	2	2
holly (seedlings)	8	56
bramble	1	0
Yorkshire fog	1	0
sedge	3	6
total (*N*)	15	64

Model sentence: I will put the figures into the formula for Simpson's Diversity Index:

$$N = 15$$

$$N - 1 = 14$$

$$N(N - 1) = 210$$

$$\Sigma n(n - 1) = 64$$

$$D = \frac{210}{64} = 3.28$$

Model sentence: The Simpson's Diversity Index for a second woodland ecosystem was calculated at $D = 1.48$. I will comment on possible differences between the two woodland ecosystems.

Communities with individuals evenly distributed between different species are said to have high 'evenness' and have high diversity as calculated by the Simpson's Diversity Index. This is because many species can coexist in the many available niches within a complex ecosystem. Communities with one dominant species have low diversity, which indicates a poorer ecosystem not able to support as many types of organism.

Model sentence: A high value of D suggests a stable and ancient site, and a low value of D suggests pollution or agricultural management.

The woodland with $D = 3.28$ could be an undisturbed ecosystem and the woodland with $D = 1.48$ could be a disturbed ecosystem. The higher value suggests a more complex ecosystem where many species can coexist. The lower value suggests a simpler ecosystem where fewer species can coexist.

Model sentence: The woodland with the higher Simpson's Diversity Index is an area that would be better for conservation. The woodland with the lower Simpson's Diversity Index is an area that would not be as good for conservation.

Hints for success: You are not required to memorize the Simpson's Diversity Index formula, but you must know the meaning of the symbols. You also need to know how the Index is significant for ecological studies: you might use it in a practical investigation, for example.

Subject vocabulary

ecosystem a community of organisms that depend on each other and the environment they live in

community a group of different species living together in a common habitat

niche where and how a species lives

Glossary

coexist live together

ancient very old

agricultural relating to farming

management actively looking after

conservation the preservation and protection of nature

Synonyms

stable.................. unchanging

significant............. important

Model sentence: Biome can be defined as a collection of ecosystems sharing similar climatic conditions.

Examples of biomes include tundra, tropical rainforest, and desert.

Model sentence: Biome distribution depends on levels of sunlight, temperature, and rainfall.

Tropical rainforest

Distribution

Tropical rainforests are found in areas with high levels of rainfall and sunlight, with warm temperatures throughout the year. Rainfall is on average over 2500 mm yr^{-1}. Tropical rainforests are found between the tropics of Cancer and Capricorn.

Structure

Tropical rainforests have a complex structure with a number of layers from ground level to canopy. They can have trees up to 50 m in height and lower layers of shrubs and vines. The thick canopy means that only 1 per cent of sunlight may reach the floor, which means the shrub layer is often sparse.

Productivity

Productivity in tropical rainforests is very high. This is because of the high levels of rainfall and sunlight, and year-round warm temperatures.

Desert

Distribution

Desert is found in areas of very low rainfall, strong sunlight, and temperatures that vary from very hot in the daytime to cold at night. Rainfall is under 250 mm yr^{-1}. Deserts are found in bands at latitudes of approximately 15–30°N and S of the equator.

Structure

Vegetation is scarce and there are no tall trees. Many of the plants, such as cacti, are adapted to dry or desert conditions. The soil has low water-holding capacity and low fertility. The soil is easily eroded by the wind. Animals are adapted to desert conditions and may spend the daytime in burrows.

Productivity

Productivity in deserts is very low due to lack of water and hot daytime conditions.

Tundra

Distribution

Tundra is found in areas with low temperatures throughout most of the year. Other conditions in tundra are low rainfall, seasonal sunlight, and short day length. They are found in high latitudes next to areas of ice.

Structure

Tundra has a simple structure. The vegetation of tundra is low **scrub** and grasses. Vegetation forms a single layer and there are no tall trees.

Productivity

Productivity in tundra is low. This is because tundra has frozen **permafrost** and soil that limits productivity. Low temperatures and low rainfall, with much water present as ice, also limits productivity. Short day length year-round also leads to low productivity, although productivity can be higher for short periods in the summer.

> **Hints for success:** As well as the three biomes covered here, you need to be able to write about one other biome. This biome may be from your local area. An example of another biome is temperate forest. The distribution of temperate forest is between 40° and 60°N of the equator, where rainfall is sufficient to establish forest (500–1500 mm yr^{-1}) rather than grassland. The structure of temperate forest is less complex than rainforest, and is often dominated by one species. There is some layering of forest, although tallest trees grow to no more than around 30 m high. The lower and less dense canopy than found in rainforest means that more light reaches the forest floor, leading to the growth of a rich shrub layer (for example brambles, bracken and ferns). The productivity of temperate forest is moderate: lower than rainforest, but higher than desert and tundra. Medium productivity is due to varying temperatures and light intensity, which vary with the seasons.

2.5.1 Explain the role of producers, consumers, and decomposers in the ecosystem

Producers

Model sentence: Producers can be defined as organisms that can make their own food.

Producers can make their own food using photosynthesis to produce glucose from water and carbon dioxide. Plants, algae, and some bacteria are all producers.

Producers support all ecosystems by constant input of energy and new biomass.

Consumers

Model sentence: Consumers can be defined as organisms that eat other organisms to obtain their food and energy.

Consumers do not contain chlorophyll and so cannot photosynthesize to make their own food.

Consumers pass energy and biomass through a food chain, from producers through to the top carnivores.

Decomposers

Model sentence: Decomposers can be defined as organisms that feed on dead organisms.

Decomposers are bacteria and fungi.

Decomposers are the basis of a food chain and feed at each trophic level. Decomposers also help make humus and improve the ability of soil to keep nutrients. They release nutrients to become ready for absorption by producers. Decomposers are essential for cycling matter in ecosystems. Matter that is cycled by decomposers in ecosystems includes elements such as carbon and nitrogen.

2.5.2 Describe photosynthesis and respiration in terms of inputs, outputs, and energy transformations

Photosynthesis

Inputs

The **inputs** of **photosynthesis** are sunlight energy, carbon dioxide, and water.

Outputs

The outputs of photosynthesis are glucose and oxygen.

Transformations

The energy transformation is from light energy into stored chemical energy (the bonds that link the carbon, hydrogen, and oxygen atoms), and thus the chemical energy is stored in **organic** matter. **Chlorophyll** is needed to capture certain visible wavelengths of sunlight energy and to allow this energy to be transformed into chemical energy.

Respiration

Inputs

The inputs of **respiration** are organic matter and oxygen.

Outputs

The outputs of respiration are carbon dioxide, water, and heat.

Transformations

The energy transformation is from stored chemical energy into **kinetic** energy and heat. Energy is released in a form available for use by living organisms, but much is also eventually lost as heat because of the **second law of thermodynamics**.

> **Hints for success:** Photosynthesis involves the transformation of light energy into the chemical energy of organic matter. Respiration is the transformation of chemical energy into kinetic energy with, ultimately, heat lost from the system.

> **Hints for success:** All organisms respire: bacteria, algae, plants, fungi, and animals.

2.5.3 Describe and explain the transfer and transformation of energy as it flows through an ecosystem

Subject vocabulary

transfer a process involving a change in location within the system but no change in state

transformation a process that leads to the formation of new products or new states

ecosystem a community of organisms that depend on each other and the environment they live in

producer an organism that makes its own food; for example, a plant that can photosynthesize

biomass living matter, made from biological molecules

photosynthesis a process that captures sunlight energy and transforms it into the chemical bonds of glucose molecules; carbon dioxide, water and light are transformed into glucose and oxygen

respiration a chemical process occurring in all cells that transforms the energy in glucose molecules into ATP, releasing energy in the process; glucose is transformed in the presence of oxygen into carbon dioxide and water

trophic level the position that an organism, or group of organisms, occupies in a food chain

consumer an organism that eats other organisms to obtain its food

food chain a simple diagram that shows feeding relationships in an ecosystem

ecological efficiency the percentage of energy transferred from one trophic level to the next

Glossary

wavelength the distance between one peak or crest of a wave of light and the next

evaporate turn from liquid into gas

reflected the return of light from a surface without it being absorbed

The flow of energy into producers

Transfers

Model sentence: **Energy enters the ecosystem as sunlight energy, some of which is captured by producers.**

A lot of the sunlight energy is not absorbed by the producers because it is the wrong **wavelength**. Other energy is not absorbed because it is used to **evaporate** water or is **reflected** off the producer. Other sunlight energy does not hit **chloroplasts** and so is **transmitted** through the leaf.

Transformations

The producers transform sunlight energy into chemical energy as **biomass**. Little of the available sunlight energy is **converted** into new biomass because producers are **inefficient** at converting sunlight energy into stored chemical energy through the process of **photosynthesis**. Only 1 per cent of the sunlight reaching the producer is turned into new biomass. Some of the energy captured that becomes new biomass is lost through **respiration**; some of it becomes the body of the producer (e.g. wood).

The flow of energy from producers to consumers

Transfers

Model sentence: **Energy is transferred between trophic levels as biomass by consumers.**

Consumers eat producers and then, further on in the **food chain**, consumers eat consumers.

Transformations

In a food chain, there is a loss of chemical energy from one trophic level to another through respiration and heat loss.

Model sentence: **All energy ultimately leaves the ecosystem as heat energy.**

Ecological efficiency can be defined as the percentage of energy transferred from one trophic level to the next. Ecological efficiency is low, with an average of one-tenth of the energy available to one trophic level becoming available to the next trophic level. Energy is lost through respiration, **inedible parts**, and faeces. All energy is ultimately lost as heat through the inefficient energy conversions of respiration. This heat is **re-radiated** to the atmosphere. Overall there is a conversion of light energy to heat energy by an ecosystem.

Diagram showing energy flow through an ecosystem

The following diagram shows the movement of energy flow through an ecosystem. Such energy-flow diagrams show the **productivity** of the different trophic levels.

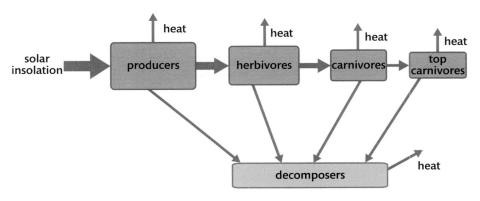

Figure 2.18 *An energy-flow diagram showing the flow of energy through an ecosystem.*

Boxes show **storages** of energy. Storages of energy are measured as the amount of energy or biomass in a specific area. The boxes are proportional in size to the amount of biomass present at each trophic level. The **flows** of energy are shown as arrows. Arrows also represent flows of productivity. Flows are measured as rates, for example J m^{-2} day^{-1}. Arrows vary in width and are proportional to the amount of energy being transferred.

Hints for success: You need to understand the difference between storages and flows of energy. Storages of energy are shown as boxes that represent the trophic level. Storages are measured as the amount of energy or biomass per unit area. Flows of energy or productivity are given as rates, for example J m^{-2} day^{-1}.

In food chains, energy flows from producer to consumer, and then from consumer to consumer. Transfer processes pass on the energy without a change in state, whereas transformation processes pass on the energy with a change in state (for example chemical energy into heat energy).

2.5.4 Describe and explain the transfer and transformation of materials as they cycle within an ecosystem

Opening sentence:

In this answer I will describe and explain how materials such as carbon, nitrogen, and water are **cycled** within an ecosystem.

These cycles involve **transfer** and **transformation** processes. The cycles involve the conversion of **organic** and **inorganic storage**.

Carbon cycle

The following diagram shows the carbon cycle:

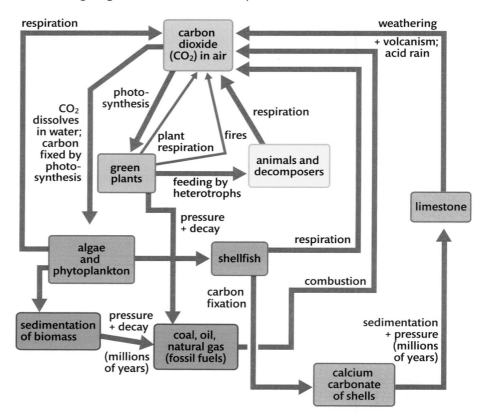

Figure 2.19 *The carbon cycle.*

Transfers in the carbon cycle

One example of a transfer process in the carbon cycle is a **herbivore** feeding on a **producer**. Another example is a **carnivore** feeding on a herbivore. Further examples of transfer processes in the carbon cycle are **decomposers** feeding on dead organic matter, and carbon dioxide from the atmosphere dissolving in rainwater and oceans.

Transformations in the carbon cycle

The process of photosynthesis converts inorganic materials into organic matter in the carbon cycle. Photosynthesis transforms carbon dioxide and water into glucose using sunlight energy trapped by chlorophyll.

The process of respiration converts organic storage into inorganic matter in the carbon cycle. Respiration transforms organic matter such as glucose into carbon dioxide and water.

Another transformation processes in the carbon cycle is **combustion**. Combustion transforms biomass into carbon dioxide and water. Biomineralization is also a transformation process. Biomineralization transforms carbon dioxide into calcium carbonate in shellfish and coral. The creation of fossil fuels is also a transformation process. Fossil fuels are made from the sedimentation of organic matter, incomplete decay, and pressure.

Nitrogen cycle

The following diagram shows the nitrogen cycle:

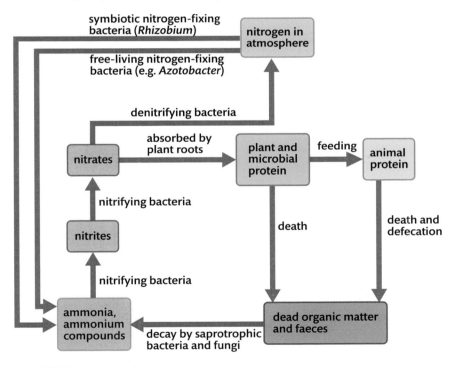

Figure 2.20 *The nitrogen cycle.*

Transfers in the nitrogen cycle

One example of a transfer process in the nitrogen cycle is a herbivore feeding on a producer. Another example is a carnivore feeding on a herbivore. Further examples of transfer processes in the nitrogen cycle are decomposers feeding on dead organic matter, and plants absorbing nitrates through their roots.

Subject vocabulary

photosynthesis a process that captures sunlight energy and transforms it into the chemical bonds of glucose molecules; carbon dioxide, water, and light are transformed into glucose and oxygen

respiration a chemical process occurring in all cells that transforms the energy in glucose molecules into ATP, releasing energy in the process; glucose is transformed in the presence of oxygen into carbon dioxide and water

biomass living matter, made from biological molecules

biomineralization the change of carbon dioxide into calcium carbonate in shellfish and coral

Glossary

chlorophyll a green-coloured molecule that can absorb sunlight energy

fossil fuel a natural fuel such as coal or gas formed from the remains of organisms

Synonyms

combustion .... burning

transformation a process that leads to the formation of new products or new states

nitrogen-fixation change of nitrogen gas in the atmosphere into ammonium ions

nitrification change of ammonium ions into nitrite and then nitrate

denitrification change of nitrates into nitrogen

deamination breaking down amino acids to form ammonia and other waste products

storage where something is kept

precipitation water travelling from clouds to the ground as rain

transfer a process involving a change in location within the system but no change in state

run-off water moves overland into rivers, lakes and seas

evaporation the change of liquid into gas

condensation the process of changing a gas into a liquid

transpiration water evaporating from a leaf

Transformations in the nitrogen cycle

The **transformation** processes in the nitrogen **cycle** involve four different types of bacteria. **Nitrogen-fixing** bacteria transform nitrogen gas in the atmosphere into ammonium ions. Nitrogen-fixing bacteria include *Azotobacter* bacteria that live in the soil and *Rhizobium* bacteria that live in plant **root nodules**. **Nitrifying** bacteria transform ammonium ions into nitrite and then nitrate. **Denitrifying** bacteria transform nitrates into nitrogen. Decomposers break down organic nitrogen into ammonia. The breakdown of organic nitrogen into ammonia is called **deamination**.

Producers convert **inorganic** materials into **organic** matter in the nitrogen cycle. Producers use nitrogen from nitrates to make amino acids and then protein.

Decomposers convert organic **storage** into inorganic matter in the nitrogen cycle. Decomposers transform protein and amino acids into ammonium ions.

Water cycle

The following diagram shows the water cycle:

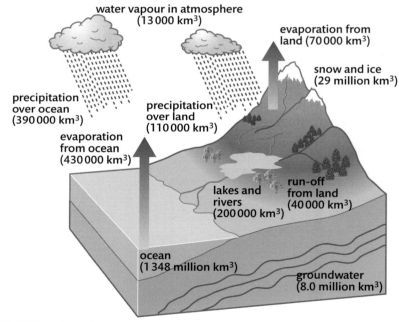

Figure 2.21 *The water cycle.*

Transfers in the water cycle

Precipitation is a **transfer** process where water falls from clouds to the ground as rain. **Run-off** is a transfer process where water flows overland into rivers, lakes, and seas. Another transfer process in the water cycle is the absorption of water by plants through their roots.

Transformations in the water cycle

Evaporation is a transformation process where water moves from the land, rivers, and oceans into the atmosphere. **Condensation** is a transformation process where water condenses from the atmosphere into clouds. **Transpiration** is a transformation process where water moves from leaves into the atmosphere.

2.5.5 Define the terms *gross productivity, net productivity, primary productivity*, and *secondary productivity*

Model sentence: A definition of gross productivity is the total gain in biomass in a specific area in a specific amount of time.

Gain in biomass could be through photosynthesis in producers or through absorption in consumers.

Model sentence: A definition of net productivity is the gain in biomass once energy from respiration has been removed. Net productivity is measured in a specific area in a specific amount of time.

Model sentence: A definition of primary productivity is the biomass gained by producers in a specific area in a specific amount of time.

Primary productivity involves the transformation of solar energy into stored chemical energy.

Model sentence: A definition of secondary productivity is the biomass gained by consumers through feeding and absorption. Secondary productivity is measured in units of mass in a specific area in a specific amount of time.

All definitions of productivity could also use energy as a measure of productivity, as well as biomass.

Hints for success: The term assimilation is sometimes used instead of secondary productivity.

Subject vocabulary

gross productivity the total gain in biomass in a specific area in a specific amount of time

biomass living matter, made from biological molecules

photosynthesis a process that captures sunlight energy and transforms it into the chemical bonds of glucose molecules; carbon dioxide, water, and light are transformed into glucose and oxygen

producer an organism that makes its own food; for example, a plant that can photosynthesize

consumer an organism that eats other organisms to obtain its food

net productivity the gain in biomass in a specific area in a specific amount of time once energy from respiration has been removed

respiration a chemical process occurring in all cells that transforms the energy in glucose molecules into ATP, releasing energy in the process; glucose is transformed in the presence of oxygen into carbon dioxide and water

primary productivity the biomass gained by producers in a specific area in a specific amount of time

transformation a process that leads to the formation of new products or new states

secondary productivity the biomass gained by consumers through feeding and absorption

absorption uptake of substances

Glossary

net productivity with energy from respiration removed from it

primary referring to the producer trophic level

secondary referring to consumer trophic levels

2.5.6 Define the terms and calculate the values of both *gross primary productivity* (GPP) and *net primary productivity* (NPP) from given data

Gross primary productivity

Gross primary productivity can be defined as the total gain by producers in **biomass** made through **photosynthesis**. **Gross primary productivity** is measured in a specific area in a specific amount of time.

Net primary productivity

Net primary productivity can be defined as the gain by **producers** in biomass once energy from **respiration** has been removed. **Net** primary productivity is measured in a specific area in a specific amount of time.

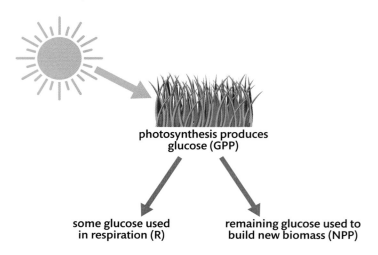

Figure 2.22 *The difference between gross primary productivity (GPP) and net primary productivity (NPP).*

How to calculate gross primary productivity (GPP) and net primary productivity (NPP)

The easiest way to measure gross primary productivity (GPP) and net primary productivity (NPP) is by using **aquatic** plants. To calculate GPP and NPP, measurements of photosynthesis and respiration need to be taken. Photosynthesis and respiration either produce or use oxygen. Measuring **dissolved oxygen** will therefore give a measurement of the amounts of photosynthesis and respiration in aquatic plants.

Net primary productivity can be calculated by measuring the increase in dissolved oxygen when aquatic plants are put in the light. In the light, both photosynthesis and respiration will be occurring but photosynthesis will be the bigger process, and therefore it produces more oxygen than the plant uses in respiration.

Gross primary productivity can be calculated using the equation: NPP = GPP − R, where R = respiratory loss.

Respiration can be calculated by measuring the decrease in dissolved oxygen when aquatic plants are put in the dark. In the dark, only respiration will occur and not photosynthesis. The equation can be rearranged to calculate GPP:

GPP = NPP + R

Example of how to calculate GPP and NPP from given data

Productivity was measured using an aquatic plant. The plant was put in light and dark conditions. Dissolved oxygen was measured before and after the plant was put in light and dark conditions. In this experiment gross primary productivity (GPP) and net primary productivity (NPP) were measured by using changes in dissolved oxygen in milligrams of oxygen per litre per hour. The results were:

Calculating NPP

Plant in the light:

Amount of dissolved oxygen at the start of the experiment = 10 mg of oxygen per litre

Amount of dissolved oxygen at the end of the experiment = 12 mg of oxygen per litre

Increase in dissolved oxygen = 2 mg of oxygen per litre

The increase in dissolved oxygen is a measure of NPP. The experiment lasted one hour and so the **NPP = 2 mg of oxygen per litre per hour**.

Calculating GPP

Plant in the dark:

Amount of dissolved oxygen at the start of the experiment = 10 mg of oxygen per litre

Amount of dissolved oxygen at the end of the experiment = 7 mg of oxygen per litre

Loss of dissolved oxygen = 3 mg of oxygen per litre per hour.

The loss of dissolved oxygen is a measure of respiration (R).

NPP = GPP − R, so GPP = NPP + R

Therefore **GPP = 2 + 3 = 5 mg of oxygen per litre per hour**.

Hints for success: The definitions of productivity must include units, i.e. the gain in biomass **per unit area per unit time**.

Gross secondary productivity

Gross secondary productivity can be defined as the total gain by **consumers** in **biomass** through **absorption**. **Gross secondary productivity** is measured in units of mass in a specific area in a specific amount of time.

Gross secondary productivity = food eaten − faecal loss

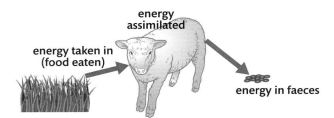

Figure 2.23 *Gross secondary productivity.*

Net secondary productivity

Net secondary productivity can be defined as the gain by consumers in biomass once energy from **respiration** has been removed. **Net** secondary productivity is measured in units of mass in a specific area in a specific amount of time.

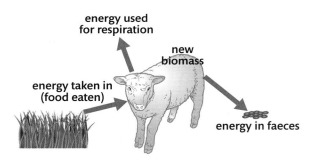

Figure 2.24 *Net secondary productivity.*

How to calculate gross secondary productivity (GSP) and net secondary productivity (NSP) from given data

The following table contains data collected from an experiment using stick insects:

	Start of experiment	End of experiment
Mass of leaves (g)	29.2	26.3
Mass of stick insect (g)	8.9	9.2
Mass of faeces (g)	0.0	0.5

A total of ten stick insects were used. They were fed privet leaves. The experiment lasted five days.

Net secondary productivity (NSP), respiration (R), and gross secondary productivity (GSP) are calculated from this data.

Calculating NSP

NSP can be calculated by measuring the increase in biomass in stick insects over a specific amount of time. The increase in biomass in stick insects (NSP) is equal to the mass of food eaten minus biomass lost through respiration and faeces.

In this experiment NSP = mass of stick insects at end of experiment – mass of stick insects at start of experiment

Over a five-day period: NSP = 9.2 – 8.9 = 0.3 g

Therefore, **NSP = 0.3/5 = 0.06 g per day**.

Calculating GSP

GSP can be calculated using the following equation: GSP = food eaten – faecal loss

Food eaten = mass of leaves at start of the experiment – mass of leaves at end of the experiment

Food eaten = 29.2 – 26.3 = 2.9 g

Also, faecal loss = mass of faeces at end of experiment = 0.5 g

Therefore, over a five-day period:

GSP = 2.9 – 0.5 = 2.4 g

Therefore, **GSP = 2.4/5 = 0.48 g per day**.

GSP represents the amount of food absorbed by the consumer.

Calculating respiration

Respiration (the loss of glucose as respiration breaks it down) can be calculated from the equation:

NSP = GSP – R, where R = respiratory loss.

The equation can be rearranged to calculate R: R = GSP – NSP

Therefore, **R = 0.48 – 0.06 = 0.42 g per day**.

2.6.1 Explain the concepts of limiting factors and carrying capacity in the context of population growth

Subject vocabulary

limiting factor factor that limits the distribution or numbers of a particular population

population a group of organisms of the same species living in the same area at the same time

competition the demand by two or more species for limited environmental resources

carrying capacity the maximum number of a species that can be maintained by an environment

Glossary

context situation in which something exists

exponentially increasingly rapid growth

barnacle a small marine animal that has a hard external shell, which attaches itself permanently to surfaces such as rocks

What are limiting factors?

Model sentence: Limiting factors can be defined as the factors that limit the distribution or numbers of a particular population.

Limiting factors restrict the growth of a population or prevent it from increasing further.

Limiting factors in this **context** include temperature, water, and nutrient availability. The main limiting climatic features are temperature and water availability. Limiting factors in plants include light, nutrients, water, carbon dioxide, and temperature. Limiting factors in animals include space, food, mates, and water.

Limiting factors and population growth

An S-shaped curve is produced when population growth is plotted against time. Here is a graph of population growth plotted against time:

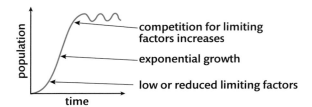

Figure 2.25 *An S population growth curve.*

The graph shows slow growth at first when the population is small. Early in the population growth curve there are few limiting factors and so the population can expand **exponentially**. **Competition** between the individuals of the population will increase as a population grows. Competition increases because individuals in the population are competing for the same limiting factors, such as resources (e.g. space on a rock for **barnacles** to attach to). Competition for limiting factors results in a lower rate of population increase later on in the curve.

What is carrying capacity?

Model sentence: Carrying capacity can be defined as the number of organisms in a population that an area or ecosystem can support sustainably over a long period of time.

Carrying capacity and population growth

The population eventually levels off when population growth is plotted against time. The population levels off when it reaches its carrying capacity. The population then **fluctuates** around a **set point** determined by the limiting factors. Changes in the limiting factors cause the population size to increase and decrease around the carrying capacity. Increases and decreases around the carrying capacity are controlled by **negative feedback** mechanisms.

The following graph shows the carrying capacity of a population:

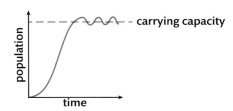

Figure 2.26 *An S population curve showing carrying capacity.*

Limiting factors are factors that limit the distribution or numbers of a particular population.

Carrying capacity is the maximum number of species that can be maintained by an environment.

Populations increase and decrease around a set point due to variations in limiting factors.

2.6.2 Describe and explain S and J population curves

S population curve

A diagram of an **S population curve**:

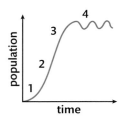

Figure 2.27 *An S population curve.*

The S population curve has four stages:

1. The **lag phase**, where **population** numbers are low leading to low birth rates.

2. The **exponential growth phase**, where the population grows at an increasingly rapid rate.

3. The **transitional phase**, when the population growth slows down considerably although continuing to grow.

4. The **stationary phase**, where the number of individuals **stabilizes** and population growth stabilizes (the graph 'flattens'). In the stationary phase the population **fluctuates** around a **set point** that represents the **carrying capacity**.

Changes in an S population curve

1. Population numbers are low in the lag phase because few individuals colonize a new area. Because numbers of individuals are low, birth rates are also low.

2. **Exponential growth** then occurs in the second stage because:

   - **limiting factors** are not restricting the growth of the population

   - there are plentiful resources such as light, space, food, and a lack of **competition** from other species.

   - There are favourable **abiotic components**, such as temperature and rainfall, and a lack of predators or disease.

   - both the numbers of individuals rapidly increases as does the rate of growth.

3. In the transitional phase, increase in number begins to slow as does the rate of growth. In addition, limiting factors begin to affect the population and restrict its growth. There is increased competition for resources because there are too many individuals in the population. An increase in predators attracted by the large population, and an increase in rate of disease and **mortality** due to increased numbers of individuals living in a small area, also cause a slowdown in growth.

4. In the stationary phase, limiting factors restrict the population to its carrying capacity (K). Changes in limiting factors such as predation, disease, and abiotic factors cause populations to increase and decrease around the carrying capacity.

J population curve

Here is a diagram of a **J population curve**:

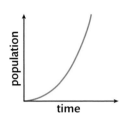

Figure 2.28 *A J population curve.*

The J population curve only shows exponential growth. Growth is slow to begin with but then becomes increasingly rapid. Growth in population does not slow down as the population increases.

Changes in a J population curve

The population is not controlled by limiting factors in the exponential growth phase. The population will suddenly decrease after reaching its peak value. Populations showing J-shaped curves are controlled by abiotic but not **biotic components**. Abiotic components cause the sudden decrease in the population. The sudden decrease in the population is called a **population crash**. The sudden decrease is shown in the following diagram:

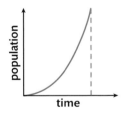

Figure 2.29 *A J population curve showing a population crash (dotted line).*

Hints for success: You need to be able to sketch and describe population curves. You also need to be able to construct and interpret population curves from given data.

2.6.3 Describe the role of density-dependent and density-independent factors, and internal and external factors, in the regulation of populations

Subject vocabulary

density-dependent factor limiting factors that are related to population density

density-independent factor factors that are non-living and do not depend on the size of the population

limiting factor factor that limits the distribution or numbers of a particular population

population density the number of individuals of a species in a specific area

biotic component a living, biological part in an ecosystem

negative feedback feedback that works against any change away from balance and stability

abiotic component a non-living part in an ecosystem

competition the demand by two or more species for limited environmental resources

parasitism interaction where one organism gets its food at the expense of another organism

predator–prey interactions how predator/prey populations affect each other

Synonyms

regulation............. control

Glossary

stability when there is no overall change in a system

mortality the occurrence of death in a population

Opening sentence:

In this answer I will describe the role of **density-dependent** and **density-independent factors** in **regulating** populations.

Density-dependent factors can be defined as **limiting factors** that depend on – are related to – **population density**. They are **biotic components** that limit population growth. Density-dependent factors lower the birth rate or raise the death rate as a population grows in size. Density-dependent factors operate as **negative feedback** mechanisms leading to **stability** or regulation of the population.

Density-independent factors can be defined as factors that do not depend on the size of the population. Density-independent factors are **abiotic components**.

Density-dependent factors

Some limiting factors are related to population density. Examples are **competition** for resources, space, disease, **parasitism**, and predation. As a population grows in size, the availability of food for each individual decreases and this can lead to a reduced birth rate and an increased death rate. Predators may be attracted to areas of high prey population density and so the **mortality** rate may increase. Disease spreads more easily in dense populations. Other density-dependent factors include the size of the breeding population and size of territory. The larger the population size, and the larger the territory, the greater the potential chance that a species has for survival.

Model sentence: Density-dependent factors operate as negative feedback mechanisms regulating the population and leading to stability.

Predator–prey relationships are a good example of density-dependent control. The following figure shows how **predator–prey interactions** regulate populations through negative feedback:

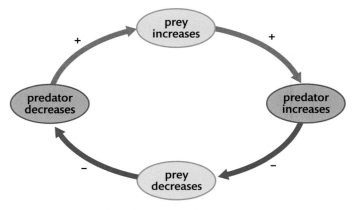

Figure 2.30 *Predator–prey relationships show negative feedback.*

When predators are low in number, the prey population begins to increase in size. As the availability of prey increases, predator numbers increase following a **time-lag**. As the number of predators increases, the population size of the prey begins to decrease. With fewer prey, the number of predators decreases. With fewer predators the number of prey may begin to increase again and the cycle continues. This can be seen in the variations of the lemming and snowy owl populations in the northern circumpolar regions, shown in the figure below:

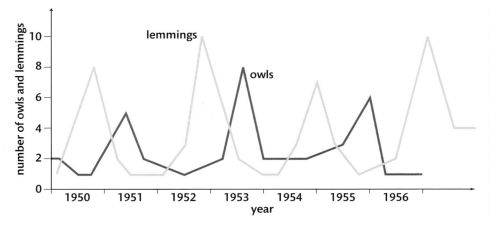

Figure 2.31 *Variations in the populations of lemmings and snowy owls.*

Density-dependent factors include **internal** and **external** factors. Internal factors include density-dependent **fertility** or size of breeding territory. External factors include predation and disease.

Density-independent factors

Model sentence: Density-independent factors are generally abiotic.

The most important ones are extremes of weather, such as drought, fire, hurricanes, and long-term climate change. Others include geophysical events, such as volcanic eruptions and tsunamis. Their impact is to increase the death rate and reduce the birth rate, especially of smaller individuals. The response depends on the frequency and **severity** of the event.

2.6.4 Describe the principles associated with survivorship curves including *K*- and *r*-strategists

Opening sentence:

In this answer I will describe the **principles associated** with **survivorship curves**

Model sentence: Survivorship curves plot the number of offspring surviving in a population over time.

Survivorship curves show changes in survivorship over the **lifespan** of the species. In these graphs, time is shown as a percentage of the total lifespan on the x-axis. Factors that affect survivorship include **competition** for resources, **predator–prey interactions**, and the amount of **parental care**. Two broad groups of species can be identified from survivorship curve graphs: *K*- and *r*-strategists.

K-strategists

Model sentence: *K*-strategists can be defined as species that usually concentrate their reproductive investment in a small number of offspring.

By investing in a small number of offspring they increase the survival rate of offspring and adapt them for living in long-term **climax communities**.

The letter '*K*' stands for **carrying capacity**. These species are called *K*-strategists because their population growth is determined by **limiting factors** and then eventually reaches a carrying capacity. *K*-strategists are controlled by **density-dependent factors**. Examples of *K*-strategists include large mammals such as rhino, whales, and humans.

r-strategists

Model sentence: *r*-strategists can be defined as species that tend to spread their reproductive investment among a large number of offspring.

By investing in a large number of offspring they ensure that offspring are well adapted to colonize new **habitats** rapidly and make **opportunistic** use of short-lived resources.

The letter '*r*' stands for reproduction. These species are called *r*-strategists because they have high reproductive rates. *r*-strategists are controlled by **density-independent factors**. Examples of *r*-strategists include cockroaches, mice, and mosquitoes.

Comparing K- and r-strategists

K-strategist	r-strategist
Larger in size	Smaller in size
Large amount of care from parents	Little or no care from parents
Few offspring	Large number of offspring
Slow development	Rapid growth and development
Longer lifespan	Short lifespan
S population growth curve	J population growth curve
Specialist species	Generalist species

K- and r-strategists represent idealized categories and many organisms occupy a place on the **continuum** between them.

Survivorship curves

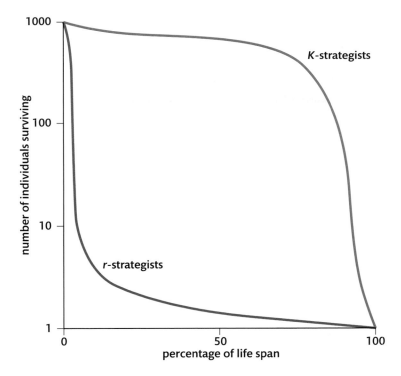

Figure 2.32 *Graph showing survivorship curves for K- and r-strategists.*

Survivorship curves for r-strategists show most individuals dying at a young age but that those surviving are likely to survive for a long time. Survivorship curves for K-strategists show almost all individuals surviving for their potential life span and then dying almost at the same time.

Synonyms

associated .... linked

surviving .... living

Glossary

continuum a continuous sequence in which elements next to each other are very similar but where the extremes are quite different

logarithmic scale axis on a graph where the increase is not linear but 1, 10, 100, etc.

Hints for success: You should be able to interpret the features of survivorship curves, including logarithmic scales. The y-axis in survivorship graphs shows the number of survivors and is shown as a logarithmic scale. A logarithmic scale is one that follows a sequence 1, 10, 100, and so on. A logarithmic scale allows very large values to be shown on the same graph as very small values.

2.6.5 Describe the concept and processes of succession in a named habitat

Subject vocabulary

succession the orderly process of change over time in a community

habitat the place where a species lives

community a group of different species living together in a common habitat

environment the external surroundings that act on an organism, population, or community and influence its survival and development

competition the demand by two or more species for limited environmental resources

sere the whole sequence of communities in a succession

seral stage the term for each stage of a succession

pioneer community the first stage of an ecological succession that contains species able to live in difficult conditions

climax community the final stage of a succession that is more or less stable/balanced

equilibrium a state of balance among the parts of a system

Synonyms

orderly................ organized/ logical

Glossary

hardy able to endure difficult conditions

> ## Opening sentence:

In this answer I will describe the processes of **succession** in temperate forest **habitats**.

What is succession?

A definition of succession is the **orderly** process of change over time in a **community**. Changes in the community of organisms cause changes in the **environment** they live in. These changes in the environment allow another community to become established and replace the one before through **competition**.

Model sentence: The whole sequence of communities in a succession is called a sere.

Each stage of a succession is called a **seral stage**. The first seral stage of a succession is called the **pioneer community**. A pioneer community can be defined as the first stage of an ecological succession that contains **hardy** species able to withstand difficult conditions. The later communities in a sere are more complex than those that appear earlier. The final seral stage of a succession is called the **climax community**. A climax community can be defined as the final stage of a succession, which is more or less stable and is in **equilibrium**.

The following table shows the differences between pioneer and climax communities:

Pioneer community	Climax community
The first seral stage of a succession	The final seral stage of a succession
r-strategists are abundant	*K*-strategists are abundant
Simple in structure with low diversity	Complex in structure with high diversity
Species can tolerate harsh conditions such as strong light and low nutrient levels	Characteristics of climax community are determined by climate and soil
e.g. community of lichens covering bare rock	e.g. community of trees and shrubs

Example of a succession in a named habitat

Model sentence: I will use the succession from bare rock to climax temperate forest community as my example.

Model sentence: Succession happens when species change the habitat they have colonized and make it more suitable for new species.

In this example, **lichens** and **mosses** are pioneer species. Very few species can live on bare rock as it contains little water and has few available nutrients. Lichens can **photosynthesize** and are effective at absorbing water. Lichens therefore do not need soil to survive and are excellent pioneers. Once established, lichens and mosses trap particles blown by the wind. When the lichens and mosses die and **decompose** they form a soil in which grasses can **germinate**. The growth of pioneers helps to **weather** parent rock, adding still further to the soil.

Model sentence: Grasses and ferns that grow in thin soil can now colonize the area.

These new species are better competitors than the **pioneer species**. Grasses grow taller than mosses and lichen, and so get more light for photosynthesis. Grass roots trap soil and stop **erosion**. Grasses have a larger photosynthetic area and so can grow faster.

Model sentence: The next stage involves the growth of herbaceous plants.

Herbaceous plants include dandelions and goose-grass, which need more soil to grow but which outcompete the grasses. These herbaceous plants have wind-**dispersed** seeds and rapid growth, and so become established before larger plants arrive.

Model sentence: Shrubs then appear, such as bramble, gorse, and rhododendron.

Shrubs are larger plants than the ones in earlier seral stages. The larger plants can grow in good soil and are better competitors than the slower-growing plants of the earlier seral stages.

Model sentence: The final stage of a succession is the climax community.

Here, trees that have grown produce too much shade for the shrubs. The shrubs are replaced by **shade-tolerant** forest floor species (species that can survive in shady conditions). The amount of organic matter increases as succession progresses because as pioneer and **subsequent** species die out, their remains contribute to a build-up of **litter** from the **biomass**. Soil organisms move in and break down litter, leading to a build-up of **organic matter** in the soil, making it easier for other species to colonize. Soil also traps water and so increasing amounts of moisture are available to plants in the later stages of the succession.

Glossary

colonize organisms becoming established in a new environment

lichen an organism that is part fungi and part algae; it is often found spreading over stone/tree surfaces

moss a small green plant that grows on wet soil/trees/rocks

decompose the decay and breakdown of organic matter

germinate when a seed begins to grow and put out roots and a stalk

weather/weathering to change through the long-term action of sun, rain, and wind

erosion gradual reduction/destruction

herbaceous plants plants that lack a permanent woody stem

dispersed spread

shrub a woody plant smaller than a tree

shade tolerant able to exist in the shade

litter dead leaves and plants

Subject vocabulary

photosynthesis a process that captures sunlight energy and transforms it into the chemical bonds of glucose molecules; carbon dioxide, water and light are transformed into glucose and oxygen

pioneer species species that are able to live in difficult conditions and are the first to appear in an ecological succession

biomass living matter, made from biological molecules

organic matter biological material in the process of decaying or decomposing

Synonyms

subsequent........... later

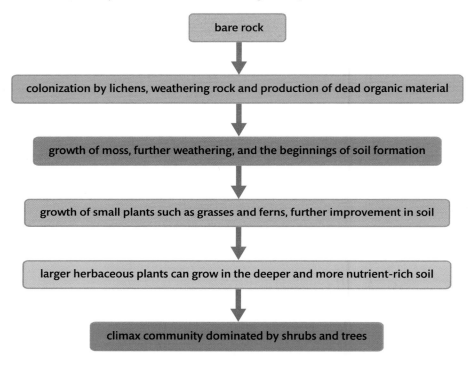

Distinguish between succession and zonation

The concept of **succession** must be carefully distinguished from the concept of **zonation**.

Succession

Model sentence: Succession can be defined as the orderly process of change over time in a community.

Changes in the community of organisms cause changes in the **environment** they live in. These changes in the environment allow another community to become established and replace the one before through **competition**.

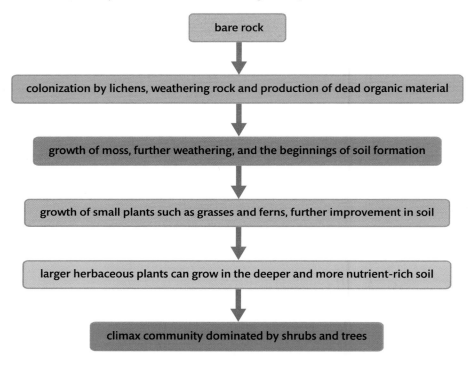

Figure 2.33 *An example of succession: the development of forest from bare rock.*

Zonation

Model sentence: Zonation can be defined as the arrangement of ecosystems into bands of different communities. The bands of different communities are formed in response to change over distance in an environmental factor.

For example, **rocky shores** can be divided into **zones** from lower to upper shore. On a rocky shore each zone can be defined by the spatial patterns of animals and plants. Seaweeds in particular show distinct zonation patterns. Seaweed species that are more resilient to water loss are found on the upper shore, such as channel wrack. Seaweed that is less resilient to water loss, such as kelp, is found on the lower shore where it is not out of water for long.

Model sentence: The main biomes show zonation in relation to latitude and climate.

Plant communities may also display zonation with altitude on a mountain. Plant zonation in response to different **altitudes** on a mountain is shown in the following figure:

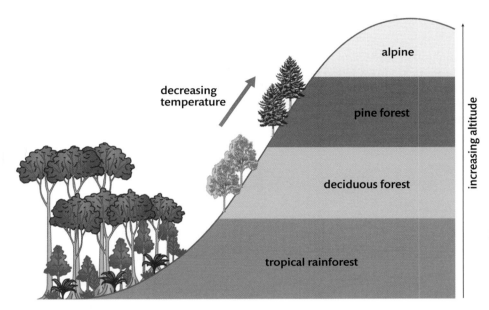

Figure 2.34 *Zonation up a mountain.*

Comparing succession and zonation

Succession refers to changes over time, whereas zonation refers to spatial patterns. An example of succession is the change over time in a forest community from a pioneer community of lichens and mosses to a climax community of mature trees and shrubs. An example of zonation is the arrangement of communities in bands on a mountain from tropical rainforest at the bottom to alpine communities at the top.

> **Hints for success:** You need to be able to refer to named examples of organisms from a pioneer community, seral stages, and climax community. You also need to be able to distinguish between the concept of succession and the concept of zonation. Succession occurs over time, whereas zonation refers to a spatial pattern.

Subject vocabulary

biome a collection of ecosystems sharing similar climatic conditions

latitude the distance north or south of the Earth's equator

climate temperature, air pressure, humidity, rainfall, sunshine, cloudiness, and winds

pioneer community the first stage of an ecological succession that contains species able to live in difficult conditions

climax community the final stage of a succession that is more or less stable/balanced

Synonyms

altitude .... height

Glossary

spatial relating to position

lichen a plant that spreads over stone/tree surfaces

moss a small green plant that grows on wet soil/trees/rocks

shrub a woody plant smaller than a tree

2.6.6 Explain the changes in energy flow, gross and net productivity, diversity and mineral cycling in different stages of succession

❝ Opening sentence:

In this answer I will explain the changes in energy flow, **gross** and **net productivity**, diversity and mineral cycling in different stages of **succession**.

A definition of succession is the orderly process of change over time in a **community**. Changes in the community of organisms cause changes in the **environment** they live in. These changes in the environment allow another community to become established and replace the one before through **competition**.

Changes in energy flow, gross productivity and net productivity

Model sentence: In early stages of a succession, the gross productivity is low because of the low density of producers.

Density of producers in the early stages of succession is low because of the lack of soil, water, and nutrients. In the early stages of a succession, the **proportion** of energy lost through community **respiration** is relatively low and so net productivity is high. When net productivity is high, the ecosystem is growing and **biomass** is **accumulating**.

In later stages of a succession, the gross productivity will be high in a **climax community** as there is an increased **consumer** community. The gross productivity is balanced by respiration in later stages of a succession, and so the net productivity will approach zero: the ratio of production to respiration therefore approaches one. The ratio of production to respiration is called the **production:respiration (P:R) ratio**. Where P:R is greater than 1, **biomass** accumulates; where P:R is less than 1, biomass is reduced. Where P:R = 1, a steady-state community results.

Changes in diversity

Model sentence: Early in the succession there is low biomass and few niches.

The plant community changes through each **seral stage**, leading to larger plants and greater complexity. As the plant community grows and complexity increases, the number of niches increases. As the number of niches increases, the **food webs** become more complex and both **habitat diversity** and **species diversity** increase.

Changes in mineral cycling

Model sentence: Mineral cycling forms an open system at early stages of succession. Elements such as carbon and nitrogen are introduced from the surrounding area to the system and can also leave the system.

Later in the succession, mineral cycling forms a **closed system**. Elements such as carbon and nitrogen remain and cycle within the system. Minerals pass from the soil into living biomass. Minerals return to the soil when organisms die and decay.

Summary

The following table summarizes differences in productivity, diversity, and mineral cycling between early and late stages of succession:

	Pioneer community	Climax community
GPP	low	high
NPP	high	low
Total biomass	low	high
Niches	few	many
Species richness	low	high
Diversity	low	high
Organic matter	small	large
Soil depth	shallow	deep
Minerals	external	internal
Mineral cycles	open system	closed system
Mineral conservation	poor	good
Role of detritus	small	large

Figure 2.35 *Succession on a shingle ridge in Devon, UK. The community changes from a pioneer community of lichens and mosses through to a climax woodland community.*

Subject vocabulary

species diversity a measurement of the number of different species in a specific area and their number/amount compared to each other

open system a system that exchanges both matter and energy with its surroundings

closed system a system that exchanges energy but not matter with its surroundings

gross primary productivity (GPP) the total gain by producers in biomass made through photosynthesis in a specific area in a specific amount of time

net primary productivity (NPP) the gain by producers in biomass once energy from respiration has been removed in a specific area in a specific amount of time

species richness the number of species in a sample or area

organic matter biological material in the process of decaying or decomposing

Glossary

in proportion (to) the correct relationship according to size, shape, or position

accumulating building up or increasing in number

detritus waste

2.6.7 Describe factors affecting the nature of climax communities

Opening sentence:

In this answer I will describe factors affecting the nature of **climax communities** such as soil, climate and human disturbance.

Ecosystems in the later stages of **succession** are likely to be more stable because **food webs** are more complex. Food webs are more complex because there are more **niches** and species **diversity** is high. This means that a species can turn to alternative food sources if one food source is reduced. By late succession, large amounts of organic matter are available to provide a good source of nutrients. Nutrient cycles are **closed systems** and self-sustaining, and so are not dependent on external influences. Closed nutrient cycles also contribute to **stability**.

Factor 1: Soil

Soils less rich in nutrients cannot support a climax community with high **biomass** and diversity. In Africa, tropical savannah grasslands grow in areas poor in soil nutrients rather than forests.

Factor 2: Climate

Climate also affects the nature of climax communities. Rainforests are an example of climax communities with high **habitat diversity**, **species diversity**, and biomass. This is because rainforests are found near the equator where the climate is warm, there is significant rainfall, and there are high levels of sunlight throughout the year. Where conditions are cold with low levels of sunlight and low rainfall, or where water is locked away as ice, **productivity** is low. Tundra is an example of climax communities in cold areas with low sunlight for most of the year; during a brief summer, however, productivity can be quite high. Tundra also has low amounts of available water.

Factor 3: Human disturbance

Human factors can affect the process of succession through disturbance. The interference stops the process of succession so that the climax community is not reached. Interrupted succession is known as **plagioclimax**. An example is the effect of footpath erosion caused by continued trampling by feet. Human activity can affect the climax community through agriculture, hunting, clearance, burning, and grazing.

The following photo shows human disturbance in the Amazon rainforest leading to a plagioclimax:

Figure 2.36 *Burning and deforestation of the Amazon forest to make grazing land.*

Burning and deforestation of the Amazon forest leads to loss of large areas of rainforest.

The nature of climax communities can be affected by different factors:

Factor 1: Soil
Soils rich in nutrients can support a climax community that is high in biomass and diversity, for example rainforest.

Factor 2: Climate
Where conditions are warm and sunny, with high rainfall, productivity can be high, leading to high biomass in the climax community.

Factor 3: Human disturbance
Continued burning and clearance leads to the establishment of grasslands. The establishment of grasslands prevents succession from occurring.

2.7.1 Describe and evaluate methods for measuring changes in abiotic and biotic components of an ecosystem along an environmental gradient

" **Opening sentence:**

In this answer I will describe and evaluate methods for measuring changes in **abiotic** and **biotic components** of an ecosystem along an **environmental gradient**.

An environmental gradient can be defined as an area where two ecosystems meet or where an ecosystem ends. Examples of two ecosystems meeting to form an environmental gradient are beaches and lake shores. An example of an ecosystem suddenly ending to form an environmental gradient are the conditions found at forest edges.

Method 1: Quadrats

Both biotic and abiotic factors vary across environmental gradients. Abiotic factors can include temperature, wind speed, and light intensity. Biotic factors can be measured across environmental gradients using **quadrats**. Quadrats can be used to measure **percentage cover**, **population density**, and **percentage frequency**. Quadrats are suitable for measuring vegetation and **non-mobile** animals.

Model sentence: Different types of quadrats can be used:

- **Frame quadrats** are empty frames of known area, such as 1 m².

- **Grid quadrats** are frames divided into 100 small squares with each square representing one percent. This helps in calculating percentage cover.

- **Point quadrats** are made from a frame with ten holes, which is placed into the ground by a leg. A pin is dropped through each hole in turn and the species touched are recorded. The total number of pins touching each species is converted to percentage frequency data; for example, if a species touched six out of the ten pins it has 60 per cent frequency.

Model sentence: It is not appropriate to place quadrats at random along an environmental gradient because environmental variables change along the gradient and all parts of the gradient need to be sampled.

Method 2: Transects

A transect is used to ensure that all parts of the gradient are sampled. Using a transect is an example of **systematic sampling**. The simplest **transect** is a **line transect**. A line transect is made by placing a tape measure in the direction of the gradient. For example, on a beach this would be at 90° to the sea. All organisms touching the tape are recorded. Many line transects need to be taken to obtain valid **quantitative** data.

Larger samples can be taken by using a **belt transect**. This is a band of chosen width, usually between 0.5 and 1 m, placed along the gradient. The following figure shows a belt transect.

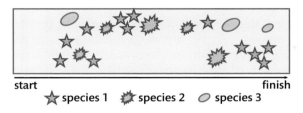

Figure 2.37 *A belt transect.*

If the whole transect is sampled it is called a **continuous transect**. If samples are taken at points of equal distance along the gradient it is called an **interrupted transect**. Horizontal distances are used if there is no visible vertical change in an interrupted transect, such as along a shingle ridge succession. If there is a climb or descent in an interrupted transect, then vertical distances are normally used, such as on a rocky shore.

Model sentence: Transects should be repeated so that data is reliable and quantitatively valid.

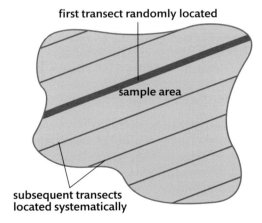

Figure 2.38 *The first transect is located randomly and then subsequent transects are located every 10 m along a line at right angles to the environmental gradient.*

Evaluation of methods

Using transects to sample an environmental gradient can give biased results if the sample is too small. It is also possible that using an interrupted transect results in some parts of the gradient not being recorded. Repeating transects and covering as large an area as possible will improve the validity of the data.

It is important that measurements from transects are carried out at the same time of day so that abiotic variables can be compared. Seasonal fluctuations mean that samples should be taken either as close together in time as possible, or throughout the whole year. Data-logging equipment allows continuous data to be recorded over long periods of time. Biotic measurements will also vary with time and so must be treated in the same way as the abiotic variables.

2.7.2 Describe and evaluate methods for measuring changes in abiotic and biotic components of an ecosystem due to a specific human activity

Model sentence: Human activities change abiotic and biotic components of ecosystems.

Human impacts include the release of **toxins** from mining activity, landfills, **eutrophication**, **effluent**, oil spills, and **overexploitation**. Changes in the ecosystem will depend on the human activity involved. Methods used for measuring abiotic and biotic components of an ecosystem must be appropriate to the human activity being studied.

Model sentence: I will use the removal of timber from a forest ecosystem as an example of a human activity.

Measurements of changes in components of an ecosystem can be made using two different methods: ground sampling and satellite images.

Method 1: Ground sampling

Both **pristine** and **logged** forest areas must be studied so comparisons can be made. **Stratified random sampling** is used in two areas because the pristine and logged forest areas are different in **habitat** quality. Sampling grids are established in both pristine and logged forest sites. Samples are collected from the grids using random sampling methods. For example, if the grid were 10 m by 10 m a random number generator could be used to choose random points to sample within the grid. Numbers generated between 0 and 1000 would provide the sample points; for example 580 would represent a point 5 m 80 cm along the bottom of the grid, and 740 a point 7 m 40 cm along the side of the grid opposite.

Abiotic and biotic measurements can be made at each sample point. Abiotic measurements can include wind, temperature, and light intensity. **Quadrats** can be used to sample biotic measurements. Biotic factors can include the species of plants and animals present, and the **population** size of selected indicator species. Mobile animals can be sampled using **capture-mark-release-recapture methods**.

Several samples are taken from each sampling grid. Sampling grids must be repeated in both pristine and logged forest areas so that data are reliable. At least five sampling grids from both pristine and logged forest are recommended.

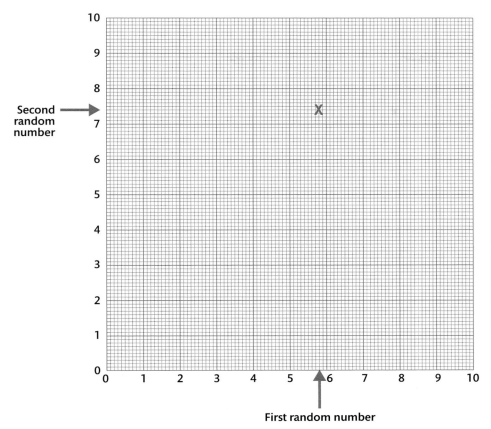

Figure 2.39 *Locating a sampling point (X) using random numbers. Numbers are generated from between 0 and 1000 using a random number generator. If the first number is 580 and the second number 740 then the sampling point is located 5 m 80 cm along the bottom of a grid, and 7 m 40 cm along the side of the grid.*

Evaluation of ground sampling

Abiotic and biotic components must be measured over a long period of time to take into account daily and seasonal variations so as to ensure data is valid. Repeating samples from both within and between sampling grids improves the reliability of the data.

Method 2: Satellite images

Satellites orbit the Earth and can be used to take photos of the Earth's surface. These images can show the effects of human disturbance on ecosystems.

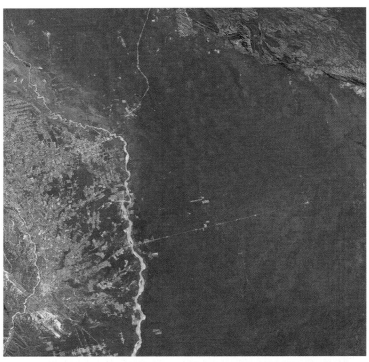

Figure 2.40 *These images show logging and the development of settlements and farming areas.*

Evaluation of satellite images

An advantage of satellite images is that they are very reliable, as they can cover a large area and monitor change over time. Another advantage is that the visible nature of the photos is useful for motivating action against logging. A disadvantage is that they can be expensive to obtain and may not be available for the area being studied. Another disadvantage is that although some biotic measurements can be taken, such as plant productivity, other biotic and abiotic components cannot be measured. Satellite images are best used in conjunction with ground studies so that the images can be matched with abiotic and biotic data from the ground.

Hints for success: Human activities can change abiotic and biotic components of an ecosystem. Human impacts can include toxins from mining activity, landfills, eutrophication, effluent, oil spills, and over-exploitation.

2.7.3 Describe and evaluate the use of environmental impact assessments (EIAs)

What is the purpose of an EIA?

An **environmental impact assessment** (EIA) must be carried out before any development project gets permission to begin. Development projects that need an EIA include airports, new housing, river dams, mines, and so on. The purpose of an EIA is to

- establish the impact of the project on the **environment**
- predict possible impacts on **habitats**, **species**, and **ecosystems**
- help decision makers decide if the development should go ahead or not.

The EIA can suggest procedures to **mitigate** any damaging effects of the development. The report should provide a **non-technical** summary at the conclusion of the EIA so that the public and the media can understand the **implications** of the study.

Model sentence: The first stage of an EIA is to carry out a baseline study.

The baseline study is undertaken because it is important to know what the environmental and biological environment is like before the project starts so that it can be monitored during and after the development. Variables measured as part of a baseline study should include:

- habitat type and **abundance**
- the number of species (animals and plants) present
- estimation of the species diversity
- the number of endangered species
- assessment of land-use type and use coverage
- assessment of **hydrological** conditions in terms of volume, discharge, flows, and water quality
- assessment of the present human **population** in the area
- assessment of soil quality, fertility, and pH.

Model sentence: The next stage of an EIA is to identify possible impacts of the development.

This is followed by predictions of the **scale** of potential impacts and then finding ways to lower the impacts. A non-technical summary is then produced so that the general public can understand the issues. Monitoring continues during the development, and continues for some time after the development has been completed.

Evaluation of EIAs

Strengths

EIAs can lead to changes in the development plans and avoid negative environmental impacts. It can be argued that any improvement to a development outweighs any negative aspects.

Limitations

It is often difficult to put together a complete baseline study due to lack of data. Sometimes not all of the impacts of the development are identified. An EIA may therefore be limited by the quality of the baseline study.

The value of EIAs in the environmental decision-making process can be compromised in other ways. Some countries include EIAs within their legal framework, with penalties and measures that can be taken if the conditions of the EIA are broken. Other countries, however, simply use the assessment to inform policy decisions and do not incorporate them into their legal framework. Some countries ignore the information and suggestions of an EIA, or put the conclusions of EIAs second place to economic concerns.

Environmental impact prediction is **speculative** due to the complexity of natural systems and the uncertainty of **feedback mechanisms**. The complexity of natural systems and the uncertainty of feedback mechanisms may mean that EIA predictions may be inaccurate in the long term.

An environmental impact assessment is a detailed survey required before a major development – the survey includes a baseline study and produces a report of its findings. Monitoring continues for some time after the development has been completed.

Glossary

speculative based on guesswork

Subject vocabulary

feedback mechanism where the results of a process influence the input of the process

3.1.1 Describe the nature and explain the implications of exponential growth in human populations

Subject vocabulary

exponential growth an increasing or accelerating rate of growth; sometimes referred to as a J-shaped curve

LEDC/less economically developed country low-income country

famine food shortage caused by decline of food or inability to buy food

malnutrition a diet that is lacking in quality of food and/or quantity of calories

MEDC/more economically developed country high-income country

dairy products foods made from milk from animals, such as butter and cheese

food chain the feeding sequence in an ecosystem

chemical fertilizers artificial sources of nutrients developed from petrochemicals that are used to help plants grow

Glossary

accelerating getting faster

stabilize to become steady or to stop changing

wealth the amount of money, land, etc., that a person owns

fossil fuels sources of energy that include oil and coal

Synonyms

consumption......... use

Model sentence: **I will describe** exponential growth.

Exponential growth refers to a growth rate that is increasingly rapid, or an **accelerating** rate of growth. The following diagram shows the exponential growth of the human population from 1800 to 1999. Growth after 1999 is not so rapid.

The world's population has grown exponentially. Most of this growth is quite recent and much of it has been in South Asia and East Asia. Up to 95 per cent of population growth is taking place in less economically developed countries (LEDCs). Rapid growth is likely to take place until at least 2050. The world's population is expected to **stabilize** at about 12 billion by around 2050–80.

The implications of exponential growth

Population growth can create:

- great pressure on governments to provide for the needs of their people
- increased risk of famine and malnutrition
- greater differences between the richer countries and the poorer countries
- increased pressure on the environment.

More resources are needed to look after the increasing number of people. The **consumption** of resources *per capita* in LEDCs is much less than the consumption of resources in more economically developed countries (MEDCs). In MEDCs, population growth rates are much lower. As the **wealth** of people in LEDCs increases, people eat more meat and dairy products. These products come from higher up the food chain. This means that more land is needed to produce the food. The increased need for food will require more land and water to produce the food. It will also require more **fossil fuels** for chemical fertilizers and for transport.

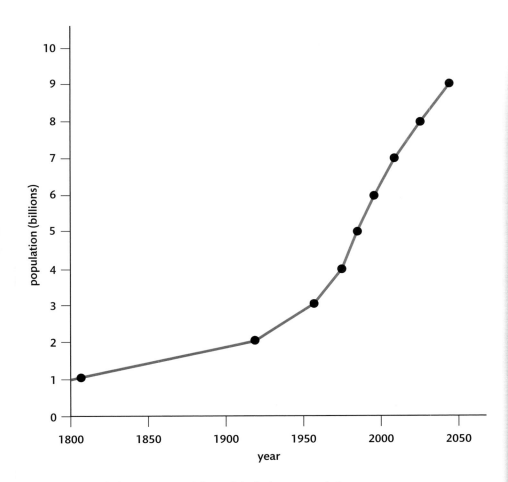

Figure 3.1 *A graph showing exponential growth in the human population.*

*Global population growth has begun to stabilize –
although it is still rapid, it is no longer exponential.*

3.1.2 Calculate and explain, from given data, the values of crude birth rate, crude death rate, fertility, doubling time and natural increase rate

Subject vocabulary

crude birth rate the number of live births per thousand people in a population

age and sex structure the composition of a population in terms of youthful, adult, and elderly people, as well as male and female

crude death rate the number of deaths per thousand people in a population

Glossary

crude a rate that does not take into account the age-structure of a population

indicator something that can be seen as a sign of something

mortality deaths

Synonyms

variation .... difference/change

trend .... a general direction in which something is changing or developing

Model sentence: I will define crude birth rate and show how it is calculated.

Crude birth rate is defined as the number of live births per thousand people in a population.

Crude birth rate is calculated as follows:

$$\text{Crude birth rate (CBR)} = \frac{\text{Total number of births}}{\text{Total population}} \times 1000$$

During 2012, there were 773,559 births in the UK out of a total population of 63,047,162. Using the above formula for the crude birth rate, we get:

$$\frac{773,559}{63,047,162} \times 1000 = 12.27 \text{ per thousand (‰)}.$$

Globally there are major **variations** in crude birth rate, with the highest rates in poorer countries and lower rates in rich countries. Crude birth rate is called crude because it does not take into account the **age and sex structure** of the population.

Model sentence: I will define crude death rate and show how it is calculated.

Crude death rate is the number of deaths per thousand people in a population.

During 2012, there were 588,230 deaths in the UK among a population of 63,047,162.

Crude death rate is calculated as follows:

$$\text{Crude death rate} = \frac{\text{Number of deaths per year}}{\text{Total population}} \times 1000$$

Using the above formula, we get:

$$\frac{588,230}{63,047,162} \times 1000 = 9.33‰$$

Crude death rate is called crude because it does not take into account the age structure of the population. Crude death rate is a poor **indicator** of **mortality trends**. This is because populations with a large number of old people will have a higher crude death rate than countries with younger populations.

Fertility

The **fertility** rate is the average number of births per woman of child-bearing age. It is the completed family size if fertility rates **remain constant**.

In general, the highest fertility rates are found among the poorest countries, and very few LEDCs have made the change from high birth rates to low birth rates. In contrast, most MEDCs have reduced their birth rates.

Natural increase and doubling time

Natural increase is the increase in population as a result of birth rates being higher than death rates. Natural increase is usually measured in per cent (%). Natural decrease occurs when death rates are higher than birth rates. Natural increase and decrease do not take into account any gains or losses from **migration**. In the UK in 2012 the crude birth rate was 12.27 per thousand and the crude death rate was 9.33 per thousand. Using these numbers, the natural increase can be calculated as follows:

Natural increase = crude birth rate – crude death rate

$$= 12.27 - 9.33$$

$$= 2.94‰ \text{ or } 0.29\%$$

Doubling time refers to the length of time it takes for a population to double in size, assuming that its natural increase remains constant.

Approximate values for it can be obtained by calculating the formula:

Doubling time (years) = 70 years ÷ natural increase in percentage

For the UK, the doubling time is 70 ÷ 0.29 = 241 years.

Hints for success: Make sure that you include units in your answer. Birth and death rates are measured in terms of per thousand (‰), whereas natural increase is measured in per cent (%). Life expectancy and doubling times are measured in years.

3.1.3 Analyse age/sex pyramids and diagrams showing demographic transition models

> **Opening sentence:**

In this answer I will analyse age/sex **pyramids** and diagrams showing **demographic transition models**.

What is a population pyramid?

A population pyramid is a bar graph on its side which shows **variations** in the age structure and sex structure of a population. The following diagrams show the population pyramids for Swaziland. Swaziland is an **LEDC** in southern Africa. The population pyramids are for the years 2000 and 2025.

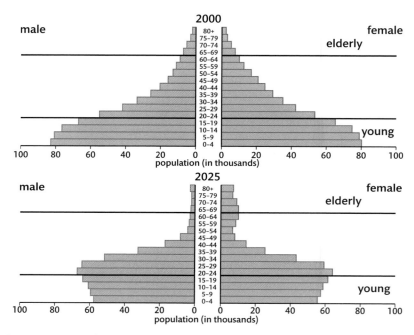

Figure 3.2 *Age–sex pyramids for Swaziland, 2000 and projected for 2025.*

The use of population pyramids

Population pyramids tell us a lot of information about the age and sex structure of a population:

- a wide base **indicates** a high birth rate – such as Swaziland in 2000
- a narrow base suggests a falling birth rate – such as Swaziland in 2025
- straight or near vertical sides indicate a low death rate – such as the under-24 year olds in Swaziland in 2025
- **concave slopes characterize** high death rates – such as Swaziland in 2000
- **bulges** in the slope suggest high rates of **in-migration**

- **gaps** in the pyramid may indicate out-migration or age-specific deaths. The relative **lack** of people over the age of 50 years in Swaziland in 2025 is predicted because of the increasing **impact** of AIDS.

The demographic transition model

The following diagram shows the main characteristics of the demographic transition model.

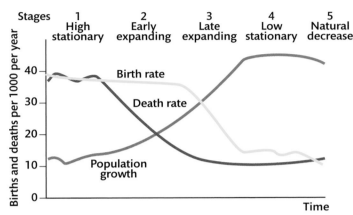

Figure 3.3 *The general demographic transition model.*

The demographic transition model (DTM) shows the change in population structure over time. It shows how population changes from when a country is an LEDC to when a country becomes an MEDC. When a country is an LEDC, it tends to have higher birth rates and higher death rates. When a country becomes an MEDC, it tends to have lower birth rates and lower death rates. It suggests that death rates fall before birth rates and that the total population **expands**. In Stage 5 there are higher proportions of elderly people and so the death rate rises.

Advantages and disadvantages of the demographic transition model

The DTM provides a model for population growth that may occur. While it is easy to understand, it has its disadvantages. The DTM is based on data from just three countries – all of them European. LEDCs take much less time than MEDCs to move through the stages of the DTM. There are alternative DTMs. Ireland's demographic transition was based on falling birth rates and rising death rates. This was as a result of out-migration following the 1845–49 famine. The next diagram shows a model for Ireland's demographic transition.

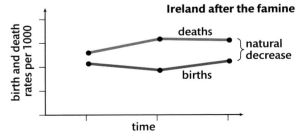

Figure 3.4 *Ireland's demographic transition model.*

3.1.4 Discuss the use of models in predicting the growth of human populations

Subject vocabulary

model a simplified description designed to show the structure and workings of a system

population projection the likely size of the population at some time in the future based on a number of factors

Synonyms

range.................. variety

Opening sentence:

In this answer I will discuss the use of **models** in predicting the growth of human populations.

A model is a simplification of reality. Models allow us to understand complex features.

The diagram below shows a **range** of **population projections** for the world in 2050.

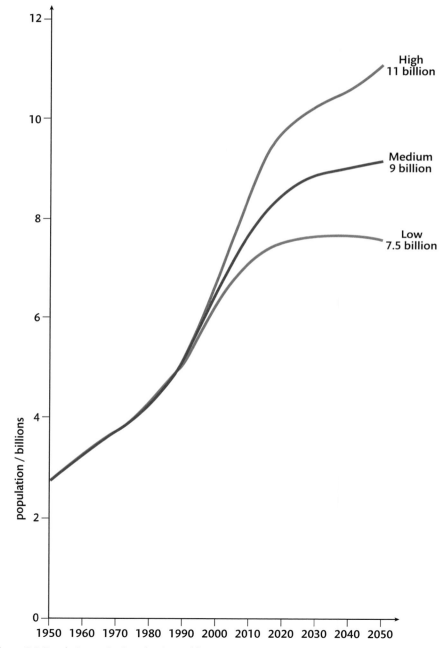

Figure 3.5 *Population projections for the world in 2050.*

The range of predictions for population growth by 2050 is very large: the high prediction is 11 billion, whereas the low prediction is 7.5 billion. The medium prediction is 9 billion. As scientists try to predict further into the future, the less certain they are. Predictions are important as they make it possible for planners to plan for the future. As there will be more people in 2050 than now, there will be greater needs. These include a need for more food and more health care. There will also be a need for more schools and more homes. Knowing whether there will be 11 billion people or whether there will be 7.5 billion people will influence what **facilities** and services need to be provided.

Variations in population projections

At the global scale, population growth is influenced by **variations** in birth rates and death rates. At a national or local scale, in-migration and out-migration is important. Population projections become less reliable the further into the future we try to predict.

Using tables of data to predict population growth

Population data for Egypt (Source CIA World Factbook)

Population aged 0–14 years	32.5%
Population aged 15–64 years	62.8%
Population aged 65 years and over	4.7%
Crude birth rate	24.2 per thousand
Crude death rate	4.8 per thousand
Infant mortality rate	24.2 per thousand
Life expectancy	72.9 years
Total fertility rate	2.94 children/woman

From this data, I can tell that:

- Egypt has a young population structure and so will continue to grow.

- It has a **moderate** birth rate but a very low death rate, which will cause it to grow.

- The total fertility rate is above the replacement level, and so the population will continue to grow.

- The life expectancy is high and the infant mortality rate is moderate, which suggest that health care and standards of living in Egypt are good.

natural resource any naturally occurring feature that provides benefit to people

natural capital the income derived from natural resources

renewable resources a natural resource that the environment continues to supply or replace as it is used

replenishable resource a non-living natural resource that can be reused, such as groundwater

natural income the benefits provided by natural resources

goods products or items that can be traded such as food

ecological services environmental benefits

climate regulation a process that reduces climate change

non-renewable resources natural resources that will eventually run out, such as fossil fuels

services benefits that are not traded, such as clean air and flood control

primary productivity plant growth

nutrient cycling the transfer of nutrients between soil, biomass, and litter

pollination transfer of pollen from one flower to another so that seeds may be produced

species diversity a measurement of the number of different species and their relative abundance in a specific area

flood regulation a process that reduces floods

habitat the place where a species lives

marketable something that can be sold

timber wood

fossil fuel energy sources from the remains of plants and animals such as oil, natural gas, and coal

income earnings

Model sentence: Natural resources are also called natural capital.

Renewable and replenishable resources can produce 'natural income' over and over again as long as they are carefully managed. Natural income is the benefit provided by natural resources. This income could be **marketable** goods, such as **timber** and grain, or it could be ecological services, such as oxygen production and climate regulation. Non-renewable resources, such as **fossil fuels**, can provide an **income** but can only be used once.

Types of ecosystem services

● Supporting services: these are the **essentials** for life and include primary productivity and nutrient cycling.

● **Regulating** services: these include climate regulation and pollination.

● Provisioning services: these are the services people get from ecosystems, such as food and water.

● Cultural services: these are produced from places when people **interact** with nature.

Woodland services		
Timber*	Climate regulation†	Recreation and tourism*
Species diversity*	Flood regulation†	Cultural heritage*
Fuelwood*	Air and water regulation†	Sense of place*

* Goods   †Services

Items in yellow are from provisioning services

Items in red are from regulating services

Items in brown are cultural services

The supporting services are not listed for the individual habitats, as they are needed to produce all other ecosystem services.

Figure 3.6 *Woodlands, such as Wytham Woods in Oxfordshire, UK, provide a range of ecological services.*

3.2.2 Define the terms *renewable*, *replenishable*, and *non-renewable* natural capital

income earnings or benefits

solar from the Sun

fossil fuel energy sources from the remains of plants and animals such as oil, natural gas, and coal

reserves supplies

Subject vocabulary

natural capital the income derived from natural resources

renewable resource a natural resource that the environment continues to supply or replace as it is used

photosynthesis a process in plants that changes light energy into chemical energy

replenishable resource a non-living natural resource that can be reused, such as groundwater

non-renewable resource natural resources that will eventually run out, such as fossil fuels

goods commodities that can be traded, such as food

services benefits that are not traded, such as clean air and flood control

nutrients chemicals, derived from the natural environment or from fertilizers, that organisms need to live and grow

Model sentence: Natural capital is the income obtained from natural resources.

There are three main types of natural capital.

- Renewable natural capital is self-producing, self-maintaining, and uses solar energy in the photosynthesis process.

- Replenishable natural capital is non-living and can be reused.

- Non-renewable natural capital can only be used once.

Forms of natural capital	Examples of goods	Examples of services	Time needed to be renewed	Living or non-living
Renewable	Living species, ecosystems, food	Climate regulation, flood control	Within a human life-time	Living
Replenishable	Groundwater and ozone	Stratospheric ozone protecting against ultra-violet radiation	Within a human life-time	Non-living
Non-renewable	Fossil fuels and mineral reserves such as uranium	Soil nutrients produced by weathering of rocks	Takes millions of years to form	Non-living

3.2.3 Explain the dynamic nature of the concept of a resource

> ## Opening sentence:

In this answer I will explain the **dynamic nature** of the **concept** of **resources**. I will show how **cultural**, **economic**, and **technological factors** influence the **status** of a resource over time and space. I will use uranium to support my answer.

Uranium is used in the **nuclear power** industry to create energy. Many factors help explain why uranium became an important resource. However, there are also reasons why the use of uranium in the future may be limited.

Dynamic nature of resource

Use of resource	Cultural factors	Economic factors	Technological factors
• Uranium has been used as a resource for less than 100 years. • It had no value until nuclear energy was developed. • Since then it has great value.	• Awareness of the role of fossil fuels in global warming may have moved interest in favour of nuclear energy for some societies. • There has been a change in values as the dangers of nuclear energy became clearer. • Nuclear weapons and nuclear disasters have turned some people against nuclear energy.	• Economic development led to increased demand for energy supply. • Nuclear energy was seen as clean and cheap. • Energy was created by nuclear fission. • Decommissioning nuclear power stations is very expensive.	• As nuclear technology has developed, the value of uranium has increased. • If nuclear fusion is developed, uranium will no longer be needed as a resource.

Glossary

dynamic constantly moving and changing

concept an idea of how something is

resource anything that is useful to people, such as fossil fuels, soil, water, wood

cultural factors aspects related to society, such as religion

economic factors aspects related to wealth

technological factors aspects related to level of technology

Synonyms

nature.................. qualities/features

status................... importance

Subject vocabulary

nuclear power energy produced by splitting uranium atoms to release heat and radiation

3.2.4 Discuss the view that the environment can have its own intrinsic value

Opening sentence:

In this answer I will discuss the view that the environment can have its own **intrinsic** value. I will show how it is difficult to **quantify** values such as **aesthetic** value, which are **qualitative in nature**.

The environment has many values. These values can be divided into two broad categories, namely use values and intrinsic values. Use values are the **benefits** derived from using the environment or the services it provides. There are a number of types of use value.

Model sentence: The economic value of an ecosystem can be quantified by the amount of money someone will pay for a good or service.

Model sentence: The ecological value of an ecosystem cannot be quantified.

Ecological values include **climate regulation** and **soil erosion control**. Experts are trying to give a value to benefits such as climate regulation. One advantage of climate regulation is a **stable** climate that allows farmers to plan for the year ahead. However, it is not possible to put a price on the benefits of climate regulation.

Model sentence: The aesthetic value of an ecosystem is the pleasure people derive from an ecosystem because of how it looks.

It cannot be quantified. The intrinsic value of an environment is the value of the environment in its own right, that is, without reference to human uses.

Model sentence: Ecosystems have a philosophical, spiritual, and ethical value even if they do not have an economic value.

Thus, they are seen to have a use value.

Figure 3.7 *Silent Valley, Dolomites, Italy – this environment has much intrinsic value as well as economic value from tourism.*

3.2.5 Explain the concept of sustainability in terms of natural capital and natural income

Model sentence: Sustainability is the use of global resources at a rate that allows natural regeneration and minimizes damage to the environment.

Sustainability means living within the **means of nature**. The concept of sustainability implies using resources at a rate at which they can be renewed by nature. It focuses on the rate of resource use.

Natural capital is renewable or replenishable. Natural income comes from natural capital. Natural income is income that nature can renew itself. It is an economic aspect of sustainability. The use of woodland for timber can be sustainable. It is sustainable if the harvesting of wood is less than the speed at which the wood regrows each year. It is unsustainable if the harvesting of wood is greater than the speed at which the wood regrows each year.

Figure 3.8 *Peat cutting in the west of Ireland.*

Any society that reduces the forms of natural capital is unsustainable. If resources are over-exploited, then future generations will have fewer resources. If human well-being depends on the goods and services provided by certain **forms** of natural capital, then long-term harvest rates should not be greater than rates of capital renewal. Sustainability means living within the means of nature. This implies living from sustainable growth generated by natural capital.

3.2.6 Discuss the concept of sustainable development

Model sentence: Sustainable development is development that meets current needs without reducing the ability of future generations to meet their own needs.

Sustainable development refers to an **approach** to development. Sustainable development suggests change that does not limit future generations. Figure 3.9 shows how sustainable development links to environmental, economic, and social factors.

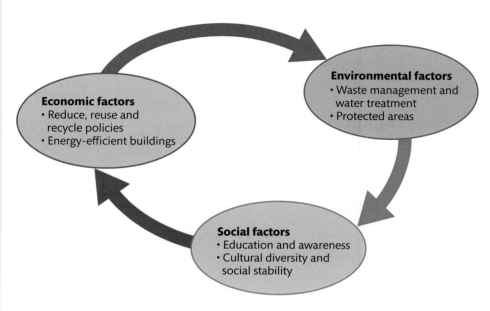

Figure 3.9 *Aspects of sustainable development.*

Sustainable development is a hard concept to define because different groups emphasize different aspects of it.

Economists refer to sustainable economic development. This means that the economy is growing at a given **rate** over a **long time**. However this may involve the **depletion** of resources.

Environmentalists also refer to sustainable development as a type of development that does not deplete resources. Other types of sustainable development include sustainable **urban** development and sustainable agricultural development.

Is sustainable development possible? Sustainable development in the long term is not possible if society depends on **fossil fuels** for its energy. Sustainable development is possible if society develops policies of reduce, reuse, and recycle. Sustainable development is possible if society develops renewable energy resources. Renewable energy resources include **hydroelectric power** and **solar power**.

There have been many international meetings to discuss how to achieve sustainable development. The Earth Summit in Rio de Janeiro in 1992 produced Local Agenda 21 plans (LA21). Local Agenda 21 plans are plans made by local communities to achieve sustainable development. Other meetings have had different aims and results. The 1997 United Nations Conference in Kyoto was aimed at reducing **emissions** of greenhouse gases. The 2002 Johannesburg Summit mainly looked at issues of **poverty**, such as access to clean water and sanitation.

Figure 3.10 *Hydroelectric power at the Marmolada Dam, Italy.*

Formulae for calculating sustainable yield (SY)

The first formula is

$$SY = ((\frac{\text{Total biomass}}{\text{energy}}) \text{ at Time } t +1) - ((\frac{\text{Total biomass}}{\text{energy}}) \text{ at Time } t)$$

If there are 11 000 fish in a lake at the end of a year and 10 000 fish at the beginning of a year, the **sustainable yield** is:

11 000 – 10 000 = 1000

The second formula is:

SY = (**annual** growth and **recruitment**) – (annual death and **emigration**)

If there is: annual growth of 2000 individuals
annual death of 1000 individuals
annual recruitment of 1500 individuals and
emigration of 500 individuals, then
SY = (2000 + 1500) – (1000 + 500)
= 3500 – 1500 = 2000.

Sustainable yield

Sustainable yield is the amount of a population (e.g. fish) that can be removed annually without the risk of **depleting** the **resource** for future generations.

Sustainable yield can be calculated as the **rate** of increase in **natural capital**, i.e. that which can be **exploited** without depleting the original stock or its potential for replenishment. The annual sustainable yield for a given crop is the annual gain in biomass through growth. **Maximum sustainable yield (MSY)** is the maximum amount of a population or crop that can be removed from the total population annually without the risk of depleting the resource for future generations.

Examples

A fish population of 10 000 produces 1000 young fish that will survive to **adulthood**. If more than 1000 fish are fished in a year, the total fish population will decrease. This is not sustainable. The maximum number of fish from this population that should be caught in any one year is 1000. The maximum sustainable yield is therefore 1000.

If fish **stock** is too low, there will not be enough adult fish to produce enough young. Fishing from a population that is too small is called over-fishing. If the fish population is too large, **reproduction rates** may be low because of competition for food.

3.3.1 Outline the range of energy resources available to society

Energy resources

Energy resources are usually divided into two main types. These are renewable energy resources and non-renewable energy resources. It takes about the same amount of time to replace renewable energy resources as it takes to extract them. A good example is biofuels. These can be renewed through photosynthesis. Replenishable energy resources may rely on solar energy in order to be restored, such as hydroelectric power and wind power. It takes a much longer time to replace non-renewable energy resources than it takes to **extract** them. Oil and coal are good examples of non-renewable energy resources. They are also called **fossil fuels**. This is because they are formed out of the **remains** of living organisms.

Cost of energy resources

The costs of energy resources may come from extraction, **production**, transport, storage, and **utilization**. Some energy sources have a high set-up cost but a low production cost. Solar energy has high set-up costs but low production costs. Some energy sources have low set-up costs but high production costs. **Peat**-burning has low set-up costs but high production costs.

Biofuel is a renewable energy resource. It has relatively low set-up costs, but production costs may be high. This is because it takes lots of effort to cut and carry the biofuel back to the house or farm.

Fossil fuels are a **form** of non-renewable energy resource. It takes a huge amount of time for them to form when compared to the amount of time it takes to extract them. Although large reserves still exist, stocks are being reduced.

Hydroelectric energy is a replenishable energy resource. It depends on solar energy for its renewal. It has high set-up costs but low production costs. How effective hydroelectric energy is depends highly on where it is located. It requires a plentiful supply of water.

3.3.2 Evaluate the advantages and disadvantages of two contrasting energy sources

Subject vocabulary

hydroelectric power energy that comes from running water

non-renewable energy source natural resources that will eventually run out, such as fossil fuels

replenishable energy source a non-living natural resource that depends on other natural sources in order for it to be restored, such as groundwater

renewable energy source a natural resource that the environment continues to supply or replace as it is used

greenhouse gases gases, such as carbon dioxide and methane, that allow incoming solar radiation to pass through the atmosphere but block a proportion of the out-going radiation from leaving the atmosphere; they can lead to global warming

habitat the place where a species lives

Glossary

fuel a substance that can be used to produce heat and energy

finite limited amount

oil spill when a large amount of petroleum accidently pours out of its container, e.g. a ship

reservoir an artificial lake that is created to supply water to people's houses

multipurpose having many aims, e.g. the generation of electricity and flood control

recreation what people do to enjoy themselves

flood a very large amount of water that covers an area which is usually dry land

displace to force to move

dam a barrier across a river which slows down the flow of water

Model sentence: In this answer I will look at the advantages and disadvantages of two different types of energy sources. I will look at oil and hydroelectric power.

Oil is a non-renewable energy source. Hydroelectric power is a replenishable energy source. Replenishable energy sources are renewable.

Advantages of oil	Disadvantages of oil
● It is a very efficient source of energy. ● It can be used as a fuel and to produce electricity. ● It is relatively cheap.	● It is a finite resource and will run out. ● Burning oil releases carbon dioxide, which is a greenhouse gas. ● Oil spills damage ecosystems.

Advantages of hydroelectric power	Disadvantages of hydroelectric power
● It is a renewable source of energy so will not run out in the future. ● Reservoirs can be multipurpose as well as having other benefits, such as recreation and fishing. ● It allows nations to control their own energy supplies. ● Once built, hydroelectric power schemes are relatively cheap to run.	● Reservoirs flood habitats and displace people. ● Dams act as barriers for species that move up and down the river.

Hints for success: If you are asked to evaluate, you must show the positive aspects and the negative aspects of something.

3.3.3 Discuss the factors that affect the choice of energy sources adopted by different societies

Factor 1: Availability of energy

The Middle East has huge reserves of oil. As a result, it relies on it as a source of energy. In contrast, Japan does not have any oil reserves so it has had to develop other sources of energy or exchange its products with other countries that can sell it energy.

Factor 2: The economy

Coal is a relatively cheap **form** of energy and so it is used a lot in developing countries. Nuclear power is a very expensive form of energy so only rich countries can afford it.

Factor 3: Culture

Many people believe that the risks of nuclear power are greater than the benefits. Fuelwood is used in many poor countries for cooking and for heating.

Factor 4: The environment

Burning fossil fuels releases greenhouse gases which are linked to global warming. Burning coal may also result in acid rain. **Disposing** of nuclear waste is very dangerous. Attempts to **extract** natural gas from shale rocks can lead to **earthquakes** and groundwater pollution.

Hints for success: You may be asked to refer to one or more societies in your answer.

Subject vocabulary

reserves the amount that could be used

fuelwood woody material used for cooking and heating

greenhouse gases gases, such as carbon dioxide and methane, that allow incoming solar radiation to pass through the atmosphere but block a proportion of the out-going radiation from leaving the atmosphere; they can lead to global warming

global warming an increase in the average temperature of the Earth's atmosphere

acid rain rain and snow that has become acidified through emissions of sulfur dioxide and oxides of nitrogen

shale a type of rock that contains natural gas

groundwater water held in rocks underground

Synonyms

form .... type

factor .... aspect

Glossary

dispose (of) to get rid of something

extract to get an energy resource out of the ground

earthquake a sudden shaking of the Earth's surface

societies groups of people sharing an easily recognized culture

3.4.1 Outline how soil systems integrate aspects of living systems

Subject vocabulary

soil a mixture of mineral particles and organic material that covers the land and in which plants grow

open system a system in which both matter and energy are exchanged with the surroundings

soil system the factors that affect soils, the processes that affect soils and the resulting soils

precipitation all forms of moisture, including rain and snow

evapotranspiration moisture loss from the ground and from vegetation

lithosphere relating to the Earth's crust and upper mantle

nutrient cycling the transfer of nutrients between vegetation, litter and soil

soil profile a vertical section through a soil, from the surface down to the parent material, which shows the soil layers or soil horizon (the horizontal layers within a soil profile)

landscape the environment including physical features, vegetation, animals and human activities

overland flow the movement of water over the Earth's surface

infiltration water seeping into the soil

groundwater flow the flow of water within bedrock

Glossary

integrate to join/link

vegetation plants in general

weather/weathering to change through the long-term action of sun, rain, and wind

Model sentence: Soil can be considered an open system.

Model sentence: Soil systems integrate aspects of living systems by being linked with the atmosphere via precipitation and evapotranspiration.

There are links between the soil, lithosphere, atmosphere, and living organisms. Soils consist of weathered rocks and organic matter. Soils also contain air and water.

Precipitation and evapotranspiration link soils with the atmosphere. Nutrient cycling links the soil and vegetation. Weathering of rocks links the soils with rocks.

Soils are often shown as a generalized soil profile. The following diagram shows how a two-dimensional soil profile fits into the landscape.

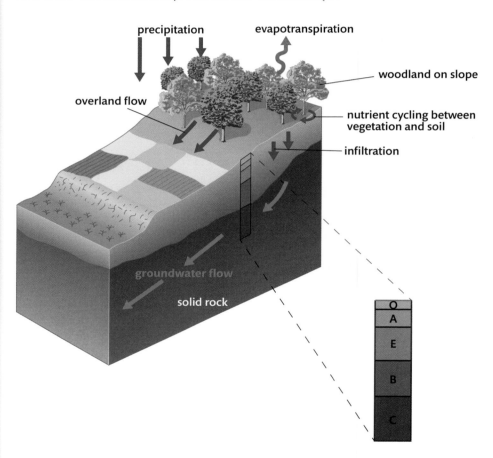

Figure 3.11 *The soil profile in the landscape.*

The next diagram shows how the processes operating in soil move materials within the soil.

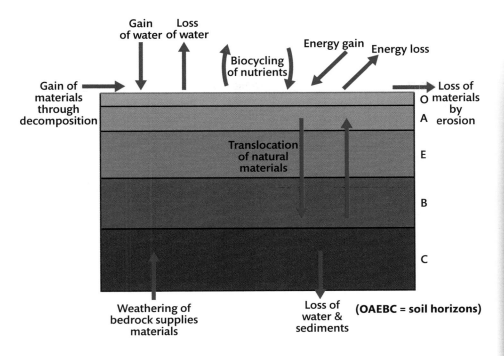

Figure 3.12 *The soil as an open system.*

Transfers and transformations

Model sentence: Transfers of material result in the reorganization of soils.

Materials can be moved up and down within the soil. There are gains and losses from the soil. Inputs include organic and parent material, water, and heat. Outputs include water, energy, particles through erosion, and **leaching**.

Model sentence: Transformations include weathering, decomposition and nutrient cycling.

Decomposition involves the breakdown of organic matter into **humus**. Nutrient cycling returns nutrients to the soil.

Soil horizons

The soil profile can be divided into soil horizons. There are five main soil horizons:

O horizon – organic horizon

A horizon – mixed mineral-organic horizon

E horizon – leached horizon

B horizon – deposited horizon

C horizon – bedrock or parent material.

3.4.2 Compare and contrast the structure and properties of sand, clay and loam soils, including their effect on primary productivity

Soil structure

Sand particles are between 0.05 mm and 2 mm in size. Clay particles are much smaller. They are less than 0.002 mm. A loam soil is a mixed soil. It can have sand and clay in it. It can also contain silt. Silt particles are between 0.002 mm and 0.05 mm in size. The following diagram shows the **range** of soil textural groups based on sand, silt, and clay.

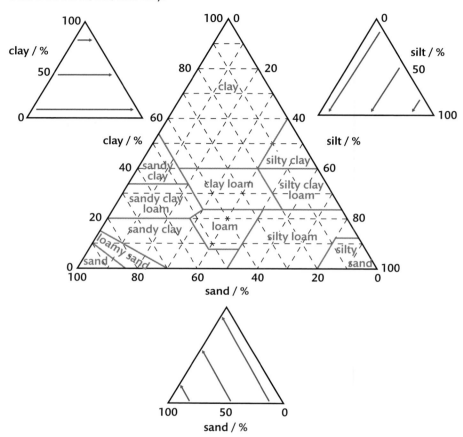

Figure 3.13 *A triangular graph that shows soil texture groups.*

Soil properties

Clay soils tend to have a high mineral content. In contrast, sand tends to have a low mineral content. A loam soil has a medium amount of mineral content.

Clay tends to hold water **readily**. However, it can become **waterlogged** quite easily. Sand **drains** very quickly because it contains large particles. Sandy soils are often quite dry. Loam soils **retain** some water, but generally do not get waterlogged.

Clay soils have limited air space. In contrast, sandy soils have a large amount of air space. Loam soils have an **intermediate** amount of air space.

Soil properties and productivity

Clay soils have a medium-low level of **primary productivity**. This is because they hold water and **nutrients**. Sometimes there may be too much water and the soil is waterlogged. Clay soils do not have much air space. Sandy soils have a low level of primary productivity. This is because they hold little water or nutrients. Loams are the most fertile soils. They are linked with high primary productivity because they retain water and nutrients. They also have air spaces allowing for plant root **respiration**.

Subject vocabulary

primary productivity the gain in biomass or energy of plants

nutrients chemicals, derived from the natural environment or from fertilizers, that organisms need to live and grow

respiration a chemical process that happens in all cells to release energy

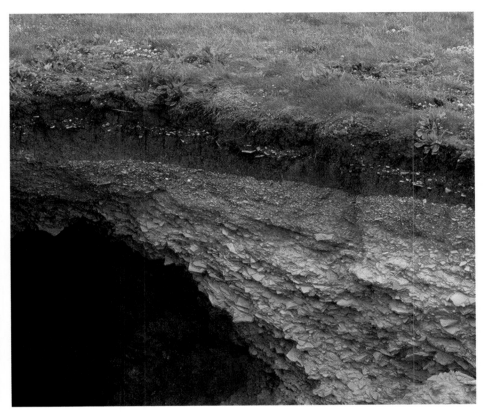

Figure 3.14 *Soil horizons.*

Subject vocabulary

soil degradation a decline in the quantity and/or quality of a soil

overgrazing too much pressure from animals eating the plants on the land

over-cultivation getting too many crops from the soil and not allowing the soil to recover

erosion the wearing away of the Earth's surface by a moving force, such as a river or the wind

salinization an increase in the amount of salts in the upper soil horizons

windbreaks trees and hedges planted to reduce the impact of wind erosion

unsustainable something that cannot be continued

desertification the spread of desert-like conditions

marginal areas poor quality land that should not be farmed

infiltration water slowly entering the soil

overland runoff water flowing over the surface of a soil

permeable a soil or rock that allows water to soak into it

eutrophication nitrate enrichment of streams and lakes

Glossary

compaction making more dense

deforestation cutting down trees and not replanting them

canopy the top of the vegetation cover

excessive too much

irrigation extra water added to a soil to encourage plant growth

toxic poisonous

yield crop productivity

enrich/enriched/enrichment to improve the quality of something

Synonyms

vulnerable .... could be easily harmed or hurt

Model sentence: Soil degradation is the decline in the amount and quality of a soil.

Soil degradation leads to a reduction in soil fertility. Soil degradation can be caused by overgrazing. Overgrazing occurs when too many animals use the land, which leads to the removal of vegetation and **compaction** of soil. Soil degradation can also be caused by over-cultivation. Over-cultivation results in the removal of specific nutrients from soils. **Deforestation** can also lead to soil degradation. Deforestation can lead to a loss of vegetation so that the soil is more easily eroded. Deforestation also removes the protection given to soils by plant roots and **canopy**.

Excessive irrigation can lead to soil degradation and to salinization. Salinization is caused by the evaporation of water from soil. Evaporating water draws salts up towards the surface. Salinization is **toxic** to plants. Removal of hedges and windbreaks can cause soil degradation. When hedges and windbreaks are removed, the soil is more **vulnerable** to wind and water erosion.

Unsustainable agricultural practices can lead to soil degradation. Unsustainable agricultural practices include the removal of the upper soil horizons and planting seeds in the B horizon.

Desertification

In extreme cases, soil degradation can be linked to desertification. Desertification is the spread of desert-like conditions into previously productive areas. Desertification may be caused by over-population. Over-population forces people to farm in marginal areas. This can cause soil degradation.

Consequences of soil degradation

- Overgrazing may lead to an increase in wind and water erosion. With less vegetation cover, the soil is compacted. This reduces infiltration and increases overland runoff.

- Deforestation also results in increased soil erosion. With less vegetation, more rain hits the soil. It compacts it and makes it less permeable. This also increases the amount of overland flow and soil erosion.

- Agricultural **yields** may decline. In order to improve yields, agricultural systems may use lots of fertilizers. This may cause the soil to be **enriched** with nitrates and phosphates. This is a form of eutrophication. Salinization is also toxic to plants. It can cause increased stress for plants and can lead to reduced agricultural yields.

- Desertification leads to a decline in plant productivity. Areas that were fertile before are no longer able to provide enough food for the people who live there.

Soil conservation is the protection of the quantity and quality of soils

Technique 1: Soil conditioning

There are a number of methods of soil **conservation**. First, I will consider soil conditioners. These include the use of lime and organic materials. Lime is used to make **acidic** soils less acidic. **Crushed** limestone can be added as a **powder** to make acid soils more fertile. Organic matter can also be added to the soil to make it more fertile. In addition, it can reduce the effect of wind erosion and it can raise the temperature of soils.

Technique 2: Wind-reduction techniques such as windbreaks and shelter belts

Windbreaks are **linear** belts of **hedges** or trees that reduce wind speed and therefore reduce the possibility of wind erosion. There are usually only one or two rows of vegetation in a windbreak. Shelter belts are similar to windreaks but generally consist of trees or shrubs spread out over three or four **rows**. In this way they reduce wind speed and provide shelter for the growing vegetation. Strip **cultivation** refers to the growing of crops in linear strips. Growing a number of different crops in strips instead of growing one crop in a large area helps reduce wind erosion. Wind speed is also reduced due to the increase in friction with the different types of vegetation.

Technique 3: Wind-reduction techniques such as terracing and contour ploughing

Cultivation techniques such as **terracing** and contour ploughing are important as they reduce the possibility of overland flow and wind erosion. Terracing involves the **levelling** of the land into a series of steps, or terraces. These help reduce soil erosion by having flat surfaces rather than a steep surface. This also reduces overland flow. Contour ploughing refers to **ploughing** around a hill rather than up and down a hill. This also reduces the amount of overland flow. This helps protect the soil.

Technique 4: Stop ploughing of marginal lands

Marginal lands are lands that are not fertile and have very limited agricultural **potential**. Using marginal lands for agriculture may lead to desertification. It may be better to use marginal lands for national parks rather than farming. National parks may earn money from tourism, whereas the farming of marginal lands generally leads to soil degradation.

Glossary

conservation protecting or preserving

acidic having a pH of less than 7

crush/crushed to press something so hard that it breaks into small pieces

powder a dry substance in the form of very small particles

linear in a straight line

hedge a row of bushes or small trees

cultivate/cultivation to grow plants and crops

terrace/terracing flat areas cut out of a hill like steps

levelling making flat

plough (to plough) to turn the earth over so that seeds can be planted in it

Subject vocabulary

soil conditioner something that is added to the soil to improve its quality

lime crushed and powdered limestone

organic matter living material

windbreak a line or two lines of vegetation planted to reduce wind speed

shelter belt three or four rows of vegetation designed to reduce wind speed and, therefore, wind erosion

friction a force resisting movement

contour ploughing ploughing around a hill (along the contours) rather than up and down a hill

overland flow the movement of water over the Earth's surface

desertification the spread of desert-like conditions

degradation a decline in the quantity or quality of soils

Synonyms

row .... line

potential .... possibility

3.4.5 Evaluate soil management strategies in a named commercial farming system and in a named subsistence farming system

Subject vocabulary

extensive farming systems that involve low inputs and outputs per unit area

wind erosion the removal of the top soil by wind

contour ploughing farming around the contours, e.g. around a hill rather than up and down

strip farming farming alternate strips of farmed land and fallow land

fallow unfarmed

cover crops crops that are planted to protect a soil from soil erosion

subsistence farming farming in which the main motive is to provide food for the famer's family

nutrients chemicals, derived from the natural environment or from fertilizers, that organisms need to live and grow

Glossary

grain the seeds of plants such as wheat and rice which are used as food

bread basket an area that is important for global production of food

tribe a population native to an area

fertile/fertility a measure of how productive a soil is

plot small piece of land

Extensive crop production involves the large-scale production of **grain** using large machinery.

In the 1930s, the southern Great Plains experienced very serious **wind erosion**. This created the Dust Bowl. In 1935, the Soil Conservation Act became US law. Many techniques of soil conservation were used.

Technique 1: Contour ploughing

Contour ploughing was introduced. Farmers ploughed around a hill rather than up and down. This reduced rates of soil erosion.

Technique 2: Strip farming

Strip farming has a strip of land with crops next to a strip of land which is **fallow**. The strips are lined up across the direction that the wind blows most of the time. This reduces wind speed and reduces soil erosion.

Technique 3: Cover crops

Farmers used **cover crops** to help hold the soil together and to reduce the impact of water erosion. Millet grows fast and so is a popular choice for many farmers.

Do these techniques work?

Many soil conservation techniques are practised on the Great Plains. There has not been another Dust Bowl like that of the 1930s, so the techniques seem to work. The USA has been one of the world's leading **bread baskets** so it is using its soils and protecting them at the same time.

Soil conservation measures in a subsistence farming system

The Kikuyu are a **tribe** in Kenya that practise bush-fallowing. Bush-fallowing is a type of **subsistence farming**. It involves clearing an area of forest or 'bush'. Farmers may burn some of the trees to provide **fertile** ash for the soil. The ash contains the **nutrients** that were contained in the trees. The farmers grow crops such as maize and sweet potatoes on the land that they have cleared. The **plot** loses its fertility after a few years and then it is abandoned. The farmers move to a new plot and they start the process again. The abandoned plot may return to forest or bush after a number of years. In this way, the Kikuyu are able to produce food and the soils are able to recover over a long period of time.

3.5.1 Outline the issues involved in the imbalance in global food supply

Model sentence: **There are large variations in global food supply.**

There are many people in LEDCs who do not have a proper diet. Many people in LEDCs do not get enough food. They suffer from under-nourishment. Others suffer from malnutrition. This means they may have a diet that is lacking in minerals or proteins. About a sixth of the world's population suffers from under-nourishment or malnutrition. These are mainly found in LEDCs. Most people in MEDCs are well-nourished. However, there are some who suffer from obesity.

Issue 1: Population changes

There are many influences on global food supply and distribution. The world's population is getting larger. This means there are more people to feed. The world's population is getting richer. This means that diets are changing. There is increased demand for meat and dairy products. It takes more land to produce meat and dairy products than it does to produce grain.

Issue 2: Subsidies and tariffs

In some MEDCs, governments provide subsidies for their farmers. Subsidies encourage farmers to produce more food. Many LEDCs cannot afford to pay their farmers subsidies. MEDCs may also charge import tariffs. This makes it more expensive to import food from foreign countries. Both of these factors make it difficult for LEDC farmers to sell their products to MEDCs.

Issue 3: Irrigation and fertilizers

To improve food supply many farmers use irrigation water and fertilizers. Irrigation can increase crop productivity. However, irrigation water may lead to salinization and falling water tables. Fertilizers can lead to increases in crop productivity. However, fertilizers can lead to eutrophication. Some crop land is being used to produce biofuels. This means that good land is taken away from agriculture. This is a problem due to the increased demand for food.

3.5.2 Compare and contrast the efficiency of terrestrial and aquatic food production systems

Similarities (compare)

Model sentence: There are similarities in the trophic levels and energy conversions in aquatic and terrestrial ecosystems.

This is due to respiration losses and waste production. There is much less energy available higher up the food web. Both terrestrial food production systems and aquatic food production systems depend on the Sun for their energy input.

Differences (contrast)

Model sentence: There are important differences in the trophic levels and energy conversions in aquatic and terrestrial ecosystems.

● In terrestrial food production systems, most food is **harvested** from low trophic levels. These are the producers and herbivores. Terrestrial food production systems that are based on crops (primary producers) are more energy efficient than those that produce livestock (herbivores).

● In aquatic food production systems, most food is harvested from higher trophic levels. At higher trophic levels the total storages are much smaller.

● Energy conversion along the food chain is more efficient in aquatic food production systems. This is because less biomass is locked up in bone and skeletal materials compared to terrestrial ecosystems. However, the initial fixing of available solar energy by primary producers tends to be less efficient in aquatic food production systems. This is because light is **absorbed** and **reflected** by water. Terrestrial food production systems have a more efficient fixing by primary producers.

3.5.3 Compare and contrast the inputs and outputs of materials and energy, the system characteristics, and evaluate the relative environmental impacts for two named food production systems

Model sentence: The two food production systems are North American cereal farming and subsistence farming in South-East Asia.

Both are arable farming types. In the North American farming system, the main crops are wheat and corn. In the South-East Asian farming system, the main crop is rice. A second crop may be grown in the dry season.

Comparing size and type of labour

Most farms in North America are very large in area. Most farms in South-East Asia are very small. Most farms in North America have large amounts of **machinery**. Much of the work on the farm is done by machine. Most farms in South-East Asia do not have much machinery. Much of the **labour** done on the farm is done by hand.

Contrast 1: Climate

North America has hot summers and cold winters. This limits the **growing season** to about six months. In South-East Asia, summers and winters are hot. There is a monsoon season in summer which causes much rainfall. Two crops are grown. One is grown in the wet season and one is grown in the dry season. Rice is the main wet season crop. Wheat is sometimes grown in the dry season.

Contrast 2: The nature of the two farming types

The North American farm is commercial. This means that it sells most of its crop for profit. The South-East Asian farm system is subsistence. This means that the crops grown are to feed the farmer's family. Usually only one type of crop is grown on the North American farms. This is called monoculture. Usually more than one crop is grown on the South-East Asian farms. This is called polyculture.

Contrast 3: Inputs into the farming system

Inputs into the North American farm include chemical fertilizers and irrigation. The farm may also use high yielding **varieties** of seed which have been genetically modified. In the South-East Asian farm, organic fertilizers are used and water is trapped by using **terraces**. Farmers may also use high yielding varieties of rice. Farming in North America is extensive. This means there are low inputs and outputs per unit area. Farming in South-East Asia is intensive. This means there are large inputs and outputs per unit area.

Many of the inputs to the North American farm are bought with money. These include seed and fertilizer. Pesticides may be used on the crops as they are growing. In the South-East Asian farm, most of the inputs are provided by the farmer. Seeds are collected from the previous year's crops. Fertilizers are collected from animals. Any **weeding** is done by hand.

Subject vocabulary

pesticide a chemical used to kill insects

efficiency (ecological) the percentage of energy transferred from one trophic level to the next

global warming an increase in the average temperature of the Earth's atmosphere

soil degradation a decline in soil quality

habitat loss a reduction in vegetation cover

biodiversity the amount of biological or living diversity in a specific area; it includes the concepts of species diversity, habitat diversity, and genetic diversity

deforestation removal of forest cover

soil exhaustion the removal of one particular soil nutrient as a result of over-cultivation

Synonyms

labour.......... work

variety .... type

impact .... effect/influence

Glossary

tractor a vehicle used in farming which can pull a plough behind it

combine harvester a machine used in farming to cut grain crops when they are ready

Contrast 4: Energy inputs and energy efficiency

The North American farm uses much energy. This is used to drive **tractors** and **combine harvesters**. Energy is also used to create chemical fertilizers and to provide irrigation water. Very little energy is used in the South-East Asian farm apart from human energy and sometimes water buffalo. The North American farm has a low energy efficiency. The South-East Asian farm has a high energy efficiency.

Contrast 5: Environmental impacts

The North American farm has many **impacts** on the environment. It contributes to global warming and it can cause soil degradation. It also causes habitat loss and reduction of biodiversity. The South-East Asian farm also has impacts on the environment. It causes deforestation and soil exhaustion. Deforestation leads to habitat loss and reduction of biodiversity.

Figure 3.15 *Labour-intensive farming (farmers resting!) at Glenore, Eastern Cape, South Africa.*

3.5.4 Discuss the links that exist between social systems and food production systems

Model sentence: Food production systems are influenced by many social factors.

In MEDCs, people have become worried about the environment and this has led to an increase in organic farming. Sales of organic food have increased in the last **decade**. People have also become worried about animal welfare and this has led to changes in the ways in which animals are farmed. There has been a growth in the number of free-range pigs and chickens.

Food production system 1: Shifting cultivation

A **link** between animism and subsistence farming is: A respect for the natural habitat, which means only what is needed is harvested.

Shifting cultivation is also known as slash-and-burn agriculture. This is because the farmers cut down an area of forest and burn the trees. This produces **ash** which **enriches** the soil. The farmers can farm the soil for a few years before it becomes infertile. Then the farmers must **abandon** their **plot** of land and move on to another one.

This system occurs in tropical rainforests where population density is low. It is a **form** of subsistence farming. The farmers grow different types of crops. This is known as polyculture. The crops grown include cassava and yams.

Many of the people who practise shifting cultivation are **animists**. They believe that everything contains a spirit or soul. This includes trees and places. Even animals have a spirit or soul. They respect all living things. Many of their sites are special to them.

Food production system 2: Wet-rice cultivation

A link between high population density and wet rice agriculture is: The increased demand for food leads to the high productivity from the fertile, flooded rice fields.

Wet-rice farming is a type of intensive subsistence farming. The inputs and outputs per unit area are high. However, the technology used is fairly simple. High population densities in South-East Asia create a high demand for food. Rice is the staple food crop. It is associated with Asian culture.

Paddy fields are located close to rivers. Clay soils retain the water. **Terraces** are built on steep **slopes**. High rainfall allows year-round growth in some areas. The soil is **fertile** because the river **floods**. This deposits nutrients in the paddy fields.

This type of farming is **under threat**. This is because soil fertility is declining and because there is less land available for this type of farming.

Food production system 3: Agribusiness

A link between agribusiness and western ideas of capitalism is: Farming is a business where food is grown for a profit. This often means more food is grown than is needed.

Glossary

slope a gentle, not steep, hill

fertility a measure of how productive a soil is

flood when a very large amount of water covers an area which is usually dry land

under threat likely to be harmed or damaged

Synonyms

dominate .... to control

mechanized . using machines

impact .... effect/influence

Subject vocabulary

commercial farming to sell products

agribusiness large-scale mechanized commercial farming

corporate capitalism farming that is controlled by large private companies and TNCs

transnational companies (TNCs) large companies that have operations in many countries

monoculture growing one type of crop

pesticide a chemical designed to eliminate pests

insecticide a chemical designed to eliminate insects

habitat loss a reduction in vegetation cover

biodiversity the amount of biological or living diversity in a specific area; it includes the concepts of species diversity, habitat diversity, and genetic diversity

eutrophication nitrate/phosphate enrichment of streams and lakes

soil degradation a decline in the quantity and/or quality of a soil

Glossary

monotonous boring/ uninteresting/all the same

In MEDCs, most food production is done for commercial reasons. There is very little subsistence farming in MEDCs. Agribusiness refers to running a farm like a business. The main aim is to maximize profit. It is **dominated** by big businesses. It is a form of corporate capitalism. Monsanto and Cargill are examples of transnational companies involved in agriculture.

Agribusinesses are usually large-scale businesses. Monoculture is also common. Large amounts of pesticides and insecticides are used. Farming is **mechanized**. Farm products are transported all over the world.

Agribusiness has many **impacts**. There are losses to habitats and biodiversity. Pollution includes eutrophication and soil degradation. Fossil fuels are used on a large scale. Small farms have been replaced by very large farms. Farm workers have been replaced by machines. Many different kinds of landscapes have been replaced by a **monotonous** landscape. The environment is used to make money. Such farmers tend to prioritize profit as achieved through crop output over concern for other species or ecological processes.

Figure 3.16 *Agribusiness leads to larger fields and a reduction in natural habitat.*

3.6.1 Describe the Earth's water budget

Model sentence: Only about 2.5 per cent of the Earth's water is fresh water.

The other 97.5 per cent is sea water. Most of the world's fresh water is in the form of ice – ice caps and glaciers. This accounts for about 70 per cent of the world's fresh water. Most of the rest of the world's fresh water is in the form of groundwater. Fresh-water lakes and rivers account for only about 0.3 per cent of the global fresh water budget. There is also some fresh water contained in the soil and in the atmosphere. The following diagram shows the distribution of fresh water resources.

Global water

fresh water 2.5%

salt water 97.5%

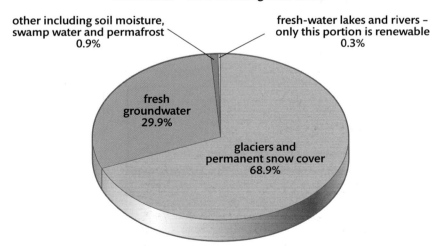

Fresh water – 2.5% of total global water

other including soil moisture, swamp water and permafrost 0.9%

fresh-water lakes and rivers – only this portion is renewable 0.3%

fresh groundwater 29.9%

glaciers and permanent snow cover 68.9%

Figure 3.17 *The Earth's fresh-water resources.*

3.6.2 Describe and evaluate the sustainability of fresh-water resource usage with reference to a case study

Fresh-water resources

All **forms** of fresh water are replenishable. However, they are replenished at different **rates**, affecting sustainability. The fresh water in ice caps may not be replenished for tens of thousands of years. The fresh water in rivers may be replenished in a matter of days. Some groundwater may not be replenished for thousands of years. Groundwater nearer the Earth's surface may be replenished in **decades**.

How much water can be considered to be renewable (or replenishable) depends on where it is found in the hydrological cycle. Renewable water resources are ones that are replenished **annually** or more frequently.

Global water scarcity

In many parts of the world there is water **scarcity**. The following diagram shows that there are different types of water scarcity in different parts of the world.

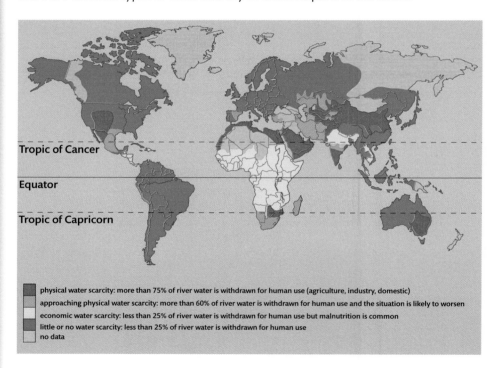

Figure 3.18 *The distribution of different types of water scarcity.*

Physical water scarcity occurs when more than 75 per cent of river water is **withdrawn** for human use. Economic water scarcity occurs when less than 25 per cent of river water is withdrawn, but malnutrition is common.

Water use in MEDCs and LEDCs

Demand for water is increasing. Water is used differently in rich countries and poor countries, as shown in the diagram below.

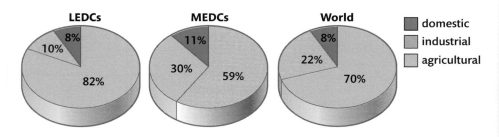

Figure 3.19 *Water use in MEDCs and LEDCs.*

In LEDCs, much more water is used in agriculture. Much water is used and lost in **irrigation**. In MEDCs, most water is used for industry. As industry develops in LEDCs they will use more water. As the world's population grows more water will be needed. As people become richer they use more water. Global warming may reduce supplies of water as some areas become hotter and drier. Although there are plentiful supplies of water, not all are usable. People are using more water than is being replenished. They are also contaminating water supplies. There could be political consequences as a result of water **shortages**.

Sustainable use of water

Sustainable use of water can be achieved in a number of ways. New buildings can be made more water efficient and recycle water. Buildings could have more water-efficient features, such as **low-flush toilets** and **dishwashers**. The use of water meters encourages people to use less water.

People in **rural** areas could use drought-resistant **crops**. **Contamination** of water supplies could be reduced by using less **fertilizer** and pesticides.

Water shortages in China

Case Study: Water shortages in China

China has major problems with the quality and quantity of its water resources. Up to 80 per cent of China's water resources are in the south of the country, but many of these are polluted. Groundwater reserves have been over-extracted and the water table is falling in many parts of the country. Water usage is expected to peak in 2030. Up to 65 per cent of the water is used for agriculture, 23 per cent for industry and just 12 per cent for domestic use.

China has been trying to increase its water supplies through dam building (e.g. the Three Gorges Dam), water transfer schemes (e.g. the South-North transfer project to divert water from the Yangtze River to the Yellow River and Beijing) and desalination plants. In addition, water conservation and recycling programmes have been introduced in a number of cities.

3.7.1 Explain the difficulties in applying the concept of carrying capacity to local human populations

What is carrying capacity?

Carrying capacity is the maximum number of a species, or 'load', that can be sustainably supported by a given area.

Difficulties applying the concept

It is difficult to apply the concept of carrying capacity to human populations for a number of reasons.

- The range of resources used by humans is usually much greater than for any other species. When a resource becomes scarce, humans show great ingenuity in substituting one resource for another. The substitution of shale gas for oil is a good example.

- Resource requirements vary according to lifestyles. These vary from time to time and from population to population. A Maasai herdsman uses far fewer resources than a person who lives in a city and is rich.

- Human populations regularly import resources from outside their immediate environment. This allows them to become larger than the carrying capacity provided by the local resources. A good example of this is the importing of food from countries such as Kenya and Zimbabwe in Africa into Europe.

By importing resources in this way, the carrying capacity for the local population can be increased. However it has no influence on global carrying capacity.

All these variables make it practically impossible to make reliable estimates of carrying capacities for human populations.

> **Hints for success:** Students commonly confuse carrying capacity with ecological footprints. The carrying capacity is the maximum number of a species that can be sustainably supported by a given environment. In this case, it is people. The ecological footprint refers to the area of land and water required to support a defined human population at a given standard of living. The measure takes into account the area required in order to provide all the resources needed by the population, and the disposal of all waste materials.

3.7.2 Explain how absolute reductions in energy and material use, reuse, and recycling can affect human carrying capacity

What is human carrying capacity?

Human carrying capacity is established by the **rate** of energy and material consumption. Carrying capacities are not **static** – they may increase or decrease over time. The **optimists'** point of view is that carrying capacity will be increased through technological improvements. Technological improvements include irrigation and fertilizers. **Pessimists** state that the Earth is a **finite** resource that can only support a certain level of population.

Synonyms

rate .... speed

Glossary

static does not change

optimist person who has an attitude that is positive

pessimist person who has an attitude that is negative

finite anything with a limited size

irrigation artificial addition of water in order to increase crop productivity

fertilizer use of materials to enrich the soil

Subject vocabulary

model a simplified structuring of reality

hydroponics growing crops in nutrient-enriched water

high-yielding varieties (HYVs) crops that produce more food than traditional varieties

The Limits to Growth model

The Limits to Growth model was developed in the early 1970s. The following diagrams shows aspects of the Limits to Growth model.

(a)

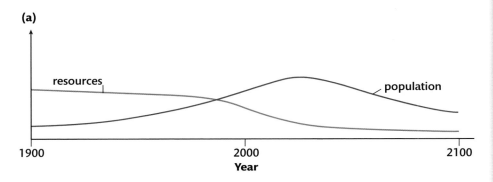

(b)

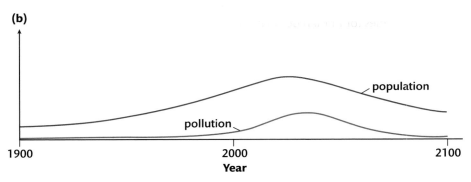

Figure 3.20 *The Limits to Growth model.*

The Limits to Growth model has a pessimistic view of population and resources. It predicts that the limits to the growth of the human population will be reached by 2100. It predicts that the human population will grow faster than the ability of the Earth to provide sufficient resources for the population.

Alternatives to the models

It is possible to produce more food. There are a number of ways in which more food could be produced. Crops could be grown in nutrient-enriched water. This is known as hydroponics. High-yielding varieties (HYVs) of plants could be used. More use of **irrigation** and **fertilizers** could increase farm production.

Subject vocabulary

shale gas natural gas that is recovered from shale rocks

hydroelectric power energy that comes from running water

recycling the processing of industrial and household waste so that the materials can be reused

reuse the use of a product many times over by returning it to the manufacturer or processor each time

reduce use less

substitution using one resource rather than another

sustainable use of global resources at a rate that allows natural regeneration and minimizes damage to the environment

Glossary

conservation protecting or preserving

fossil fuels energy sources from the remains of plants and animals such as oil, natural gas, and coal

fertilizer use of materials to enrich the soil

Synonyms

link .... to be connected with

There have also been new developments in energy resources. New energy sources have been developed. Shale gas is a good example. There has been increased development of renewable energy. Renewable energy includes hydroelectric power and wind energy. Increased energy conservation reduces consumption.

The effect of pollution

Pollution is the addition to an environment of a substance or an agent (such as heat) by human activity, at a rate greater than that at which it can be rendered harmless by the environment. It also has a negative effect on the organisms within the environment.

Humans cause pollution, which damages natural systems. Global life-support systems include a clean atmosphere and clean water. Clean air and clean water are needed for a healthy population and a healthy planet.

Types of pollution include air pollution and water pollution. Air pollution can be caused by the burning of fossil fuels. Water pollution can be caused by soil erosion and when agricultural fertilizer is allowed to enter water systems. Some air pollution is linked to global warming. As global warming continues, there will be less food production in some areas. In addition, some areas will have water shortages if there is less fresh water as a result of global warming.

Reuse and recycling

Recycling is the processing of industrial and household waste so that the materials can be reused. Paper and glass can be recycled. There are a number of materials that can be recycled. Such recycling reduces the need to consume more material (such as trees) to make the product (such as paper).

Reuse is using a product many times by returning it to the manufacturer or processor. The reuse of glass milk bottles is a good example. Reuse of goods reduces the need to get new raw materials.

Reducing the amount of energy used means less energy resources are needed. Turning off lights when they are not needed is a good example.

Substitution is using one resource rather than another. The use of renewable energy sources rather than non-renewable energy sources is more sustainable.

3.8.1 Explain the concept of an ecological footprint as a model for assessing the demands that human populations make on their environment

What is an ecological footprint?

The ecological footprint of a population is the area of land that would be required to provide all the population's resources and assimilate all its wastes. It is useful as a model because it is able to provide a quantitative estimate of human carrying capacity. It is the opposite of carrying capacity. It refers to the area required to sustainably support a given population rather than the population that a given area can sustainably support.

Components of the ecological footprint

The ecological footprint consists of four main categories as shown below:

1. Energy land: land used for fossil fuel energy use

2. Consumed land: land that has been built on

3. Currently used land: farmland, forests, and gardens

4. Land of limited availability: unused forests and deserts.

Advantages of ecological footprints as a model

Ecological footprints have many advantages as a model:

● they are a useful snapshot of the sustainability of a population's lifestyle

● they provide a way for individuals or governments to measure their impact and to identify possible changes in lifestyle

● they are a symbol for raising awareness of environmental issues.

Disadvantages of ecological footprints as a model

There are many disadvantages of using ecological footprints:

● Ecological footprints do not include all information on the environmental impacts of human activities

● It is only a model so it simplifies information and is not exact

● It does not use actual figures so the calculations are not precise.

Subject vocabulary

ecological footprint the area of land and water required to support a defined human population at a given standard of living; the measure takes into account the area required to provide all the resources needed by the population, and the disposal of all waste materials

carrying capacity the maximum number of a species, or 'load', that can be sustainably supported by a given environment

sustainability use of global resources at a rate that allows natural regeneration and minimizes damage to the environment

model a simplified description designed to show the structure of a system and how it works

Glossary

assimilate to absorb/to take in and use

quantitative numerical or size of

fossil fuels energy sources from the remains of plants and animals such as oil, natural gas, and coal

snapshot a picture showing the conditions at a particular time

symbol something that represents an idea

raise awareness to improve people's knowledge of something

Synonyms

given .... particular

impact .... effect

Calculating the ecological footprint of a country

The accurate calculation of an ecological footprint is very complex, but an **approximation** can be made using *per capita* land requirements for food production and *per capita* land requirements for **absorbing** waste. These are given in global hectares (gha). The following formula is used:

per capita land requirement for food production (ha) =

$$\frac{per\ capita\ \text{food consumption (kg yr}^{-1})}{\text{mean food production per hectare of local arable land (kg ha}^{-1}\ \text{yr}^{-1})}$$

and:

per capita land requirement for absorbing waste CO_2 from fossil fuels (ha) =

$$\frac{per\ capita\ CO_2\ \text{emission (kg C yr}^{-1})}{\text{net carbon fixation per hectare of local natural vegetation (kg C ha}^{-1}\ \text{yr}^{-1})}$$

Data for ecological footprints for an LEDC and an MEDC

	Per capita food (grain) consumption (kg/year)	Mean food (grain) production per hectare of local arable land (kg/ha/year)	Per capita CO₂ emissions (kg C/year)	Net carbon fixation per hectare (kg C/ha/year)
LEDC	250	2900	1900	10 000
MEDC	750	3030	17 200	4000

The LEDC's ecological footprint is thus:
$(250 \div 2900) + (1900 \div 10\,000) = 0.09 + 0.19 = 0.28$ gha

The MEDC's ecological footprint is
$(750 \div 3030) + (17\,200 \div 4000) = 0.25 + 4.25 = 4.50$ gha

The total ecological footprint can be calculated as **the sum of** these two *per capita* requirements multiplied by the total population. These are very simplified footprints because they only take into account two categories. The actual ecological footprints for both types of country would be much larger. It ignores the land or water required to provide any **aquatic** and atmospheric resources. It also ignores the assimilation of wastes other than CO_2 from fossil fuels. It does not take into account the land lost due to **urbanization**. Thus this calculation is only an approximation.

3.8.3 Describe and explain the differences between the ecological footprints of two human populations, one from an LEDC and one from an MEDC

Opening sentence:

In this answer I will describe and explain the difference between the ecological footprints of an **LEDC** (Bangladesh) and an **MEDC** (United States).

Differences in the ecological footprint of an LEDC and an MEDC

The **ecological footprint** of MEDCs is greater than the ecological footprint of LEDCs. The USA is an example of an MEDC. The ecological footprint of the USA is 7.17 **gha**. Bangladesh is an LEDC. The ecological footprint of Bangladesh is 0.63 gha. The following diagram shows the **composition** of the ecological footprints for the USA and Bangladesh.

	United States	Bangladesh
Size of ecological footprint in gha/ Rank in world (out of 149 countries	Carbon 4.87 gha/4	Carbon 0.15 gha/112
	Grazing 0.19 gha/82	Grazing 0 gha/144
	Forest 0.86 gha/10	Forest 0.07 gha/137
	Fishing 0.09 gha/49	Fishing 0.02 gha/96
	Cropland 1.09 gha/16	Cropland 0.32 gha/127
	Built-up land 0.07 gha/48	Built-up land 0.07 gha/48
	Total 7.17 gha/5	Total 0.63 gha/144

Figure 3.21 *Ecological footprints for the United States and Bangladesh (Source Living Planet Report, 2012).*

There are major differences between them. The largest **contribution** to the USA's ecological footprint is carbon. This is nearly 70 per cent of the US footprint. Carbon is less than 25 per cent of the ecological footprint in Bangladesh. **Cropland** is the largest contribution to Bangladesh's ecological footprint. This is just over 50 per cent of the ecological footprint of Bangladesh. In the USA, cropland is only 15 per cent of the ecological footprint. Forests and fishing make up a similar contribution to the ecological footprints of both the USA and Bangladesh.

Explaining the differences in the ecological footprints of an LEDC and an MEDC

There are a number of **models** that help explain the differences in the ecological footprints of populations in LEDCs and MEDCs. Ecological footprints can also be linked to stages of the **demographic transition model** (DTM). Generally, there is an

Subject vocabulary

LEDC less economically developed countries/low-income countries

MEDC more economically developed countries/high-income countries

ecological footprint the area of land and water required to support a defined human population at a given standard of living; the measure takes account of the area required to provide all the resources needed by the population, and the disposal of waste materials

gha global hectares

cropland land that is used for growing crops, i.e. arable land

model a simplified description designed to show the structure of a system and how it works

demographic transition model a general model describing the changing levels of fertility and mortality in a human population over time; it describes the changes experienced as countries pass through the processes of industrialization and urbanization

Glossary

composition the way something is made up of different parts

contribution the share of the total

Subject vocabulary

energy efficiency strategies attempts to reduce the amount of energy used, such as public transport systems and turning off appliances when not in use

vegetarian a person who does not eat meat

trophic level the feeding level in an ecosystem

carbon emissions the release of carbon dioxide into the atmosphere through the burning of fossil fuels and deforestation

Glossary

raise to look after animals

appliances electrical or mechanical equipment that provides a function, e.g. fridges and computers

consumption the use of

fossil fuels energy sources from the remains of plants and animals such as oil, natural gas, and coal

increase in the ecological footprint with each stage of the DTM. Some MEDCs may now be reducing footprints through energy efficiency strategies.

How does diet affect the ecological footprint?

Model sentence: People in MEDCs tend to eat more meat than people in LEDCs.

Animal products provide about twice as much energy in the diet of people in MEDCs than for people in LEDCs. The ecological footprint for a meat eater is generally much larger than the ecological footprint for a vegetarian. It requires more energy to produce meat than to grow crops. Meat eaters are eating at a higher trophic level, which means more land is required to create feed for livestock and for raising livestock.

How does the use of energy affect the ecological footprint?

Model sentence: Energy use will be much greater in MEDCs as people have more appliances.

Greater wealth allows higher consumption of goods. In addition, people in MEDCs travel more. This increases carbon emissions. In MEDCs, more goods are imported. This also increases carbon emissions. Populations in MEDCs are more dependent on fossil fuels. This results in higher CO_2 emissions.

Figure 3.22 Solar panels, seen here on Ærø Island, Denmark, reduce the ecological footprint of a country.

3.8.4 Discuss how national and international development policies and cultural influences can affect human population dynamics and growth

National and international policy

Some **policies directly** influence population dynamics and growth. Other policies **indirectly** influence population growth. Population policies can be described as pro-natalist when they try to increase the birth rate, or anti-natalist when they try to reduce population growth.

Population policies

The most famous anti-natalist policy is China's one-child policy. It was introduced in 1979 and limits most Chinese families to one child. China's population would now be 400 million people larger if the one-child policy did not exist. Some critics believe that China's fertility would have come down even if there had not been the one-child policy. They believe that urbanization and industrialization would lead to reduced population growth. In particular, they believe that improved female education and more working women would lead to reduced birth rates.

Example: Singapore

Singapore is an example of a country that had an anti-natalist policy and then changed to a pro-natalist policy. It changed because its fertility rate had dropped to below 1.25 and the workforce was decreasing in size. The government offered **incentives** to families to have three or more children if they could afford them. Singapore's fertility rate has remained low despite the incentives. Women continue to play an active role in the workforce and are choosing jobs rather than having children.

National and international policies

In 2000, the United Nations announced the Millennium Development Goals (MDG). The aim of the Millennium Development Goals is to solve the problems of poverty and inequality. Many of them deal with population growth directly. These include MDG 4: Reduce child mortality and MDG 5: Improve maternal health.

National and international development policies may encourage **rapid** population growth by lowering **mortality** without having a significant effect on fertility. Agricultural development and improved public health may lead to population growth by lowering mortality without having a significant effect on fertility. Birth rates often fall following urbanization. There is less demand for children and more women have jobs in the formal and informal sectors. Policies aimed at female education and female **participation** in the job market are believed to be the most effective method for reducing population pressure.

Glossary

policy a way of doing things that has been agreed by a government or governments

direct in this example, a policy aimed at reducing or increasing population growth

indirect in this example, a policy that influences population growth through a different factor, such as improved diet

incentive something that motivates people to do something

mortality death

participation take part in

Subject vocabulary

population dynamics the changes in population as a result of birth rates, death rates, and migration

pro-natalist in favour of increasing the birth rate

birth rate the number of live births per 1000 people per year

anti-natalist against raising the birth rate

urbanization the increase in the proportion of people living in urban areas

fertility rate the average number of children a woman will have over the course of her life

public health developments such as clean water and sanitation that reduce death rates and increase chances of survival

formal sector jobs that are regulated and taxed

informal sector the job market that is unregulated and pays no taxes; there is no legal basis for such jobs

population pressure the increasing pressure placed upon resources as a result of population growth

Synonyms

rapid .... fast

Cultural factors

Parents may rely on their children for support in their old age. This may create an incentive to have many children. Boys are more valued than girls in some cultures. This can lead to an increase in fertility so that more boys are born. Cultural or religious influence on contraception can also influence fertility. Education about birth control encourages family planning.

Figure 3.23 *Population policy: AIDS awareness in St Lucia.*

3.8.5 Describe and explain the relationship between population, resource consumption, and technological development, and their influence on carrying capacity and material economic growth

Population, resource consumption, and technological development

As countries develop and improve, their resource consumption increases. The use of technology leads to the consumption of resources. In MEDCs and in newly industrializing countries (NICs), the use of cars and electrical goods has increased. This increases the demand for more energy resources. MEDCs have about 20 per cent of the world's population, but use over 50 per cent of the world's resources.

The world has been described as a 'globalized consumer culture'. Resources are extracted and manufactured into goods. They are then transported and stored in warehouses and shops. These goods are sold and eventually thrown away. The demand for consumer goods has increased dramatically in the last 30 years and this has put the world's resources under great pressure. Many believe that the world is reaching its carrying capacity.

Carrying capacity

The carrying capacity is the maximum number of a species, or 'load', that can be sustainably supported by a given environment.

The IPAT model

The IPAT model, which describes the environmental impact of a population, is
I = P × A × T, where:

I = Environmental impact

P = Population size

A = the affluence of the population

T = the environmental effects of the technologies used to obtain and use the resources. This includes the resources needed to produce goods and get rid of the waste that is produced.

As population size increases, the impact on the environment will increase. However, of more importance is the affluence of the population. Wealthy populations have a far greater environmental impact than poorer populations. The role of technology is contradictory. It might be expected that as technology increases, the impact on the environment increases. However, technology may reduce environmental impact by increasing efficiency.

The influence on carrying capacity and material economic growth

Increased material economic growth may lead to a reduced carrying capacity. Increases in the population size, levels of wealth, and the availability of technology may be expected to reduce carrying capacity. This is because more resources

Subject vocabulary

resource consumption the use of resources, such as oil and coal

MEDCs more economically developed countried/high-income countries

newly industrializing countries (NICs) countries with an increasing share of the world's industrial output

globalized consumer culture the interconnected global trade arrangement based on the manufacture, buying and selling of consumer goods

carrying capacity the maximum number of a species, or 'load', that can be sustainably supported by a given environment

IPAT model a model that describes the environmental impact of a population based on population size, wealth, and the technology it uses

material economic growth the growth of the economy through the development of consumer goods and resources

Glossary

extract/extraction to get the energy resource out of the ground

manufactured made into finished and semi-finished goods

warehouse a large building where lots of products can be stored

affluence the level of wealth of a population

Synonyms

given .... particular

are being used up. However, technology may lead to greater efficiency and new technologies that can harvest renewable resources, such as solar power and wind power.

Many economists state that human carrying capacity can be increased through technological developments. The Earth can hold more people if we learn to use energy and resources more efficiently. Technocrats believe that difficult situations encourage people to find answers to problems and that human **adaptability** and intelligence will find a solution.

Model sentence: **Many of the 'solutions', such as** hydroelectric power **and nuclear energy, require huge amounts of fossil fuels to be used in order to build power stations.**

Many **forms** of sustainable development are very expensive. Sustainable **urban** development can be very expensive.

Governments and oil companies will continue to choose to make less difficult decisions as long as it is cheaper to extract fossil fuels than develop alternative technologies. Governments face many pressures and there are many demands on their resources. Governments know that spending money on technologies that might not **pay back** for many years is not popular with the people.

Figure 3.24 *Soil degradation, seen here at Breakfast Vlei, Eastern Cape, South Africa, reduces carrying capacity.*

Subject vocabulary

technocrats people who believe that technology has the answers for human resource problems

hydroelectric power (HEP) energy that comes from running water

sustainable development development that meets current needs without compromising the ability of future generations to meet their own needs

alternative technologies technologies that do not rely on fossil fuels, e.g. HEP and wind power

Glossary

adaptability being able to change successfully

pay back to make a profit

Synonyms

form .... type

urban .... of a town/city

4.1.1 Define the terms *biodiversity*, *genetic diversity*, *species diversity*, and *habitat diversity*

Biodiversity

Model sentence: Biodiversity is the amount of biological or living diversity in a specific area. It includes the concepts of species diversity, habitat diversity, and genetic diversity.

Figure 4.1 *Rainforests are high in biodiversity as they are rich in resources, such as food and space. There are many different niches in rainforests and so many species can live together.*

Genetic diversity

Genetic diversity is the **range** of **genetic material** which is present in a **species**.

Species diversity

Model sentence: Species diversity is a measurement of the number of different species and how abundant they are compared to other species in a specific area.

habitat the place where a species lives

conservation the preservation and protection of nature

habitat diversity the range of different habitats in an ecosystem

species diversity measurement of the number of different species and their number/amount compared to one another in a specific area

genetic diversity the range of genetic material present in a species

Glossary

to preserve to save something from destruction

Habitat diversity

Model sentence: Habitat diversity is the range of different habitats in an ecosystem.

Figure 4.2 *Ecosystems such as deserts have low habitat diversity and low species diversity because there are fewer opportunities for species to live together.*

Conservation of habitat diversity usually leads to species diversity and genetic diversity being protected and preserved.

Hints for success: You must include the words 'in a specific area' in your definitions of biodiversity and species diversity.
Species diversity does not mean the number of species in an area. The definition of the number of species in an area is species richness. Species richness is the number of species in a specific area, whereas species diversity also includes a measure of the relative abundance of each species.

4.1.2 Outline the mechanism of natural selection as a possible driving force for speciation

Model sentence: Speciation is the process by which new species form. Natural selection works with isolating mechanisms as a driving force to produce new species.

What is the role of natural selection in the formation of new species?

The theory of **evolution** by natural selection was first developed by Charles Darwin. Darwin published his book *On the Origin of Species* in 1859. The book explained and provided evidence for the theory of evolution by natural selection.

Natural selection is the process where organisms that are better adapted to their surroundings are more likely to survive and produce more **offspring**. All species show **variation** and all species show **over-reproduction**. Variation is caused by **genetic diversity**. Over-reproduction leads to **competition** for limited resources and there is a '**struggle for existence**'. Because species show variation, those individuals that have adapted best to their surroundings (i.e. that fit their environment) survive. The individuals who are fittest and survive can then go on to reproduce. The **genetic characteristics** of an individual help determine whether it will survive or not. The genetic characteristics that are successful are passed on to the next generation when an individual reproduces. Over time, there is a gradual change in the genetic characteristics of a species and this leads, eventually, to the formation of new species.

Figure 4.3 *Charles Darwin about 20 years after the voyage of the* Beagle, *when he was in his forties and accumulating evidence in support of his theory of evolution.*

4.1.3 State that isolation can lead to different species being produced that are unable to interbreed to yield fertile offspring

Opening sentence:

In this answer I will show how **isolation** can **lead to** different **species** being produced that are unable to **interbreed** to produce **fertile offspring**. I will use examples to illustrate my answer.

Speciation can occur as a result of different **isolating mechanisms**. Speciation can occur as a result of **geographical isolation** or **reproductive isolation**.

Model sentence: Geographical isolation is isolation caused by a barrier that results in populations becoming separated.

Separation may occur when new land or water barriers **form**.

Model sentence: Reproductive isolation is isolation caused by processes that prevent the members of two different species from producing offspring together.

Reproductive isolation may be caused by ecological, behavioural, or **anatomical** differences between populations.

Geographical isolation

Model sentence: Two examples of geographical isolation are the islands of the Galápagos and the East African Rift.

1. The islands of the Galápagos

The islands are **volcanic** and were created as a result of **plate tectonic** activity beneath the sea. Animals and plants on the islands arrived from mainland South America. The separation of the islands caused the animal and plant populations that arrived from mainland South America to become geographically **isolated** from each other. Because the local conditions on each island were different, **natural selection** resulted in different species evolving on different islands.

2. The East African Rift

An example of a geographical barrier is rift valleys that form when tectonic plates move apart. The East African Rift is an example of a rift valley formation. Some of the East African **rift valley** has filled with water to form lakes, such as Lake Malawi, Lake Tanganyika, and Lake Victoria. Another example of a geographical barrier is a **mountain range** such as the Himalayas. The following diagram shows how the formation of a geographical barrier can lead to speciation.

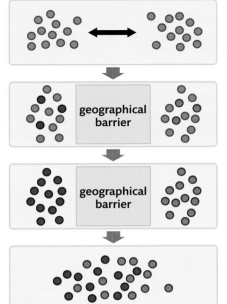

two populations of one species can interbreed and mix genes (gene flow occurs)

populations separated by a geographical barrier cannot interbreed; each develops its own variations (gene flow interrupted)

eventually two separate species develop in response to different selection pressures

even without a geographical barrier, the two species remain genetically distinct

Figure 4.4 *How geographical barriers can lead to speciation. Geographical barriers include mountains, water (sea, river, or lake), or hostile environments.*

Reproductive isolation

1. Ecological causes

An ecological cause of reproductive isolation is **environmental isolation**. Environmental isolation is the separation of populations that have the same geographic ranges but whose **niches** are different in some way. An example of environmental isolation is **temporal isolation**. Temporal isolation is the separation of populations that have the same **geographic ranges** but whose times of activity are different. An example of temporal isolation is the American toad (*Bufo americanus*) and the Fowler's toad (*Bufo fowleri*). The American toad and the Fowler's toad have been mated in the laboratory, but mating does not happen in the wild because of differences in mating times. The American toad mates early in the summer while the Fowler's toad mates in late summer.

2. Behavioural causes

Behavioural isolation is when differences in the behaviour of two populations result in speciation.

An example of behavioural isolation is differences in **courtship display**. An example of behavioural isolation is shown by the **birds of paradise**. Male birds of paradise have bright and colourful feathers which they use to attract females. Different species have different patterns. Dancing displays also vary between different species. Changes in the appearance or behaviour of populations may result in males and females of those populations no longer being attracted to each other and therefore not breeding together.

4.1.4 Explain how plate activity has influenced evolution and biodiversity

Model sentence: Evolution is the cumulative and gradual change in the genetic characteristics of successive generations of a species.

These cumulative gradual changes eventually give rise to species different from the common ancestor.

Model sentence: Biodiversity is the amount of biological or living variety in a specific area.

Biodiversity includes the concepts of species diversity, habitat diversity, and genetic diversity.

Model sentence: Plate activity has resulted in changes in the genetic characteristics of species and to the formation of new biodiversity.

New biodiversity is formed by the process of speciation. Speciation takes place when populations are separated into new surroundings and then natural selection occurs when the populations adapt to their new surroundings.

Model sentence: The movement of tectonic plates causes populations to be separated and creates the conditions for natural selection to take place.

How does plate activity lead to speciation?

The formation of geographical barriers such as mountains and rift valleys

1. The formation of new mountain or rift valleys forms a barrier between two populations.

2. New habitats are created.

3. The increase in habitat diversity leads to an increase in species diversity as the number of available niches increases.

4. The geographical barrier could separate species and put them in two different ecosystems with climates that might be completely different.

5. Separated populations would adapt to their new surroundings and eventually evolve into new species.

Model sentence: The separation of land by rift valleys can lead to speciation on each side of the valley.

When rift valleys fill with water, new aquatic habitats are created that lead to the formation of new biodiversity.

Model sentence: An example of geographical isolation is the formation of the East African rift valley created Lake Tanganyika, which has a large number of endemic cichlid fish species.

The following diagram shows the role of plate tectonics in the formation of geographical barriers:

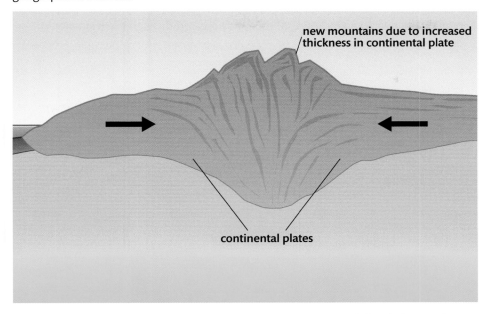

new mountains due to increased thickness in continental plate

continental plates

Figure 4.5 *Continental plates colliding. This leads to an increase in continental plate thickness and eventually to new mountain ranges, such as the Himalayas, where the Indian plate is being pushed against the large Asian plate.*

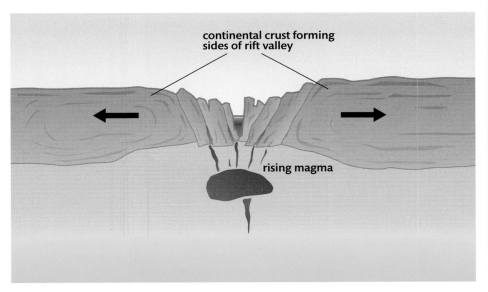

continental crust forming sides of rift valley

rising magma

Figure 4.6 *Continental plates moving apart cause rift valleys. Deep lakes may form in these valleys, such as the world's deepest lake, Lake Baikal, in Siberia, Russia.*

The separation of land by rift valleys can lead to speciation on each side of the valley. When rift valleys fill with water, new aquatic habitats are created that lead to the formation of new biodiversity. For example, the formation of the East African rift valley created Lake Tanganyika, which has a large number of endemic cichlid fish species.

Island formation

The following figure shows how islands can be created through plate activity:

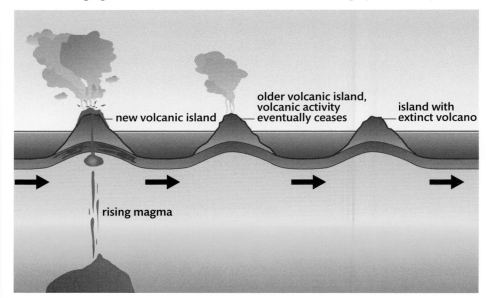

Figure 4.7 *In some areas, hot liquid rock rises from deep in the Earth and breaks through the outer rocks. The movement of tectonic plates over these 'hot spots' creates chains of islands.*

Examples of islands formed in this way are the Galápagos Islands and Hawaii.

Populations that are located on islands can result in speciation.

1. The formation of **volcanic** islands creates new environments

2. Animals and plants **colonize** the new islands

3. The animals and plants **adapt** to local conditions

4. This leads to speciation and increased regional **diversity**.

Summary

In each of the examples above, **isolation** can lead to behavioural or **ecological differences** that in turn lead to **reproductive isolation**. Reproductive isolation means that members of two different species cannot produce offspring together, as their **genetic material** has become too different.

In addition, when **tectonic plates collide** it leads to a **convergence** of land masses which produces a mixing of genetic material. The joining of land masses encourages new ecological links and there may also be **interbreeding** between the populations that have come together. The joining of new land masses can also lead to new **habitat diversity** as well as to new **species diversity**.

Model sentence: Plate activity creates geographical isolation, which can lead to ecological and behavioural differences between populations.

Geographical and reproductive isolation cause new species to be formed as the two groups lose the ability to produce **fertile offspring** together.

Evolution is the cumulative and gradual change in the genetic characteristics of successive generations of a species.

Biodiversity is the amount of biological or living variety in a specific area.

Plate movement leads to evolution and an increase in biodiversity because:

- *The collision of plates can lead to uplift leading to mountain formation.*
- *The collision of plates can cause the spread of species through the creation of land bridges.*
- *Plate movements cause the separation of continental plates leads to isolation of populations.*
- *Plate activity can create new islands, usually through volcanic activity.*
- *The movement of plates to new climate regions leads to evolutionary change to adapt to new conditions.*

Plate movement leads to an increase in biodiversity because:

- *New habitats form, with populations adapting to new environments.*
- *Populations separate, leading to speciation.*

Hints for success: You do not need to have a detailed understanding of the mechanism of plate tectonics. You do need to be able to explain how plate movement has resulted in evolution and biodiversity.

geographical isolation a physical barrier that causes populations to become separated

behavioural difference differences between organisms in the way that they act/behave

Glossary

fertile able to produce young/babies

offspring the young/children

4.1.5 Explain the relationships among ecosystem diversity, stability, succession and habitat

Subject vocabulary

succession the orderly process of change over time in a community

community a group of different species living together in a common habitat

diversity variety; the meaning depends on the situation in which it is used

species diversity a measurement of the number of different species and their number/amount compared to one another in a specific area

habitat diversity the range of different habitats in an ecosystem

genetic diversity the range of genetic material present in a species

stability when there is no overall change in a system

ecosystem community of organisms that depend on each other and the environment they live in

seral stage the term for each stage of a succession

nutrients chemicals, derived from the natural environment or from fertilizers, that organisms need to live and grow niche where and how a species lives

niche where and how a species lives

species a group of organisms that mate/breed and have young able to breed/mate and have their own young

genetic material each cell in an organism contains the molecule DNA, which is a set of instructions for particular characteristics in a species

climax community the final stage of a succession that is more or less stable and is in equilibrium

pioneer community the first stage of an ecological succession that contains hardy species which are able to survive difficult conditions

food web a diagram that shows food chains in an ecosystem and how they are linked together

Model sentence: Succession **is the orderly process of change over time in a community.**

Model sentence: Diversity **can be defined as variety, but the meaning depends on the context in which it is used. In this answer I will refer to species diversity, habitat diversity, and genetic diversity. Stability is a situation where there is no overall change in a system.**

How does diversity and stability change during succession?

As a succession progresses, the complexity of an ecosystem increases. As complexity increases, diversity becomes greater:

1. Each seral stage of succession helps create a deeper soil with more nutrients, which allows larger plants to grow.

2. Changes in the plant community increase habitat diversity.

3. This leads to greater species diversity and genetic diversity.

4. Greater habitat diversity leads to an increase in niches, which allows more species to live together.

5. Greater species diversity increases genetic diversity because there is a greater range of genetic material in the greater number of species.

6. Climax communities have a more complex system and so are more stable than earlier seral stages, such as pioneer communities.

Model sentence: **A complex ecosystem has more food webs and so the loss of one species can lead to it being replaced by another species and this leads to stability.**

Model sentence: **A complex ecosystem has a variety of nutrient and energy pathways which provide stability.**

How do human activities alter succession?

Model sentence: **Human activities alter succession, for example through logging, grazing, and burning.**

Human activities can replace complex ecosystems with simpler ecosystems. When human activities simplify ecosystems they make them **unstable**. An ecosystem's ability to survive change depends on diversity, resilience, and inertia. Resilience is the ability of an ecosystem to recover after it has been disturbed. Inertia is the resistance of an ecosystem to being altered. For example, wheat farming has replaced the original **native** tall grass **prairie** ecosystems with a monoculture.

Tall grass prairie has high diversity with complex food webs, which maintains stability. Complex **nutrient cycles** in this ecosystem also maintain stability. The increase in organic matter leads to deep, nutrient-rich soils. The soils encourage new growth which allows this ecosystem to recover quickly after the fires that pass through prairies from time to time. Tall grass prairies therefore have low inertia because they burn very easily but have high resilience because they recover quickly after fire.

Low diversity in wheat fields means that they are likely to suffer from crop pests. Wheat fields are also more likely to suffer damage by fire. They do not recover well after they have been disturbed due to low diversity, low inertia, and soils that need to be looked after **artificially** through the addition of nutrients.

Model sentence: Because wheat fields do not recover well after they have been disturbed, they have low resilience.

An ecosystem's ability to survice depends on diversity, resilience, and inertia:

- *Diversity is the variety of living things in an area.*

- *Resilience is the ability of an ecosystem to recover after it has been disturbed.*

- *Inertia is the resilience of an ecosystem being altered.*

Hints for success: Make sure you know and understand the differences between inertia and resilience, as they are difficult terms. Inertia is the resistance of an ecosystem to being changed. In contrast, resilience is its ability to recover after it has been disturbed.

4.2.1 Identify factors that lead to loss of diversity

Model sentence: I will identify two different factors that lead to the loss of diversity. Loss of diversity can be due to natural events or it can be due to human actions.

Factor 1: Natural events

Natural events, such as **volcanoes**, drought, **ice ages**, and **meteor impact**, have led to loss of diversity. The **eruption** of **Krakatau** in 1883 caused a cloud of smoke and dust that reduced the amount of sunlight reaching large areas of the Earth's surface and which led to a fall in surface temperatures. Changes in the Australian **climate** as the result of movements in **tectonic plates** and **global warming** have caused an increase in the **frequency** of fires and a general drying of the continent. The increasingly dry climate in Australia has led to the **prevalence** of **drought-tolerant** species and the **extinction** of other species.

Changes in the **orbit** of the Earth and its **tilt**, along with **plate tectonic** movement, have led to many **long-term** cold periods. These have resulted in the selection of species **adapted** to colder conditions and the extinction of less-adapted species. One reason for the success of **mammals** is their ability to produce their own heat and control their temperature, which has made it possible for them to survive in colder environments.

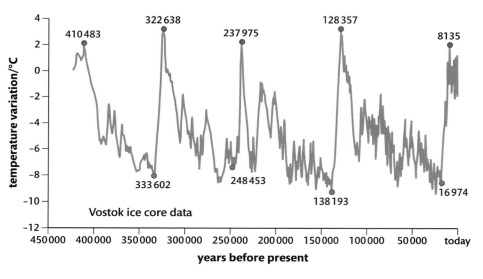

Figure 4.8 *Variation in the temperature of the Earth, shown through data taken from ice in the Antarctic. Major ice ages have occurred about every 100 000 years.*

Volcanic activity has also led to **mass extinctions**. Mass extinctions have also been caused by other factors, such as meteor impact. Both meteor impact and volcanic events led to **climate change** that destroyed a large proportion of the Earth's **biodiversity**. Climate change meant that many species were no longer adapted to their surroundings and were not able to adapt fast enough in order to survive.

Factor 2: Human actions

Losses to diversity as a result of human actions include **habitat degradation**, **fragmentation**, and loss. Some agricultural methods are a threat to **native** species. These methods include the introduction of **monocultures**, and the use of **pesticides** and **genetically modified (GM) species**. Native species are less able to compete with **species** that are introduced through agriculture. Monocultures mean a large loss of diversity compared to the native **ecosystems** that they replace. **Non-specific pesticides** can destroy native as well as imported pest species and this leads to a loss of diversity. If GM species are allowed to escape and reproduce, they might eventually get rid of all less-competitive native species.

Loss of diversity in a particular area can be caused by droughts, floods, habitat loss, disease, or the evolution of a superior competitor.

Mass extinctions are caused by global catastrophic events such as volcanic activity, meteor impact, and glaciation events causing changes in sea level.

Hints for success: The rate at which biodiversity is lost may vary from country to country depending on the ecosystems which are found there. The rate of biodiversity loss may also vary because of differences in protection policies, monitoring, environmental viewpoints, and stage of economic development.

Glossary

drought-tolerant able to survive times when there is not enough water for plants and animals

orbit the curved path of the Earth around the Sun

tilt the rotation of the Earth relative to the Sun

long-term over a long period of time

mammal the type of animal that drinks milk from its mother

native originally found in a country

Synonyms

adapt........... change successfully

Subject vocabulary

habitat degradation decrease in the quality and complexity of the area where organisms live

fragmentation when habitat is divided into smaller areas that are separate from each other

monoculture growing one type of crop

pesticide a chemical substance that kills unwanted pests

genetically modified (GM) species species in which new genetic material has been introduced from other organisms

species a group of organisms that mate/breed and have young able to breed/mate and have their own young

ecosystem a community of organisms that depend on each other and the environment they live in

non-specific pesticide a chemical substance that kills lots of different pests and is not a targeted pesticide

4.2.2 Discuss the perceived vulnerability of tropical rainforests and their relative value in contributing to global biodiversity

Opening sentence:

In this answer I will discuss why tropical rainforests are **perceived** to be **vulnerable**. I will also discuss their value in contributing to **global biodiversity** when compared to other **biomes**.

Why are tropical rainforests vulnerable?

Figure 4.9 *Tropical rainforest showing its layered structure. Photo taken near Kuranda, Queensland, Australia.*

Tropical rainforests are vulnerable because they are under constant threat from **logging** or the removal of forest for other land use, such as agriculture. An average of 1.5 hectares (the size of a football pitch) of tropical rainforest is lost every four seconds. Deforestation and forest degradation occur as the result of external demands for timber, beef, soya, and **biofuels**. External demands for beef and soya lead to the destruction of trees to create farmland.

Rainforests have thin, nutrient-poor soils. The poor soils have implications when forests are cleared. Because there are not many nutrients in the soil, it is difficult for rainforests to regrow once they have been cleared. Studies in the Brazilian Atlantic Forest have shown that certain aspects return surprisingly quickly, within 65 years, but for the forest to fully recover, more time is needed. It can take up to 4000 years for cleared tropical rainforest to fully recover. Recovery depends on the level of disturbance. A large area of cleared land will take a lot longer to grow back than small areas which have been used for **shifting cultivation**. A forest which has been **selectively logged** can grow back if not too much timber has been removed. If too much timber is removed from selectively logged forests, the forest never fully recovers because fast-growing, light-loving species, such as vines and **creepers**, block out the light for slow growers. As a result, the forest remains at a sub-climax level.

What is the relative value of tropical rainforest in contributing to global diversity?

Tropical rainforests cover only 5.9 per cent of the Earth's land surface, but may contain up to 50 per cent of all species. Tropical rainforests are found in South America, Africa, and South-East Asia. Temperatures vary from 20°C at night to 35°C at midday, and levels of sunlight and temperature do not vary throughout the year. Rainfall is high in tropical rainforests. The constant warm temperatures, high levels of sunlight, and high rainfall lead to high levels of **photosynthesis** and high **net primary productivity**. High net primary productivity leads to high **biomass**. High biomass leads to **abundant** resources, such as food. Rainforests are **complex ecosystems** with many **layers**: the tops of the tallest trees, the **canopy** layer, the understorey, and finally the ground layer. The complex layered structure of rainforests increases **habitat diversity** and allows them to support many different **niches**. They are one of the two most species-rich and biodiverse ecosystems on Earth (**coral** reefs are the other). Many contain **biological hotspots**, which contain large numbers of species, often **endemic** to the area. Over 50 per cent of the world's plant species and 42 per cent of all land **vertebrate** species are endemic to 34 identified biodiversity hotspots, most of which are in rainforests.

What is the role of deforestation in the development of green politics?

Green politics is a political viewpoint that places an importance on ecological and environmental goals, and **sustainable development**. The Green movement aims to reduce deforestation and increase **reforestation**. The Green movement started in part as a result of the threats to tropical rainforests. Many politicians get involved because they know it is an important and popular topic for many voters. **Anti-capitalism** is an important feature of Green politics: it focuses on the way in which people are destroying nature for personal gain.

4.2.3 Discuss current estimates of numbers of species and past and present rates of species extinction

What is the current estimate for the numbers of species on Earth?

The total number of **species** on Earth today is still not well understood. Estimates of the **current** number of species on the planet **range** from 5 million to 100 million. So far, science has identified about 1.8 million species. It is impossible to get an accurate count of the number of species because many species have not been discovered yet. Many species that have not yet been discovered are very small, such as insects, bacteria, and other **microbes**. There are areas of the Earth that we still know little about, such as the **canopy** of rainforest and the deep ocean, where many undiscovered species may live. Without a **reliable** estimate of the number of species, it is difficult to calculate **extinction** rates.

What are the past and present rates of species extinction?

The **fossil record** shows that there have been five periods of **mass extinction** in the past. Mass extinctions are when species disappear in a **geologically** short time period, usually between a few hundred thousand to a few million years. Figure 4.10 on page 145 shows the periods of mass extinction over **geological time**.

Model sentence: Past mass extinctions have natural, abiotic causes.

Causes of mass extinction include **meteorite strikes** and huge **volcanic eruptions**. Animals and plants died from both the initial event and the events that followed. Events that followed meteorite strikes and massive volcanic eruptions include **climate change** and **planetary cooling**.

Model sentence: Scientists believe that the Earth is currently experiencing a sixth mass extinction, caused by human activities (i.e. biotic causes).

The sixth mass extinction is therefore the first mass extinction event to have biotic, rather than abiotic, causes.

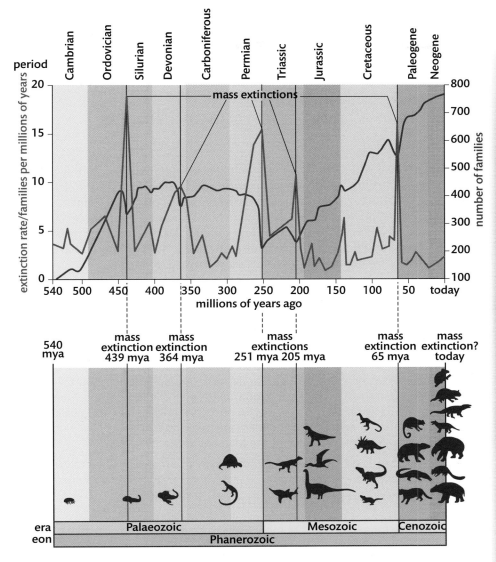

Figure 4.10 *The five mass extinctions that have wiped out 99 per cent of all species that have ever existed on Earth.*

Model sentence: Current extinctions are occurring at a faster rate than past mass extinctions because human activity is rapidly damaging ecosystems.

Mass extinctions of the past took place over geological time, which allowed time for new species to **evolve** to fill the gaps left by the extinct species. Current changes to the planet are occurring much faster, over the period of human lifetimes. **Over-population**, **invasive species**, and **overexploitation** are making the extinction worse. **Pollution** and **global warming** are also speeding up changes to the planet. The changes to the planet do not allow time for species to **adapt** and evolve, which increases extinction rates. Some scientists have predicted that 50 per cent of all species could be extinct by the end of the 21st century.

Hints for success: You need to be able to compare and contrast the possible causes of mass extinctions in the past to present-day extinctions. For example, past mass extinctions had abiotic causes. In contrast, current extinctions have a biotic cause.

4.2.4 Describe and explain the factors that may make species more or less prone to extinction

Not all **species** are equally **vulnerable** to **extinction**. Certain animals and plants, through their ecology or behaviour, are more at risk.

Model sentence: I will now describe and explain each factor in turn.

Factor 1: Small population size and limited distribution

Species with small **population** sizes and limited **distribution** are more likely to become extinct than common and **widespread** species. For example, the slender-billed grackle (*Cassidix palustris*) was a bird that once occupied a single **marsh** near Mexico City and became extinct through human activity. Species with small populations are also more likely to have low **genetic diversity** and their inability to **adapt** to changing conditions can be **fatal**. Many of the large cat species have low genetic diversity, for example the cheetah, snow leopard, and tiger.

Factor 2: Degree of specialization

Specialist species are more likely to become extinct than **generalist species**. **Specialized** species have a narrow **niche** so, if their surroundings change, they may not be able to adapt and change. For example, a species' food resources may be very specialized, such as the giant panda, which mainly eats bamboo. Some animals can live only on certain tree species, such as the Palila bird (a Hawaiian honeycreeper), which depends on the Mamane tree (*Sophora chrysophylla*) for its food and is therefore losing habitat as the Mamane tree is cut down.

Factor 3: Reproductive potential

Species that live for a long time are more likely to have a low **reproductive rate** and this makes them vulnerable to extinction. If there is a change in **habitat** or a **predator** is introduced, the population drops and there are not enough reproductive adults to support and maintain the population. Because they are slow-reproducing, any loss in numbers means a fast decline. The Steller's sea cow was heavily hunted and unable to replace its numbers fast enough. Animals with long **gestation** times, for example elephants and rhinos, are also prone to low rates of reproduction, and it can take many years to recover from any reduction in population numbers.

Factor 4: Poor competitors

Species that show weak **interspecific competition** are more likely to become extinct than good **competitors**. **Flightless** and slow-moving birds, such as the great auk, great elephant bird, and the dodo, are helpless under the pressures of hunting and **predation**. Their lack of **mobility** and poor **defensive instincts** mean that they are easily preyed upon. Animals that have **evolved** in areas where they have no predators, such as the dodo on Mauritius, are prone to extinction when a predator is introduced.

Factor 5: Trophic level

Top predators are **sensitive** to any disturbance in the food chain. Any reduction in numbers of species at lower trophic levels can have dramatic consequences. Top predators are more likely to be rare because energy is lost through food chains. This means that there is little energy left by the end of the food chain. Top carnivores are therefore particularly sensitive to hunters and reductions in population size.

It is also possible that species in high trophic levels may **accumulate toxins**, such as the American bald eagle.

Factors that make a species more prone to extinction include:

- *Factor 1: Small population size*

- *Factor 2: Limited distribution*

- *Factor 3: Being a specialist species*

- *Factor 4: Low reproductive potential*

- *Factor 5: Being a poor competitor*

- *Factor 6: High trophic level*

Hints for success: If an exam question asks you to outline factors that make a species prone to extinction, use factors from this page. Do not talk about general causes for the loss of biodiversity such as floods, droughts, volcanic activity, and so on.

Synonyms

adapt .... change successfully

fatal .... result in death

flightless .... unable to fly

mobility .... ability to move

sensitive .... easily damaged by something

Subject vocabulary

food chain a simple diagram that shows feeding relationships in an ecosystem

trophic level the position that an organism, or group of organisms, occupies in a food chain

carnivore an organism that eats other animals

Glossary

accumulate build up

toxin a poisonous substance

4.2.5 Outline the factors used to determine a species' Red List conservation status

Opening sentence:

In this answer I will outline the factors used to determine a species' Red List conservation status.

For over 40 years, the International Union for the Conservation of Nature (IUCN) has published documents called the Red Data Books. These **assess** the conservation status of a particular species in order to **highlight** species that are threatened with extinction, and to encourage their conservation. The Red List is a record of all threatened species. The plants and animals on the Red List are an **irreplaceable** resource that the IUCN hopes to **conserve** by increasing awareness of them.

Model sentence: A range of factors are used to determine the conservation status of a species on the Red List. I will outline these in turn and give an example of an animal or plant for each factor.

Factor 1: The population size of a species

Smaller **populations** are more likely to **go extinct**.

Example of Red List species: *Puya raimondii*, also known as 'Queen of the Andes'. This is a spectacular plant found high in the Andes Mountains in Peru and Bolivia. It is **isolated** and has a very small population size.

Factor 2: Reduction in population size

A reduction in population size may **indicate** that a species is under threat.

Example of Red List species: the European eel (*Anguilla anguilla*).

European eel numbers are at their lowest levels ever in most of its range and it continues to decline.

Factor 3: The numbers of mature individuals

Species with few mature individuals have lower **reproductive rates**.

Example of Red List species: orang-utan (*Pongo pygmaeus*).

Orang-utans have one of the slowest reproductive rates of all **mammal** species. They give birth to a single offspring only once every 6 to 8 years. With such a low reproductive rate, even a small decrease in numbers can lead to extinction.

Factor 4: Geographic range

Species with a limited geographic range may be under greater threat from extinction.

Example of Red List species: the peacock parachute tarantula (*Poecilotheria metallica*).

The peacock parachute tarantula is found in only a single location in the Eastern Ghats of Andhra Pradesh in India.

Factor 5: Degree of fragmentation

Species in **fragmented habitats** may not be able to maintain large enough population sizes.

Example of Red List species: the Sumatran rhinoceros (*Dicerorhinus sumatrensis*).

Fragmentation of tropical rainforest in South-East Asia has led to a reduction in habitat area for this species.

Factor 6: Quality of habitat

Species that live in habitats that are poorer in quality are less likely to survive than species in habitats that are better in quality.

Example of Red List species: the fishing cat (*Prionailurus viverrinus*).

The fishing cat is found in South-East Asian **wetland** areas where it is a **skilful** swimmer. **Drainage** of wetlands where it lives for agriculture has led to a reduction in habitat quality.

Factor 7: Area of occupancy

Species that live in a smaller area are under greater threat from extinction than more **widespread** species. Loss of the area they live in will lead to loss of the species.

Example of Red List species: golden lion tamarin (*Leontopithecus rosalia*).

Golden lion tamarin monkeys are only found in one small area of Brazil, and are therefore especially **prone** to extinction.

> **Hints for success:** You do not need to know the definitions of the Red List conservation status categories, such as 'threatened' and 'least concern'. You do need to be aware that a sliding scale is used.

Glossary

case history/case study a detailed account of someone or something over a period of time

intervention involvement in a situation in order to improve it or prevent it from getting worse

native originally found in a country

mammal the type of animal that drinks milk from its mother

burrow a passage dug in the ground where animals live

ground-nesting birds birds that make their nests on the ground

settler people who move a long way from their homes to live in a new place

scrub an area of poor soil with low bushes and trees

Subject vocabulary

species a group of organisms that mate/breed and have young able to breed/mate and have their own young

extinction/extinct the loss of species from the Earth

critically endangered a species that still exists in nature but is listed as being at the highest risk for extinction

conservation status a measure of how endangered a species is; a sliding scale runs from 'least concern' to 'extinct'

predator an animal that hunts and eats other animals

habitat the place where a species lives

Synonyms

tame.................... not wild

seashore.............. beach

Opening sentence:

In this answer I will describe the **case histories** of three different **species**. One species has become **extinct**, another is **critically endangered**, and the third has had its **conservation status** improved by **intervention**.

A species that is extinct

Model sentence: I will describe ecological and other factors that caused a species' extinction. I will describe the species' ecological role and the possible consequences of its disappearance. For my case study, I will use the example of the Falkland Islands wolf.

The Falkland Islands wolf was the only **native** land **mammal** of the Falkland Islands. In 1833, Charles Darwin visited the islands and described the wolf as 'common and **tame**'.

Ecological role

The Falkland Islands wolf is said to have lived in **burrows**. It is probable that its diet was **ground-nesting birds**, such as geese and penguins. The Falkland Islands wolf may have eaten insects, and also animals on the **seashore**.

Pressures

Settlers of the Falkland Islands from Scotland, France, and England thought that the Falkland Islands wolf was a threat to their sheep. A large-scale operation of poisoning and shooting began with the aim of removing the wolf completely from the island. The operation was successful very rapidly. It was easy to kill the wolf because there were no forests, the animal was tame, and it had no **predators**.

Consequences of disappearance

The Falkland Islands wolf was not particularly threatening, nor was it a significant predator. However, the removal of a top predator would have had an impact on the rest of the food chain.

A species that is critically endangered

Model sentence: I will describe ecological and other factors that have caused the species to become critically endangered. I will describe the species' ecological role and the possible consequences if it becomes extinct. For my case study I will use the example of the Iberian Lynx.

The Iberian lynx (*Lynx pardinus*) is also known as the Spanish lynx and is native to Spain and Portugal. It is smaller than northern lynxes, such as the Eurasian lynx, and so it usually hunts smaller animals that are generally no larger than hares. It also differs in **habitat** choice. It lives in open **scrub**, whereas the Eurasian Lynx lives in forests.

Ecological role

The Iberian lynx is a specialist species; rabbits make up 80–100 per cent of its diet. Lynx often kill other animals, such as wild cats and foxes, but they do not eat them.

Pressures

The lynx's very specialized diet makes it a **vulnerable** species. The rapid decline in rabbit populations since the 1950s has had a direct impact on lynx numbers. The Iberian lynx lives only in very small, **isolated** areas in Spain and possibly Portugal. Habitat destruction and deterioration have had a negative impact on the lynx for centuries. Some lynxes are still shot and killed in **traps and snares** that are intended for smaller predators.

Possible consequences of disappearance

Species at the trophic level below the lynx may become more numerous as they are subject to less predation. The shortened food chain could produce **imbalances** at other trophic levels. Removal of the lynx could result in sick or weak animals lower down the food chain, usually eaten by the lynx, not being killed. Less fit individuals lower down the food chain could survive and **breed**.

A species whose conservation status has been improved by intervention

Model sentence: **I will describe ecological and other factors that caused a species to become critically endangered. I will describe the species' ecological role, measures, and interventions that have been taken to restore populations. For my case study I will use the example of the American bald eagle.**

Ecological role

Bald eagles live near large areas of open water, such as lakes, and **nest** in tall trees. They mainly feed on fish, but also eat small animals and occasionally **carrion**.

Pressures

It has been estimated that there were around 300 000 to 500 000 bald eagles in the early 1700s. Their population fell to less than 10 000 nesting pairs by the 1950s. Their population fell to less than 500 pairs by the early 1960s. This population decline was caused by the large-scale shooting of eagles, the use of **pesticides** on crops, and the destruction of habitat. The **contamination** of waterways and food sources by a wide range of poisons and other harmful chemicals also caused population decline. The use of **DDT** on crops caused eagle egg shells to become thinner and they often broke during **incubation**.

Methods of restoring population

The use of DDT became illegal in the USA in 1972 and in Canada in 1973. This action greatly helped in saving the bald eagle. Laws for protecting bald eagles include the Endangered Species Act and the Bald and Golden Eagle Act. Bald eagle numbers have increased throughout the USA since the early 1960s.

Hints for success: You need to know the ecological, socio-political, and economic pressures that caused or are causing a species' extinction. You should also understand the species' ecological roles and the possible consequences of their disappearance.

Subject vocabulary

specialist species species that have a narrow niche

habitat destruction the complete removal of a habitat so that it no longer exists

habitat deterioration the gradual reduction in quality/complexity of a habitat

trophic level the position that an organism, or group of organisms, occupies in a food chain

food chain a simple diagram that shows feeding relationships in an ecosystem

pesticide a chemical that kills unwanted pests

DDT Dichloro-diphenyl-trichloroethane, a man-made pesticide that is not very soluble in water but is very soluble in fats; it lasts a long time, so builds up in the fatty tissue of organisms

Glossary

vulnerable something that can easily be harmed

isolated being far from other people and places

traps and snares pieces of equipment used for catching animals

breed mate and produce young

interventions involvement in a situation in order to improve it or prevent it from getting worse

to nest to build a place where birds live and lay their eggs

carrion dead and rotting animal flesh

contamination make something impure by adding a pollutant

incubation the time when a bird sits on its eggs to keep them warm

Synonyms

imbalance .... uneven distribution

measures ...... steps

restore .... return to its previous state

4.2.7 Describe the case history of a natural area of biological significance that is threatened by human activities

Synonyms

significance..... importance

vulnerable...... something that can easily be harmed

unintentional .. unplanned

mass.............. large scale

prey on .... hunt and eat

Glossary

mammal the type of animal that drinks milk from its mother

coral a hard stony substance secreted by polyp animals as an external skeleton, typically forming large reefs in warm shallow seas

souvenir an object that reminds you of a special place that you have visited

diver a person who swims underwater using special equipment to breathe

fin a long rubber shoe that you use to swim faster

anchor a piece of heavy metal used to stop a boat from moving

sugar plantation a large area of land where sugar is grown

run-off water moving over land

sedimentation the slow build-up of small pieces of dirt and rock that settle at the bottom of seas, rivers, and lakes

mangroves an area of tropical trees that live in or near water

bleaching loss of colour due to death of algae

Subject vocabulary

biodiversity the amount of biological or living variety in a specific area. It includes the concepts of species diversity, habitat diversity, and genetic diversity

ecosystem a community of organisms that depend on each other and the environment they live in

Opening sentence:

In this answer I will describe the Great Barrier Reef as my example of a natural area of biological **significance** that is threatened by human activities.

The Great Barrier Reef is the world's biggest single structure that is made by living organisms. It is large enough to be seen from space.

The Great Barrier Reef has high levels of biodiversity. It is found along the Queensland coastline of eastern Australia. It is home to 1500 species of fish, 215 bird species, and more than 30 species of sea **mammals**, including **vulnerable** dugongs (sea cows). In addition, there are thousands of different sponges, worms, and crustaceans, and 800 species of echinoderms (starfish, sea urchins).

Model sentence: There are many and varied threats to this ecosystem.

Ecological, socio-political, and economic pressures are causing the destruction of the **coral** reef. The destruction of the coral reef is threatening the biodiversity of the area. Threats include:

- Tourists damage the coral when they break bits off as **souvenirs**.

- The coral is very fragile and is easily damaged by **divers' fins**.

- Over-fishing can disturb the balance of species in the food chain.

- There is accidental damage from **anchors** and pollution from boats.

- Fishing for prawns along the sea bed results in the **unintentional** catching of other species and the destruction of the sea bed.

- **Sugar plantations** have replaced forests that once grew along the coast of Queensland. The plantations use a lot of fertilizers. **Run-off** from the soil into the sea has led to high levels of nutrients in the water and to algal blooms. Algal blooms cause eutrophication.

- **Sedimentation** has increased due to the deforestation of **mangroves** as land has been cleared. Land has been cleared to make space for tourist developments, housing, and farming. Sedimentation reduces coral reef productivity as it blocks sunlight from reaching the reef.

- Global warming is also having an effect on the reef. Increases in sea temperature through global warming have caused two **mass** coral **bleaching** events. Bleaching events kill the reef, which leads to a loss of biodiversity.

- Climate change may be causing some fish species to move away from the reef in order to find waters that are at a temperature they prefer. This leads to increased deaths in seabirds that **prey on** the fish. The habitat available for sea turtles will also be affected, which will lead to a reduction in population numbers.

What are the natural threats to the Great Barrier Reef?

Human impacts make the coral even more vulnerable to natural threats, such as disease and natural **predators**. One such predator is the crown-of-thorns starfish which preys on the **polyp** animals that form the coral reef. Sudden increases in the number of these starfish are thought to be natural, but the frequency and size of these **outbreaks** has increased as a result of human activity.

Storms and cyclones can cause **structural** damage to the coral. Changes in sea water temperature can also affect the coral. **El Niño events** occur when there are variations in the temperature of surface waters of the tropical eastern Pacific Ocean and these lead to increases in sea temperature across the east-central and western Pacific Ocean area, including Australia. Increased sea temperature can lead to coral bleaching. Coral bleaching affects fish species that depend on the reef for food and protection.

What are the consequences of the threats to the Great Barrier Reef?

Coral reefs are able to resist some threats, but the **current** combined effect of human and natural processes can lead to **irreversible** damage to the reef and the species that depend on it. These effects can lead to the breakdown of the reef ecosystem. When a **critical threshold** is reached, the problems may become irreversible and the ecosystem will not recover even if the threats stop. Loss of biodiversity and the valuable role that the ecosystem provides will **inevitably** lead to a reduction in its value as an economic resource.

Hints for success: You need to know the ecological, socio-political, and economic pressures that are causing the degradation of a natural area of biological significance. You also need to know the threat to biodiversity that has been caused by the degradation.

Subject vocabulary

fertilizer a chemical or natural substance added to soil to help plants grow

nutrients chemicals, derived from the natural environment or from fertilizers, that organisms need to live and grow

algal bloom a fast increase in the build-up of algae in an aquatic/water environment

eutrophication the natural or artificial enrichment of a body of water that results in the depletion of oxygen in the water

global warming an increase in average temperature of the Earth's atmosphere

climate change change in the Earth's climate due to an increase in the average atmospheric temperature

habitat the place where a species lives

predator an animal that hunts and eats other animals

critical threshold a point above which an important ecological change will take place, and below which this change will not take place

Glossary

polyp a small animal with a cylindrical body and a mouth at the top surrounded by tentacles

outbreak sudden increase in population size of a species

structural concerning the way something is connected or built

El Niño event a change in the weather in the Pacific Ocean that happens every three to seven years

Synonyms

current .... present

irreversible ..... when something cannot be changed to the way it was before

inevitably .... certain to happen

Model sentence: There are many arguments for preserving species and habitats. These arguments can be divided into four groups:

Argument 1: Ethical reasons

Everyone has a responsibility to protect resources for future generations. **Ethical** reasons also include the idea that every species has a right to survive.

Argument 2: Aesthetic reasons

Species and habitats are pleasant to look at and provide beauty and **inspiration**.

Argument 3: Economic reasons

Species and habitats provide financial income. Species should be preserved to maintain **genetic diversity**, so that genetic resources will be available in the future. An example of why genetic diversity is important is that it will allow crops to be improved in the future. Other reasons for preserving **biodiversity** are that commercial resources, such as new medicines, are still waiting to be discovered. **Ecotourism** is successful when habitats are preserved that are high in biodiversity, which attracts people to see them.

Argument 4: Ecological reasons

Rare habitats should be **conserved** as they may contain **endemic** species that require specific habitats. In addition, **ecosystems** with high levels of biodiversity are generally more **stable** and more likely to survive into the future. Healthy ecosystems are also more likely to provide **ecosystem services** such as **pollination** and **flood prevention**. Species should be preserved because if they disappear they could have effects on the rest of the **food chain** and ecosystem.

Model sentence: I will use tropical rainforest to show the arguments for preserving species and habitats. I will also explain why some arguments are easier to give a value to than others.

The value of biodiversity can be difficult to **quantify**. Products that are **harvested** from an ecosystem are easier to give value to than **indirect values**, such as the **aesthetic** or cultural aspects of an ecosystem. For example, it is easy to value rainforest in terms of the amount of **timber** in it because this has direct monetary value. But rainforests that have not been affected by human activity also provide **invaluable** ecosystem services for the local, national, and **global** communities. Rainforests are essential to the water cycle. Rainforests also **stabilize** some of the world's most **fragile** soils by preventing **soil erosion**. They are also responsible for controlling temperature and weather patterns in the areas that surround the forest.

In addition, they **isolate** and **store** large amounts of carbon from the atmosphere. They cool and clean the world's atmosphere. They are a huge source of the world's biodiversity. Rainforests provide fresh water; for example, the Amazon provides 20 per cent of the world's fresh water.

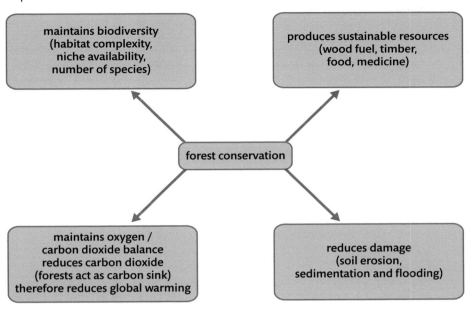

Figure 4.11 *The biological significance of a forest.*

Most of the benefits listed above are difficult to give monetary value to. Every person on the planet benefits from these services, but none of us pay for them. From the point of view of ecotourism, rainforests have value because untouched rainforests are aesthetically pleasing and this makes people want to visit them. It can also be stated that we have an ethical responsibility to conserve them because rainforests contain such a high percentage of the existing global biodiversity.

The value of ecosystems depends on cultural background as well as economic status. The value of a rainforest to someone who lives in and relies on it for their livelihood is very different from its value to an outsider who does not have these concerns.

Model sentence: In summary, it is easier to give value to some aspects of biodiversity than others.

It is easier to give commercial value to resources such as timber, medicine, and food. It is more difficult to give value to ecosystem services, **cultural services**, and ethical and aesthetic factors.

4.3.2 Compare and contrast the role and activities of intergovernmental and non-governmental organizations in preserving and restoring ecosystems and biodiversity

What are intergovernmental and non-governmental organizations?

Model sentence: An intergovernmental organization (IGO) is an organization that is established through international agreements in order to protect the Earth's natural resources.

Examples of IGOs include the United Nations Environment Programme (UNEP) and the European Environment Agency (EEA).

Model sentence: A non-governmental organization (NGO) is an organization that is not run by the governments of any country.

NGOs are not **funded** or influenced by governments in any way. Examples of NGOs are Greenpeace and the World Wide Fund for Nature (WWF).

Model sentence: I will now compare and contrast IGOs and NGOs in terms of use of the media, speed of response, diplomatic constraints, and political influence.

Similarities

Similarities between IGOs and NGOs are:

- They look to resolve concerns that affect the world.
- They use the media to get their message across and to influence decision making.
- They operate both locally and globally to **preserve** and **restore ecosystems** and **biodiversity**.
- They publish reports and articles about their activities.

Differences

The following table summarizes the differences between IGOs and NGOs:

	IGOs (e.g. UNEP)	NGOs (e.g. WWF, Greenpeace)
Use of media	• Professional media liaison; officers prepare statements • International news clips and informative videos released	• Advertise on popular channels, using footage of own protest activities • Leaflets and events such as 'Earth Hour' • Produce press packs
Speed of response	• Fairly slow – many countries involved in reaching a consensus • Must meet legal requirements in many countries	• Can be rapid and regular. Organizations are independent and can make own decisions
Diplomatic constraints	• Cannot give opinion without consulting lawyers and other countries because they represent many nations • International disagreements can cause serious constraints	• Relations are with international non-profit-making companies and generally unaffected by politics • Activities may be illegal although this is generally discouraged
Political influence	• Great – direct access to the governments of many countries	• No direct political influence but Green politics may establish environmental concerns as part of the political process
Enforceability	• Through international agreements and laws (e.g. UNEP can pass laws within Europe to address environmental issues)	• Rely on public pressure rather than legal power to influence governments; no power to enforce laws

Table 4.1 *Comparison of the differences between IGOs and NGOs*

IGOs are more likely to have a more **conventional** approach to **conservation** and are not likely to be **controversial**. NGOs are more likely to be **radical** in order to get their message across to the public. NGOs are also more likely to be **field-based**, gathering information to support their **arguments**. IGOs are more likely to gather information from scientific research which they pay for. Table 4.1 summarizes important differences between IGOs and NGOs:

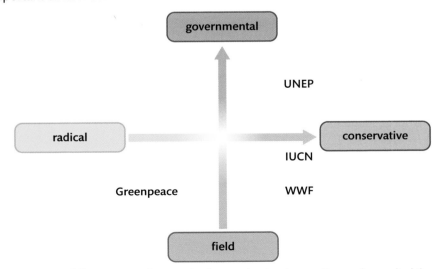

Figure 4.12 *How different conservation organizations can be placed on continuums from radical through to conservative, and from field-based through to governmental.*

Glossary

conventional a way that has been used for a long time and is considered to be the usual way

controversial may cause a lot of disagreement

radical new and very different

field-based mainly working outside in natural systems carrying out research and so on, rather than office-based

argument a reason that shows that something is correct

conservative holding traditional attitudes and being cautious about change

continuum a continuous sequence in which elements next to each other are very similar but where the extremes are quite different

Subject vocabulary

conserve/conservation preserve and protect nature

Model sentence: International conventions have been influential in developing attitudes towards sustainable development. They include:

UN Conference on the Human Environment

The UN Conference on the Human Environment took place in Stockholm in 1972. The conference was the first time that the international community had met together to discuss the **global** environment and development needs together. The conference led to the Stockholm Declaration which played an essential role in setting targets for sustainable development both locally and internationally.

UN Rio Earth Summit

The 1992 UN Rio Earth Summit was attended by 172 governments. The Earth Summit **set the agenda** for the sustainable development of the Earth's resources. The conference resulted in the Rio Declaration and Agenda 21. The Earth Summit led to agreement on **legally binding** conventions. One of the legally binding conventions was the UN Convention on Biological Diversity (CBD). The CBD is governed by the Conference of the Parties (CoP) which meet either **annually** or **biennially** in order to **assess** the success and future directions of the Convention. For example, CoP 11 of the CBD took place in India in 2012. In 1997, a **follow-up** meeting to the Earth Summit took place in New York to consider the success of the Earth Summit and to discuss future directions.

Rio +20

A conference took place in Rio in 2012, 20 years after the first Earth Summit. This meeting was known as Rio +20. One of the conference aims was to obtain political commitment from nations to sustainable development. Another aim was to assess how much progress there had been on internationally agreed commitments, such as CO_2 reductions. The conference also discussed new and **emerging challenges**.

The World Conservation Strategy

The World Conservation Strategy (WCS) was established in 1980 by the International Union for the Conservation of Nature (IUCN). The WCS consisted of three factors:

- Maintaining essential life support systems (climate, water cycle, soils) and ecological processes

- **Preserving genetic diversity**

- Using **species** and **ecosystems** in a sustainable way.

The WCS recommended that each country should prepare its own national strategy for conserving natural resources for the long-term good of humanity. The WCS emphasized how important is was that the users of natural resources became their protectors. The WCS recognized that conservation plans can only succeed if they are supported and understood by local communities.

The WCS focused on specific factors for preserving biodiversity. It focused on these issues because they are the ones that people with different environmental viewpoints are more likely to agree on. Ethical and aesthetic arguments are more difficult to define and may vary between different communities. These arguments used by the WCS are also more scientifically verifiable than ethical or aesthetic arguments. Most nations place more value on scientific validity than other arguments.

> **Hints for success:** You need to know about recent international conventions on biodiversity.
> - *Stockholm Declaration*: a statement produced by the UN Conference on the Human Environment in Stockholm, 1972, with the declaration playing an essential role in setting targets and forming action concerning sustainable development at both local and international levels.
> - *Earth Summit*: the first ever UN conference to focus on sustainable development, which took place in Rio de Janeiro, Brazil, in 1992.
> - *Rio Declaration*: a document produced at the Earth Summit that outlined future sustainable development around the world.
> - *Convention on Biological Diversity (CBD)*: an international legally binding agreement made at the Rio Earth Summit, which has three main goals:
>   1. The conservation of biodiversity;
>   2. The sustainable use of its components;
>   3. The fair and equitable sharing of the benefits arising from genetic resources.
> - *Rio +20*: a meeting that took place 20 years after the first Earth Summit.
> - *World Conservation Strategy*: an international agreement that set the priorities of the maintenance of essential life support systems, the preservation of genetic diversity and the need to use species and ecosystems in a sustainable way.

Intergovernmental and non-governmental organizations have been involved with the planning and implementation of international conventions on biodiversity, such as the Rio Earth Summit (1992) and subsequent updates.

What are protected areas?

Most countries have large areas of land that have been cleared of **native habitat** for development purposes (e.g. cities). The remaining areas of native habitat can be made into **protected areas**. Protected areas are often **isolated** and in danger of becoming islands within areas of disturbance, such as cleared land. When protected areas become islands, they will normally lose some of their **diversity**.

Model sentence: The principles of island biogeography can be applied to the design of reserves.

Island biogeography theory predicts that smaller islands of habitat will contain fewer **species** than larger islands. Size, shape, the **impact** of **edge effects**, and whether reserves are linked by **corridors** are all factors to consider when designing reserves. Figure 4.13 shows different **criteria** that can be used to design reserves:

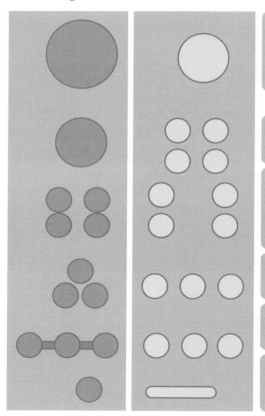

Large is preferable to small because more habitats and species are included and populations are bigger. Ideal for large mammals. There is less edge effect.

One large is preferable to several small because populations are bigger. There is less edge effect.

If several small reserves are unavoidable, close is preferable to isolated because animals can disperse and recolonize if a reserve loses stock through disturbance such as fire or disease.

Clumped is preferable to spread out because animals can disperse and recolonize as necessary.

Corridors are preferable to no corridors because animals can migrate.

Round is preferable to any other shape because there is less edge effect. Poaching is reduced because the centre is less accessible.

Figure 4.13 *The shape, size, and connectivity of reserves are important in the design of protected areas.*

Model sentence: I will now explain how each criterion helps to protect biodiversity in protected areas.

Area

If the habitats which are to be **preserved** are not all reasonably close together then several small reserves may be necessary. However, in general it is better to have larger reserves, as one large area can support more species than several smaller areas. This is because large reserves have more habitats and can support more top carnivores. Larger reserves have higher population numbers of each species and greater productivity at each trophic level. This results in longer food chains and greater stability. Several large reserves would allow protected habitats to be replicated, protecting against the possible effects of fire or a disease. Fire or disease in one reserve could lead to the extinction of species in that reserve.

Edge effects

At the edge of a protected area there is a change in abiotic components. This change includes more wind, more warmth, and less humid conditions compared to the interior of the reserve. These are called edge effects. Edge effects will attract species that are not found deeper in the reserve but that survive successfully in the edge conditions. Edge effects may also attract exotic species from outside the reserve. Larger reserves have fewer edge effects as they have a low perimeter to area ratio. Fewer edge effects will mean that less of the area is disturbed.

Shape

The best shape for a reserve is a circle because this has the lowest edge effects. Long thin reserves have large edge effects. In practice, the shape is determined by what is available and where the habitats to be conserved are located. Parks are more likely to be irregular shapes.

Corridors

Corridors join up areas of a reserve that are surrounded by disturbed areas. Corridors have many benefits. Corridors allow gene flow through movement of animals in and out of the area. They allow movements of animals that would otherwise end up restricted in one area of a reserve. Corridors also allow the movement of large mammals and top carnivores between separated parts of the reserve. There are some disadvantages of corridors. Fire or disease can move between areas of a reserve. Illegal hunters can also more easily move from one reserve to another. Corridors may be narrow, leading to a big increase in edge effects and causing them to be unsuitable for species that normally avoid edge habitat. It is also possible for corridors to become barriers to some species when they are protected by fences.

Buffer zones

Areas around protected areas are called buffer zones. They contain habitats and may be either managed or undisturbed. These areas minimize disturbance from outside influences such as people, agriculture, or the sudden arrival of diseases or pests. For example, a nearby town or extensive disturbance such as logging can directly impact a protected area if it is not surrounded by an area that buffers it from the effects of the disturbance.

Subject vocabulary

carnivore an organism that eats other animals

productivity the amount of living matter generated by photosynthesis in a certain amount of time

trophic level the position that an organism, or group of organisms, occupies in a food chain

food chain a simple diagram that shows feeding relationships in an ecosystem

stability when there is no overall change in a system

extinction the loss of species from the Earth

abiotic component a non-living part in an ecosystem

exotic species a species that is not native to an area

perimeter to area ratio the quantitative relationship between the boundary of an area and the size of the area itself; it is the number of times one value contains, or is contained within, the other

gene flow the movement of genes within and between populations

buffer zone land that surrounds protected areas and contains habitats that are either managed or undisturbed; they minimize disturbance in the protected area from outside influences

pest small animals/insects that destroy crops/food

logging removal of trees from forests for commercial purposes

Glossary

conserve protect for the future

barrier a physical object that keeps things two or more things apart

4.3.4 Evaluate the success of a named protected area

Opening sentence:

In this answer I will evaluate the success of a named protected area. I will use the Danum Valley Conservation Area in Malaysia as an example of a protected area.

Figure 4.14 *Danum Valley Field Centre, Malaysia. Research at the centre focuses on local primary forest ecology as well as the effect of logging on rainforest structure and communities.*

The Danum Valley Conservation Area (DVCA) is a **protected area** located in the Malaysian state of Sabah on the island of Borneo, at **latitude** 5° North. The DVCA and surrounding areas is a **model** of how effective **conservation** can be **matched** with local economic needs.

Strengths of Danum Valley

Funding from the government

The DVCA needs **significant** **funding**. The land is owned by Yayasan Sabah, which opened a field centre on the edge of the protected area in 1986. Yayasan Sabah is a state foundation funded by the Sabah Government and Federal Government of Malaysia. The surrounding area contains **commercial** forest also owned by Yayasan Sabah. Funds from the commercial forest and other sources have helped to fund the conservation area.

Involvement of government agencies

Danum Valley is controlled by a management committee made up of all the relevant local institutions, including wildlife, forestry, and commercial concerns. These agencies help to develop and monitor the management programme for the DVCA.

Subject vocabulary

protected area area that aims to preserve the greatest amount of natural habitat and species within an ecosystem

latitude the angular distance north or south of the Earth's equator, measured in degrees

conserve/conservation preserve and protect nature

Synonyms

model .... a successful example

match .... connect to

significant .... large amounts of

Glossary

fund provide money for an organization

commercial sold to make money

The presence of high-profile animals

The DVCA and surrounding forest is an important protected area for orang-utan. The forests are particularly rich in other large **mammals** including the Asian elephant, Malayan sun bear, clouded leopard, bearded pig and several **species** of deer. The area also provides one of the last **refuges** in Sabah for the **critically endangered** Sumatran rhino. Overall, the DVCA contains more than 120 mammal species including ten species of **primate**.

Scientific research programme

In 1986, a scientific research programme was set up at Danum Valley. Research of the **primary rainforest** within the DVCA has demonstrated the biological importance of the **native** forest and has been a source of **inspiration** for conservation in the region. Research has also provided important scientific information about the forest and what happens to it when it is disturbed through **logging**.

Tourism

An **ecotourism** hotel opened on the northeastern edge of the DVCA in 1996. The hotel has allowed tourists to visit the area and see the unique forest. As well as earning money for the local area, ecotourism has increased international attention on the area as an important centre for conservation and research. The number of visitors is controlled to stop disturbance.

Local support

The local community has supported Danum Valley by running the various facilities in the protected area itself and in local towns, and this has also been important in making the project a success. Visitors from within Sabah and more widely within Malaysia have also added to the success of the protected area.

Limitations of Danum Valley

- Oil palm plantations are being grown near to the northern border of the DVCA. This could affect the ecotourism potential of Danum Valley as tourists do not want to see agricultural areas so close to a protected area. The presence of people so near to the conservation area may also lead to increased poaching activity or illegal logging activity.

- The funding that supports the DVCA has been raised by logging and conversion of land once covered by rainforest to forest plantation. Some conservationists may see a conflict between the activities that have provided revenue for the DVCA and the aims of a protected area.

- The DVCA and surrounding area is currently designated a conservation area, but a change of leadership within those involved with the DVCA could see this designation changed. The establishment of the DVCA as a World Heritage Site would give international protection to the DVCA and ensure its long-lasting protection.

Hints for success: Even when a species or ecosystem has been given protected status, this is no guarantee of protection unless there is community support, adequate funding, and proper research. You need to be able to evaluate the success of a specific local protected area.

4.3.5 Discuss and evaluate the strengths and weaknesses of the species-based approach to conservation

Subject vocabulary

captive breeding the process of raising animals outside of their natural surroundings in controlled environments such as zoos

reintroduction programme a scheme in which animals raised or looked after in zoos are released into their natural habitat

species-based approach to conservation a method which focuses on specific individual species that are vulnerable with the aim of attracting interest in their conservation

species a group of organisms that mate/breed and have young/ babies able to breed/mate and have their own young/ babies

conservation the preservation and protection of nature

habitat loss the permanent damage or removal of natural areas where organisms live population a group of organisms of the same species living in the same area at the same time

extinction the loss of species from the Earth

Glossary

aesthetic relating to beauty and the study of beauty

vulnerable something that can easily be harmed

fund/funding provide money for an organization

preserve save something from destruction

legally binding an agreement that cannot be stopped or avoided

enforce make people/ organizations obey the law

fine money you pay as a punishment

poaching illegal hunting

smuggling bringing things into a country illegally

Synonyms

specimen....... example

In my answer I will consider the relative strengths and weaknesses of the Convention on International Trade in Endangered Species (CITES), captive breeding and reintroduction programmes, and zoos, and contrast aesthetic values with ecological values.

What is the species-based approach to conservation?

The species-based approach to conservation is an approach that focuses on specific individual species that are vulnerable. The aim is to attract interest in their conservation. The species-based approach attracts attention, and therefore funding for conservation, and can successfully preserve a species in zoos and botanic gardens.

Evaluation of CITES

CITES is an international agreement between governments that aims to ensure that international trade in wild animals and plants does not threaten their survival. Trade in animal and plant specimens and parts, in addition to factors such as habitat loss, can seriously reduce their wild populations and bring some species close to extinction.

Some strengths of CITES include:

- It is supported by many countries (178) and it protects many species (ca. 35 000).
- It is legally binding and so countries that have signed the convention must accept its conditions.
- The treaty works across international borders.

Limitations of CITES include:

- It does not replace national laws; countries that have signed the agreement must make their own laws to ensure that CITES is put into practice at national level.
- It is difficult to enforce.
- Fines are relatively small and may not stop poaching and smuggling.
- In some countries it is only weakly supported and is not very effective. Despite the agreement, illegal hunting still occurs.

However, taken overall, CITES has been responsible for preventing the international trade in endangered animals and plants.

Evaluation of captive breeding, reintroduction programmes, and zoos

There are many strengths to modern zoos:

- Education of the public about species and conservation
- Research in zoos increases the knowledge of individual species

- There is **genetic monitoring**, which makes it possible for the **genetic diversity** of species to be maintained

- Zoos allow species to be held while **habitats** are being restored.

Weaknesses of zoos include:

- Possibility that captive animals may be unable to adapt to being back in the wild

- Some people object to animals being kept in captivity for profit

- A species can be **artificially** preserved in a zoo while its natural habitat is destroyed. For example the Sumatran tiger is being kept in zoos while its rainforest habitat in Sumatra is disappearing.

Model sentence: Captive breeding and reintroduction programmes are organized by zoos.

Strengths of captive breeding programmes include:

- They can improve **reproductive success**

- Populations can build up quickly as habitat and food are **abundant**

- Captive breeding allows individual animals to be exchanged between zoo collections in order to prevent **inbreeding** and to maintain genetic diversity; successful examples of captive breeding include the Arabian oryx and golden lion tamarin.

Weaknesses of captive breeding and reintroduction programmes include:

- They do not directly conserve natural **habitat diversity** of the species

- Not all species **breed** easily in captivity, for example giant pandas

- Captive animals released into the wild may be easy **prey** for **predators**.

Model sentence: I will contrast the aesthetic value of species conservation with its ecological value.

With a species-based approach to conservation the focus is more likely to be on the conservation of **high-profile**, **charismatic** species that catch the public's attention. Popular, charismatic species may be conserved, whereas less charismatic animals may not be. For example, **endemic** Madagascan hissing cockroaches play an important role in **nutrient** cycling in forests but do not attract the same level of interest as Madagascan lemurs. Charismatic species help to attract the public, and zoos use the money obtained to pay for the other species.

5.1.1 Define the term *pollution*

Model sentence: Pollution is the addition of a harmful substance or agent (such as heat) to an environment which has a noticeable effect on the organisms within that environment.

Pollution can be natural or the result of human activities. It can also be a combination of the two. An example of a natural source of pollution is a volcanic eruption. Volcanoes **emit** large quantities of sulfur dioxide, which can cause **acid rain**. The following photograph shows trees that have died as a result of heat and sulfur dioxide emitted from the Soufrière volcano, Montserrat.

Figure 5.1 *Tree die-back on Soufrière Hills, Montserrat.*

Other types of pollution are related to human activities including **acidification** of forests and buildings, and **eutrophication** of streams and ponds.

Pollutants only become pollutants when there is too much. Not all **fertilizer** or **manure** causes pollution. Fertilizers that are used by plants do not cause pollution. Spreading manure on fields does not cause pollution if the amount spread can be used by plants.

5.1.2 Distinguish between the terms *point source pollution* and *non-point source pollution*, and outline the challenges they present for management

Point source pollution

Point source pollution refers to the release of pollutants from a single site.

This could be a factory chimney or the waste disposal pipe from a **sewage works** into a river. The photograph on the right shows point source pollution. The pollution enters the stream from the pipe on the right.

Figure 5.2 *Point source pollution.*

Non-point source pollution

Non-point source pollution refers to the release of pollutants from a number of widely **dispersed** origins, such as the gases from the exhaust systems of many vehicles.

A type of pollution can sometimes be point source and at other times non-point source. If there is only one source of the pollution, then it is point source pollution. It is possible that many potential sources could be involved when the pollution is located at a distance from the possible source of pollution. This makes it non point-source pollution.

Challenges

Point source pollution is generally more easily managed because its impact is more localized. This makes it easier to control **emission**. It is also easier to identify the source of the pollutant and the polluter. This makes it easier to take legal action.

Non-point source pollution is much harder to control. Many polluters emit sulfur dioxide and oxides of nitrogen. The main sources are power stations and vehicles. These contribute to acid deposition. It is impossible to blame the effects of **acid deposition** on emissions from one particular power station or vehicle. It is impossible to blame it on the emissions from one particular country. Therefore, it is very difficult to manage the problem.

5.1.3 State the major sources of pollutants

The main sources of pollutants include the burning of **fossil fuels** and domestic waste. Other sources include industrial waste and waste from manufacturing and agricultural systems.

Source 1: Fossil fuels

The burning of fossil fuels releases carbon dioxide and sulfur dioxide. It can also release oxides of nitrogen and **particulate matter**. These can contribute to many impacts, such as **acidification** and **global warming**. In some cases they may have an effect on human health.

Source 2: Domestic waste

The main pollutants from domestic waste include solid domestic waste and **sewage**. Solid domestic waste includes paper and glass. Solid domestic waste can cause the release of methane gas from landfill sites. Sewage can cause **eutrophication**.

Source 3: Agriculture

The main pollutants from agriculture include **run-off** of **manure** and **fertilizers**. This may cause eutrophication. The use of **pesticides** can also cause pollution. The use of pesticides may eventually kill animals though **biomagnification** and **bioaccumulation**.

Source 4: Manufacturing industry

The main pollutants from the manufacturing industry include solid waste and industrial dumping. These may result in land **contaminated** with heavy metals, such as cadmium and copper.

5.2.1 Describe two direct methods of monitoring pollution

Method 1: Air pollution

There are many pollutants that can be monitored or measured. These include chemicals and **particulate matter**. Chemicals include SO_x and NO_x. Particulate matter includes **dust**. There are a number of ways in which these can be measured. These include:

- use of a **monitor** or **probe**
- use of **filter paper** in a container
- weighing the filter paper before and after collection
- taking the material filtered for chemical analysis.

Method 2: Particulate matter

It is possible to monitor particulates such as dust in different parts of a city or neighbourhood. **Contrasting** sites should be chosen. These could include some areas that are close to a main road and some areas that have much less traffic. Small containers can be left attached to structures, e.g. lamp posts. The containers should ideally be at least 2 m off the ground so that they cannot be reached and disturbed. The containers can be taken down after a set amount of time. The particulate matter is then weighed. Another way of doing this is to cover cards with a sticky substance. The cards are then hung at different locations. Using a magnifying glass, it is possible to estimate the density of dust after a set amount of time.

Method 3: Water pollution

Water quality can be measured using standard water testing kits. These kits include tests for phosphates and nitrates. The readings can then be compared with a table of **critical values**. Clean water has less than 5 mg dm^{-3} of nitrates. Polluted water contains 5 to 15 mg dm^{-3}.

Subject vocabulary

particulate matter tiny pieces of solid/liquid matter held in the atmosphere

SO_x oxides of sulfur, in particular sulfur dioxide (SO_2) typically released/produced by coal-burning power stations

NO_x oxides of nitrogen produced by vehicles, for example

monitor an instrument to measure the amount of different pollutants

probe a physical device that uses electronic test equipment to measure a substance

filter paper special paper that will allow a liquid to pass through but will trap solids including particulates

critical values significant levels of a substance as defined by an organization

Glossary

dust very fine particles in the atmosphere made up of particulate waste, from vehicles and volcanoes for example

Synonyms

contrasting … differing

The following table shows typical values of nitrates and phosphates in clean water and polluted water:

	Clean water	Polluted water
Phosphates	Clean water contains < 5 mg dm^{-3}	Polluted water contains 15–20 mg dm^{-3}
Nitrates	Clean water contains 4–5 mg dm^{-3}	Polluted water contains 5–15 mg dm^{-3}

Method 4: Soil pollution

Soil pollution refers to a **decline** in soil quality. Changes that occur in soil as it becomes polluted include changes in **organic content** and **chemical content**. When monitoring soil pollution, it is important to have a reference soil. When examining the impact of **trampling** on soils, it is important to take samples at regular distances from the centre of the footpath. The organic content of soil can be found by taking samples of soils. These are weighed and then baked in an oven for 24 hours at 100°C. This removes the moisture from the soil. They are then reweighed. Then they are burnt over a Bunsen burner for 15 minutes. Then they are reweighed. The difference in the weight of the soil before and after burning gives us the weight of the organic content of the soil.

Figure 5.3 *Monitoring water quality using indicator species.*

Synonyms

decline.........fall

Subject vocabulary

organic content living matter in soils, such as plant roots and worms

chemical content the chemical composition of a soil, including its pH

Glossary

trampling the impact on the ground of heavy footfall/lots of walking

5.2.2 Define the term *biochemical oxygen demand* (BOD) and explain how this indirect method is used to assess pollution levels in water

Biochemical oxygen demand (BOD)

Biochemical oxygen demand (BOD) is a measure of the amount of dissolved oxygen required to break down the organic material in a given volume of water through aerobic biological activity.

Using BOD to assess pollution levels in water

Aerobic organisms use oxygen in respiration. When there are more organisms and a faster rate of respiration, more oxygen will be used. The biochemical oxygen demand at any point is affected by two main factors. These are:

1. The amount of aerobic organisms

2. Their rate of respiration.

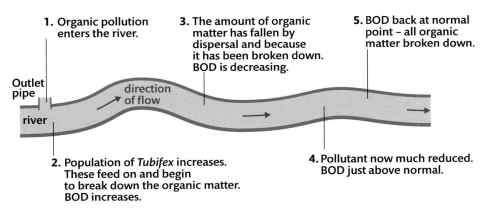

1. **Organic pollution enters the river.**

2. **Population of *Tubifex* increases. These feed on and begin to break down the organic matter. BOD increases.**

3. **The amount of organic matter has fallen by dispersal and because it has been broken down. BOD is decreasing.**

4. **Pollutant now much reduced. BOD just above normal.**

5. **BOD back at normal point – all organic matter broken down.**

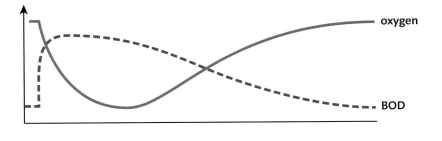

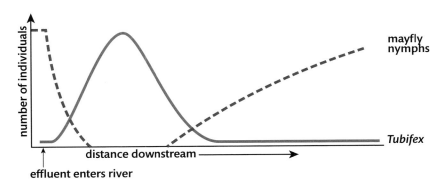

Figure 5.4 *Organic pollution and variations in BOD.*

Subject vocabulary

biochemical oxygen demand (BOD) a measure of the amount of dissolved oxygen needed to break down the organic material in a given volume of water through aerobic biological activity

dissolved oxygen the amount of oxygen in water

pollution adding a substance/agent (such as heat) to an environment faster than it can be made harmless by the environment, and which has a noticeable effect on the organisms within it

aerobic organisms organisms that use oxygen in respiration

Glossary

aerobic using/needing oxygen for respiration reactions

respiration a chemical process that happens in all cells to release energy

outlet pipe a pipe that carries sewage including where it is released into a river

Sewage is an organic pollutant. The presence of an organic pollutant causes an increase in the population of organisms that feed on the pollutant, breaking it down. Figure 5.4 shows how organic pollution in a stream causes variations in BOD.

Organic pollution and *Tubifex* worms

Organic pollution causes a high BOD. *Tubifex* worms are **tolerant** of organic pollution and the low oxygen content **associated** with it. Mayfly nymphs are associated with clean water. Where there are high levels of pollution there are high levels of BOD. *Tubifex* is associated with high levels of BOD. Where there are low levels of pollution there are low levels of BOD. Mayfly nymphs are associated with low levels of BOD. The following diagram shows how *Tubifex* and mayfly nymph can be used to show levels of BOD.

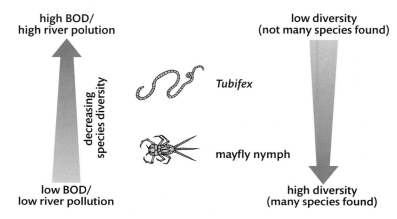

Figure 5.5 *BOD, water pollution, and the presence of* Tubifex *worms and mayfly nymphs.*

Species diversity in polluted and non-polluted water

Species diversity is low in highly polluted rivers and streams. However, the populations of certain species may be high. The population of *Tubifex* is very high in polluted streams. Mayfly nymphs are not found in polluted streams. They are only found where there are low levels of pollution.

Subject vocabulary

tolerant able to survive under certain conditions, e.g. high levels of BOD

species diversity a measurement of the number of different species and their number/ amount compared to one another in a specific area

Synonyms

associated .... linked

5.2.3 Describe and explain an indirect method of measuring pollution levels using a biotic index

Measuring pollution using a biotic index

When using a **biotic index** it is important to compare a polluted and an unpolluted site, such as upstream and downstream of a **pollution** source. Seasonal changes may also be important. The **Trent Biotic Index** is based on the disappearance of certain **indicator species** as the levels of pollution increase. Changes in the amount of light and **dissolved oxygen** cause less-tolerant species to die out. As pollution increases, diversity decreases. The Trent Biotic Index ranges from 0 to 10. The highest maximum value for the Trent Biotic Index is 10. A stream containing mayfly nymphs will have a Trent Biotic Index of between 6 and 9. A stream containing *Tubifex* worms will have a Trent Biotic Index of between 1 and 4.

Explanation

Certain species have different levels of **tolerance** to environmental conditions and change. Mayfly nymphs are found in non-polluted water. *Tubifex* worms are found in polluted water. *Tubifex* worms can tolerate high levels of pollution, such as organic matter. Mayfly nymphs cannot tolerate high levels of pollution. The presence or absence of indicator species can be used to **indirectly** suggest conditions in the water.

In a polluted stream there might be very large numbers of *Tubifex* worms. This is because very few organisms can tolerate the highly polluted conditions. *Tubifex* worms can tolerate the high levels of pollution and so become abundant. Thus, the stream has a low level of **biodiversity** but a high level of species abundance.

Many species can survive in a non-polluted stream. They can tolerate the low levels of pollution. Therefore the stream has a high level of biodiversity. No single species will be very abundant. Thus, the non-polluted stream has high biodiversity and low levels of species abundance.

Other indicator species

Other examples of indicator species include **lichens** and nettles. Certain lichen species indicate very low levels of sulfur dioxide in the atmosphere. Nettles indicate high phosphate levels in the soil.

5.3.1 Outline approaches to pollution management with respect to Figure 5.6

Pollutants are produced through human activities and create long-term effects when released into ecosystems.

Strategies for reducing these impacts can be directed at three different levels in the process. These strategies are shown in the following diagram.

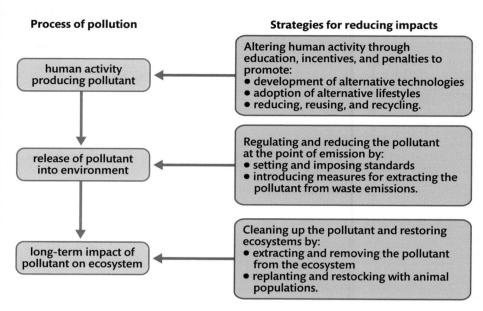

Figure 5.6 *Approaches to pollution management.*

The first strategy is altering human activity. The second strategy is **regulating** and reducing quantities of pollutant released at the point of emission. The third strategy is cleaning up the pollutant and **restoring** ecosystems after pollution has occurred.

Factors affecting the choice of **pollution**-management strategy also vary at local and national levels. Local attitudes and the **enforcement** by local authorities may influence the choice of pollution-management strategies at a local scale. Economic resources and national legislation may influence such choices at a national scale.

It is cheaper and more efficient to alter human activities. Most action over pollution is treating the effects of pollution rather than altering behaviour and the causes of pollution. Treating pollution is very costly and wasteful.

Strategies that alter human activity

There are a number of ways of changing human activities that produce pollutants. A good example is **CFCs** and **ozone depletion**. The use of CFCs has been reduced by using alternative gases/substitutes. This has occurred because scientists have developed alternative technologies. There has also been an international treaty that bans the use of CFCs. This treaty is known as the Montreal Protocol.

The main advantage of this strategy is that it prevents the effects of ozone depletion from happening in the first place. Most countries did not start reducing ozone-depleting substances until after the impacts were seen and understood.

Strategies that manage the release of a pollutant

There are a number of ways in which it is possible to manage the release of a pollutant. CFCs are the pollutant that destroys ozone. It is possible to recycle CFCs from disused refrigerators. Emission regulations have been developed that limit the amount of CFCs that may be used. More efficient technology is now being used so less ozone-depleting substances (ODS) are used.

Trying to get different countries to agree to regulations on emissions is very difficult to achieve. LEDCs believe that they have not had the benefit from the pollutant. They believe that rich countries have benefited from the pollutant and that it has helped them to develop. If agreement can be reached it may reduce the long-term impacts of ozone depletion.

Strategies that manage the long-term impact of a pollutant on the ecosystem

There are many ways in which it is possible to manage the long-term impact of a pollutant on the ecosystem. The removal of CFCs from the atmosphere is not possible. Alternative strategies are needed. To protect against increased UV radiation, people need to protect their skin with sunscreen and/or protective clothing. People should also avoid being outside during the hottest part of the day. It is possible to develop protective materials using UV resistant technologies. GM crops could be developed with improved UV resistance.

The major disadvantage with these strategies is that they are tackling the effects of ozone depletion rather than preventing them from happening. An advantage is that the technology is now available that will help develop resistance to the impacts of increased UV radiation.

Conclusion

There are a range of strategies that can be used to manage pollution. There are advantages to altering human activities over strategies that manage the release of pollutants and managing the long-term impacts on the ecosystem.

Subject vocabulary

recycling the processing of industrial/household waste so that the materials can be used again

emissions regulation laws to control the release of a substance, such as CFCs

UV radiation ultraviolet or short-wave radiation; it is harmful to humans, some animals and some plants

Glossary

disused no longer in use

resistance able to fight the effects of something

5.3.2 Discuss the human factors that affect the approaches to pollution management

Model sentence: There are a number of human factors that affect approaches to pollution management.

These include cultural values, political systems, and economic systems. These influence the choice of pollution-management strategies and their effective implementation.

Human Factor 1: Cultural values

Areas with a low population density might not consider pollution to be a problem if people are not negatively affected by it. Pollution tolerance levels vary from society to society. Some LEDCs accept the waste of other countries for recycling. Bangladesh accepts many old ships for recycling. Some types of pollution are more tolerated than others by a particular culture. Noise or visual pollution may be tolerated in a rapidly urbanizing city. Cultural perspective can be altered through education.

Human Factor 2: Political systems

LEDCs are often willing to allow pollution to encourage local industry. Mexico's *macquiadoras* industries are a good example. They attract investment from the USA. The dumping of toxic waste from MEDCs in LEDCs is sometimes allowed by the governments. Lower standards for pollution may encourage industry into certain countries. Some footwear companies in LEDCs may have dangerously high levels of glue in the workplace. Governments may choose to ignore this if the industry is profitable, paying taxes, and creating jobs. Apple's use of Hon Hai's Foxconn factory in China is a good example of a firm from an MEDC using an LEDC company to carry out some of their production. LEDCs often do not have the resources to enforce the laws that they do have in place.

Human Factor 3: Economic systems

Capitalist societies often consider the economic profit over the environmental damage of pollution. Often they would rather treat the symptoms (effects) of pollution rather than address the causes of pollution. Treating the impacts of soil acidification is a good example.

Subject vocabulary

cultural values the commonly held standards of a society, e.g. what is right or wrong?

political systems the way in which a country is governed, e.g. democracy or state-control

economic systems the way in which the economy is run, e.g. capitalist or socialist

pollution management attempts to control pollution through changing human activities, controlling emissions or cleaning up the environment

pollution adding a substance/agent (such as heat) to an environment faster than it can be made harmless by the environment, and which has a noticeable effect on the organisms within it

LEDC less economically developed country/low-income country

recycling the processing of industrial/household waste so that the materials can be used again

MEDC more economically developed country/high-income country

capitalist an economic system that aims to maximize profit

acidification an increase in the acidity of precipitation (rain and snow), in freshwater (lakes and streams), in soil, in oceans, and dry deposition on buildings

Synonyms

strategies...... approaches/methods

toxic .... harmful/poisonous

Glossary

tolerance the ability to withstand/live with certain conditions/situations without being harmed

Many MEDCs have a 'throwaway' society and so generate a large amount of waste and pollution. Increasingly in high-income countries people value a clean and tidy environment so pollution is not tolerated. All three steps of the pollution model (Figure 5.6 on page 174) are likely to be carried out. In many MEDCs the most common pollution-management strategy may be the second one, as the rich society may want to keep the pollution-causing industry but regulate it. Although many high-income countries invest in pollution prevention technologies, they are still responsible for a large amount of the world's pollution. This is created through travel and transport, as well as the import of goods produced for their benefit.

LEDCs often recycle large amounts of waste through informal waste pickers. The Zabbaleen waste collectors in Cairo, Egypt, recycle up to 80 per cent of the waste they collect. Many LEDCs can only afford old, polluting equipment and have limited resources for technology to clean up pollution.

In some cases UN protocols are not signed as countries fear it may slow the economy. The USA's failure to sign up to the Kyoto Protocol is a case in point. As countries develop there is a tendency to spend more money on pollution prevention.

Model sentence: **Pollution-management strategies are affected by a number of human factors. One of the most important appears to be the distinction between MEDCs and LEDCs. Political systems and cultural values also affect pollution-management strategies.**

Figure 5.7 *Rubbish generated by tourists, Tenerife.*

5.3.3 Evaluate the costs and benefits to society of the World Health Organization's ban on the use of the pesticide DDT

> **Opening sentence:**
> In this answer I will evaluate the costs and benefits to society of the World Health Organization's ban on the use of the **pesticide** DDT.

Benefits of DDT

DDT is a man-made pesticide. It has many advantages and disadvantages. Its main advantages are in the control of disease and in improving farm yields. During the 1940s and 1950s, it was used **extensively** to control lice and mosquitoes. Lice spread the disease typhus and mosquitoes spread the disease malaria. Today there are about 250 million cases of malaria each year. DDT was also used as a pesticide in farming. This helped to raise **agricultural yields**.

The costs of DDT

In the 1960s, public opinion turned against DDT. This was largely as a result of the publication of the book *Silent Spring* by Rachel Carson. Carson claimed that the large-scale spraying of pesticides was killing **top predators**. It affected top predators because of **bioaccumulation** and **biomagnification**. Bioaccumulation refers to the build up of non-**biodegradable** or slowly biodegradable chemicals in the body. Biomagnification refers to the process whereby the **concentration** of a chemical substance increases at each **trophic level** – the end result is that a top predator may have an accumulation that is thousands of times greater than that of a primary producer.

DDT can cause cancer in humans. There are also links between DDT and **premature** births. DDT has also been linked to low birth weight and reduced mental development.

Recent developments in the management of DDT

In the 1970s and 1980s, the use of DDT in farming was banned in many **MEDCs**. In 2001, the Stockholm Convention on **persistent organic pollutants (POPs)** **regulated** the use of DDT – it was banned for use in farming but was permitted for disease control. Cases of malaria increased in South America after countries stopped spraying DDT. Cases of malaria in Ecuador decreased by over 60 per cent following an increase in the use of DDT.

In 2006, the WHO changed its recommendations. It recommended the use of DDT for regular treatment in buildings and in areas with a high **incidence** of malaria. WHO still aims for a total **phase out** of the use of DDT by the early 2020s.

Conclusion

Thus, there are many advantages and disadvantages in using DDT. As the WHO is suggesting the total phase out of DDT by the early 2020s, it suggests that they believe the disadvantages outweigh the advantages.

5.4.1 Outline the processes of eutrophication

> ## Opening sentence:

In this answer I will outline the process of **eutrophication**. Eutrophication refers to the enrichment of water bodies with **nitrates** and **phosphates**.

There are many natural and human causes of eutrophication. These are shown in the following diagram.

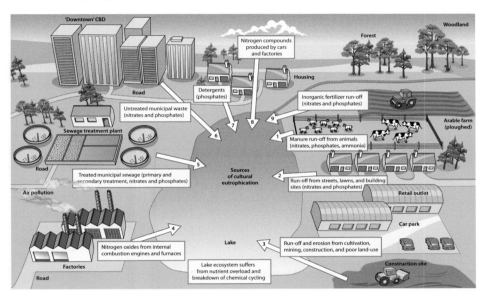

Figure 5.8 *Natural and human causes of eutrophication.*

Natural cycles of eutrophication may include nutrients added from **decomposing biomass** and run-off from surrounding areas. In some coastal areas **upwelling ocean currents** bring nutrients to the surface. Human causes include **run-off** of fertilizers or **manure** from **agricultural** land. Domestic wastewater may contain phosphates from **detergents**. Non-treated sewage may also lead to eutrophication. Eutrophication as a result of human activity happens a lot faster than natural eutrophication. It also occurs on a larger scale.

Natural and human causes of eutrophication are the result of an increase in nitrates and/or phosphates. This leads to the rapid growth of **algae**. This causes an **accumulation** of dead organic matter and a high rate of decomposition. Eventually it causes a lack of oxygen.

Impact 1: Eutrophication and feedback cycles

Positive feedback

Positive feedback occurs in the process of **eutrophication**. Algae increase as more nutrients are added to the system. Decomposition of the increased algae leads to further nutrients in the system. This is an example of positive feedback.

The growth of algae also blocks light, causing underwater plants to die. These add more nutrients to the system as they decompose. More nutrients leads to further growth of algae so again there is positive feedback.

Negative feedback

Negative feedback can also occur during the process of eutrophication. The increase in nutrients promotes the growth of plants that store the nutrients in biomass. This leads to a reduction in nutrients so balance is restored. The increase in algae will lead to an increase in species that feed on algae. This may lead to a decrease in algal populations so balance is restored.

Figure 5.9 *Algal bloom.*

Impact 2: The impact on the environment

Positive changes

Human and natural eutrophication leads to an increase in biomass of algae. The algae increase turbidity, reducing the light that reaches underwater plants. The increased death of algae and underwater plants leads to an increase in dead organic matter. Bacteria begin to break down the dead organic matter.

Negative changes

The increase in the amount of bacteria increases biochemical oxygen demand, which leads to a lowered oxygen content of water. The reduced oxygen content of water is known as hypoxia.

Reduced oxygen leads to the death of many organisms. Net primary productivity is usually higher in eutrophic streams compared with unpolluted water. Increased net primary productivity may result in extensive algal blooms. The diversity of primary producers changes and finally decreases. Figure 5.9 shows an algal bloom in a stream.

Eutrophication leads to a change in species composition rather than removing all species. Surface-dwelling organisms are favoured rather than bottom-dwelling organisms, with the exception of bacteria that decompose the dead organic matter.

The length of the food chain decreases as algae lock up the nutrients. Algae also blocks sunlight from reaching the river bed. Thus there is less light and fewer nutrients available. This causes the varied species diversity to be replaced by cyanobacteria (blue-green algae) and a less varied food chain. Fish populations are negatively affected by reduced oxygen availability. The fish community becomes dominated by surface-dwelling coarse fish including pike and perch. Macrophytes (submerged aquatic plants) disappear because they are unable to photosynthesize as less sunlight penetrates the water. In theory, the submerged macrophytes could also benefit from increased nutrient availability. However, they are shaded by the free-floating microscopic organisms.

Most lakes are naturally oligotrophic (nutrient poor) – once eutrophication starts to occur, productivity increases as nutrient enrichment occurs.

Impact 3: The impact of eutrophication on society

Eutrophication also has impacts on human populations. One is financial. The loss of fertilizers from fields may reduce crop productivity and therefore farm yield and profit. The cost of treating nitrate-enriched water is expensive. In the UK, it costs between £50 million and £300 million to treat nitrate-enriched water each year. There are also health risks. Nitrate-enriched water is associated with higher rates of stomach cancer and 'blue baby syndrome' (methaemoglobinaemia – not enough oxygen in pregnant women's blood). However, many other factors are likely to be involved.

Model sentence: **There are many impacts of eutrophication on the environment and on society. The impacts are mostly negative.**

Subject vocabulary

algae a wide range of autotrophs, from single-celled organisms to large seaweeds

turbidity a measure of how clear water is

biochemical oxygen demand (BOD) a measure of the amount of dissolved oxygen needed to break down the organic material in a given volume of water through aerobic biological activity

hypoxia reduced oxygen availability

net primary productivity the gain by producers in biomass once energy from respiration has been removed

algal bloom a fast increase in the build-up of algae in an aquatic/water environment

producer an organism that makes its own food

food chain a simple diagram that shows feeding relationships in an ecosystem

macrophytes underwater plants

photosynthesis a process that captures sunlight energy and transforms it into the chemical bonds of glucose molecules; carbon dioxide, water, and light are transformed into glucose and oxygen

oligotrophic nutrient poor

Glossary

composition the way something is made up of different parts

diversity including many different types

Synonyms

dwelling .... living

dominated .... overpowered

submerged ... underwater

penetrates .... gets through

yield .... production/output

Pollution-management strategies with respect to eutrophication

There are three main approaches to **pollution-management strategies** with respect to **eutrophication**. These are shown in Figure 5.6 on page 174.

- The first pollution-management strategy is **altering** the human activity that produces pollution.

- The second pollution-management strategy is **regulating** and reducing pollutants at the point of **emission**.

- The third pollution-management strategy is clean-up and **restoration** after pollution.

Strategy 1: Altering human activity

There are many ways of altering human activity to reduce eutrophication. These include:

- use fewer **chemical fertilizers**

- use organic **fertilizers** (**manure**) on agricultural fields as these contain less phosphorus than most chemical fertilizers

- avoid spreading fertilizers in winter when the soil is bare and **run-off** may wash fertilizers into rivers and streams

- use autumn-sown crops as a cover crop during the winter

- use less fertilizer if the previous year was dry as more will be left in the soil

- use **mixed cropping** or **crop rotation** so fewer fertilizers are needed

- do not use fertilizers in fields that are next to streams and rivers.

Strategy 2: Regulating and reducing pollutants

Regulating and reducing pollutants at the point of emission can be illustrated by sewage treatment processes that remove **nitrates** and **phosphates** from waste. These can be done in many ways:

- reduce use of fertilizers in fields and gardens

- only use washing machines with a full load of washing

- use zero- or low-phosphorus detergents

- use **phosphate stripping** to remove phosphorus from **sewage treatment works**.

Strategy 3: Cleaning and restoring ecosystems

There are many ways in which ecosystems can be cleaned and restored after they have become eutrophic:

- removal of nutrient-rich **sediment** by pumping sediment out of lakes

- pumping air through lakes to increase oxygen levels

- removal of **biomass**, such as algae

- reintroduction of plant and animal species into the ecosystem

- using barley bales to lock up nitrates in the water, since barley takes in nitrogen in its inorganic form (nitrates or ammonium)

- using a solution of aluminium or ferrous salt to **precipitate** phosphates.

Figure 5.10 *Restored meander ecosystem – the River Cole in Oxfordshire.*

Problems for pollution-management strategies and eutrophication

There are many potential solutions to the problem of eutrophication. However, it is not always possible to solve the problem. This is because it can be **non-point source pollution** and there are many different causes of eutrophication.

It is cheaper and more efficient to alter human activities than to regulate and reduce pollutants at the point of emission. It is also cheaper and more efficient to alter human activities than to clean up and restore ecosystems following eutrophication, for example by dredging or removing sediment.

Conclusion

Most action over pollution is treating the effects of pollution rather than altering behaviour and the causes of pollution. Treating pollution is very costly and wasteful. Not every country has the resources to implement these strategies.

Types of solid domestic waste

There are many types of solid **domestic waste**. In an **MEDC**, solid domestic waste consists of the following (typical percentage volumes are shown in brackets):

- organic waste from kitchen or garden, including waste wood (20–50 per cent)

- paper/packaging/cardboard (20–30 per cent)

- glass (5–10 per cent)

- metal (less than 5 per cent)

- plastics (5–10 per cent)

- **textiles** (less than 5 per cent)

- electrical appliances, such as computers and fridges (less than 5 per cent)

- nappies (diapers) (2 per cent)

- rubble/bricks (less than 1 per cent)

- ash (less than 1 per cent).

Nappies are a form of solid domestic waste, but **faeces** is not. Some domestic waste is **biodegradeable**. The following photograph shows electrical and electronic waste that has been made into a sculpture – a form of reuse.

Figure 5.11 *The WEEE man – a robotic figure weighing over 3 tonnes and formed of **w**aste **e**lectrical and **e**lectronic **e**quipment.*

The following diagram shows the **composition** of solid domestic waste in a high-income household.

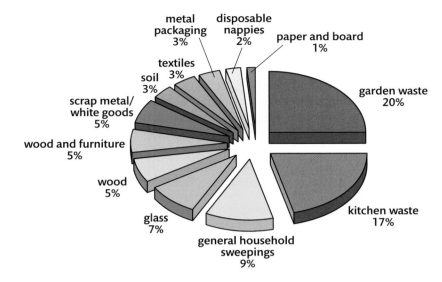

Figure 5.12 *Solid domestic waste in a typical MEDC household.*

The amount will vary from place to place, and over time. The total volume of waste **generated** can be over 800 kg/person/year.

Hints for success: You should consider your own, and your community's, generation of waste. Keep a record of your waste for a week. Use a table to organize your results. The following table shows an example of such a record.

Record of solid domestic waste	
Materials	**Amount (kg/week)**
Paper	
Glass	
Plastics	
Organic waste*	
Packaging	
Total waste	

*Organic waste includes kitchen and garden waste.

Subject vocabulary

pollution-management strategies attempts to control pollution through changing human activities, controlling emissions, or cleaning up the environment

recycling the processing of industrial and household waste so that the materials can be reused

incineration the burning of waste

composting the breakdown/natural decay of organic material and its use as a fertilizer in soil

landfill the disposal/getting rid of waste on to or into the land

biodegradable can be broken down naturally by bacteria into substances that do not harm the environment

fertilizer a chemical/natural substance added to soil to help plants grow

Glossary

toxic harmful/poisonous

ash grey powder produced from burning something

decomposition decay/breakdown of natural things through a natural chemical process

Synonyms

construction.. building work

Types of pollution-management strategies

The main **pollution-management strategies** for solid domestic and industrial waste include: **recycling, incineration, composting,** and **landfill**

Strategy 1: Recycling

Recycling is the processing of household and industrial waste so that it can be used again. There are many advantages and disadvantages of recycling. The advantages include:

- a reduction in the amount of resources used
- a reduction in the amount of material in landfill sites
- the use of recycled materials to make new products.

However, there are disadvantages. These include:

- the transport of heavy goods, which requires lots of energy
- the production of **toxic** waste.

Strategy 2: Incineration

Incineration is the burning of household and industrial waste so that it is reduced in volume. There are many advantages and disadvantages of incineration. Advantages include:

- the reduction of the volume of waste, thereby reducing the need for landfill
- the production of energy from waste
- the production of **ash** that can be used in **construction**.

However, there are disadvantages. These include:

- the production of greenhouse gases
- the release of toxic chemicals
- people may object to the building of new incinerators in their neighbourhood.

Strategy 3: Composting

Composting is the **decomposition** of **biodegradable** material and its use as a fertilizer in soil. There are many advantages and disadvantages of composting. Advantages include:

- the production of organic **fertilizer**
- a reduction in the use of chemical fertilizer
- a reduction in the volume of organic waste.

However, there are disadvantages of composting. These include:

- the production of unpleasant smells
- the attraction of **vermin** if not done properly
- it is a slow process.

Strategy 4: Landfill

Landfill is the **dumping** of material in a hole in the ground or on the ground. There are many advantages and disadvantages to landfill. Advantages include:

- the production of energy in the form of methane gas
- the amount of time and labour that are required are relatively small
- it is a cheap and easy means of waste disposal.

However, there are disadvantages of landfill. These include:

- the production of methane, which is a greenhouse gas
- the pollution of watercourses and groundwater by **leachate**
- the increase of vermin, which can spread diseases.

Factors affecting the choice of waste disposal

A number of factors affect the choice of waste disposal. These include:

- government policy, for example a **strategy** to encourage recycling
- international agreements to cut greenhouse gases or dumping at sea
- population density and the amount of land available for landfill.

Many poorer communities are much better at recycling materials than richer communities. Recycling forms the basis of many industries in Cairo, Egypt. Up to 80 per cent of waste material in Cairo is recycled by the Zabbaleen community.

Glossary

vermin small animals/birds/insects that destroy crops/food and spread disease

dumping getting rid of/leaving dangerous waste material in places that are not safe

Subject vocabulary

leachate water that has passed through soil or rock and picked up material

Synonyms

strategy......... method/approach

Glossary

composition the way something is made up of different parts

soot black powder produced from burning something

Synonyms

varies...........changes/differs

Subject vocabulary

trace gases gases that are found in very small quantities but which are very important, such as ozone and carbon dioxide

aerosols tiny solid materials held up in the atmosphere

weather the state of the atmosphere over a short time-scale such as a few days; it includes temperature, rainfall, cloud cover, humidity, and wind speed and direction

ozone a molecule made up of three atoms of oxygen

The structure and composition of the atmosphere

The structure and **composition** of the atmosphere **varies** with height. The atmosphere is a mixture of solids, liquids, and gases that are held to the Earth by its gravitational force. The atmosphere is quite similar in composition up to a height of about 80 km. It consists mainly of nitrogen (78 per cent), oxygen (21 per cent), and argon (0.9 per cent). There are also a variety of other **trace gases**, such as carbon dioxide and ozone. There is also water vapour and solids (**aerosols**), such as dust and **soot**.

There is no outer limit for the atmosphere, but most **weather** occurs in the lowest 16–17 km. This part of the atmosphere is known as the troposphere. Temperatures decrease with height in the troposphere. The changes in temperature and density are shown in Figure 5.13.

Layers of the atmosphere

The troposphere is the lowest part of the atmosphere. The next upper part of the atmosphere is the stratosphere. It is separated from the troposphere by the tropopause. Above the stratosphere is the mesosphere. The mesosphere is separated from the stratosphere by the stratopause. The highest layer of the atmosphere is the thermosphere. It is separated from the mesosphere by the mesopause.

Certain gases are concentrated at height. **Ozone** occurs in the stratosphere. It is mostly found at around 10–50 km above the Earth. It is important for the filtering of harmful ultraviolet radiation.

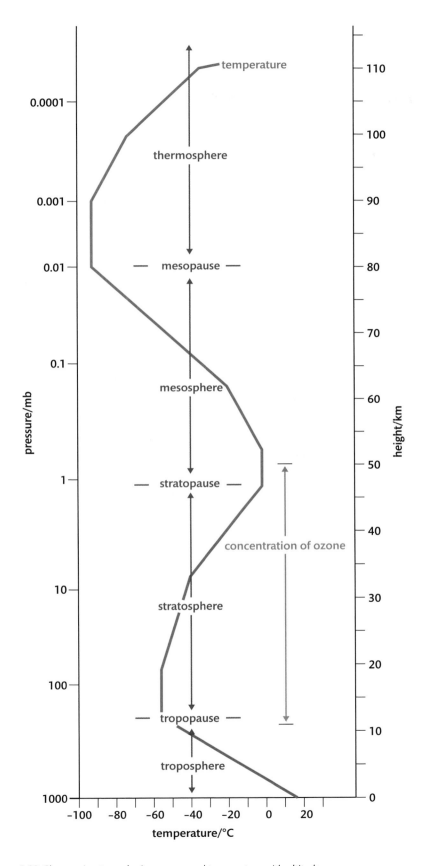

Figure 5.13 *Changes in atmospheric pressure and temperature with altitude.*

Synonyms

altitude .... height

5.6.2 Describe the role of ozone in the absorption of ultraviolet radiation

The importance of ozone

The ozone layer shields the Earth from harmful radiation that would otherwise destroy most life on the planet. **Ultraviolet radiation** is **absorbed** by **ozone**. Ozone also absorbs some out-going, **long-wave radiation**, so it is a greenhouse gas too.

How ozone is formed and destroyed

Ozone is created by oxygen rising up from the top of the **troposphere** and reacting with sunlight. Ultraviolet radiation (short-wave radiation) breaks down oxygen molecules (O_2) into two separate oxygen atoms. The oxygen atoms (O) **combine** to form ozone (O_3). Thus natural processes create ozone. Human activities can destroy ozone. Human production of **chlorofluorocarbons (CFCs)** is linked to a decrease in ozone. The following diagram shows how natural processes and human processes combine to **destroy** ozone.

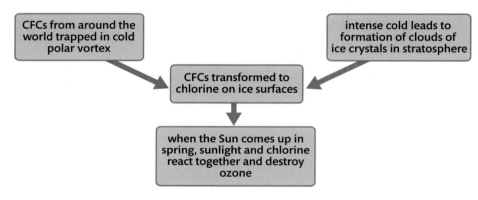

Figure 5.14 *Human and natural processes and the destruction of ozone.*

Hints for success: Memorization of chemical equations relating to ozone and ultraviolet radiation is not required.

5.6.3 Explain the interaction between ozone and halogenated organic gases

Ozone and halogenated organic gases

The chemicals that cause stratospheric ozone **depletion** include halogenated organic gases. Halogenated organic gases (halogens) include chlorofluorocarbons (CFCs). These are found in many products, including aerosol sprays and refrigerators. They can also be found in air conditioners, foamed plastics, pesticides, fire extinguishers, and solvents.

Halogenated organic gases are very stable under normal conditions but can release halogen atoms when exposed to ultraviolet radiation in the stratosphere. Halogen atoms react with monatomic oxygen and slow the rate of ozone reformation.

Pollutants and the 'ozone hole'

Pollutants such as CFCs increase the destruction of ozone, changing the **equilibrium** of the ozone production system. They cause 'holes' in the ozone layer. The ozone hole is a thinning of the **concentration** of ozone in the stratosphere. Figure 5.15 shows the thinning of ozone over Antarctica between 1980 and 1991.

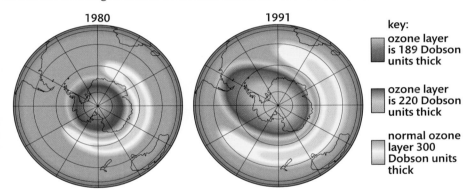

Figure 5.15 *Change in the 'ozone hole' over Antarctica between 1980 and 1991.*

The 'ozone hole' lets more ultraviolet radiation pass through the Earth's atmosphere.

Seasonal changes

There is a clear seasonal pattern to the concentration of ozone. Each spring there is a decrease in the amount of ozone over Antarctica. It recovers when summer comes. This is because, in winter, air over Antarctica becomes cut off from the rest of the atmosphere. The intense cold allows the **formation** of clouds of ice particles. Chemical reactions in these ice particles release single chlorine molecules. Chlorine may come from CFCs. Each spring, when the ice particles melt, the chlorine atoms break ozone down into oxygen gas and other particles. By summer the ice clouds have disappeared and monatomic chlorine is converted to other compounds; thus there is less destruction of ozone.

5.6.4 State the effects of ultraviolet radiation on living tissues and biological productivity

Subject vocabulary

ultraviolet (UV) radiation
also known as short-wave radiation, i.e. radiation at the wavelength 0.1–0.4 μm, which is harmful to humans, some animals, and some plants

genetic mutation a permanent change in DNA structure

photosynthesis a process in plants that changes light energy into chemical energy

plankton any organism that lives in the water and is incapable of swimming against the current

marine phytoplankton sea-water plankton that live close to the water's surface where there is sufficient light to photosynthesize

biological productivity the amount of biomass created by photosynthesis in a certain amount of time

biosphere the part of the Earth inhabited by organisms

Synonyms

subsequent..... later

aquatic........... water/marine

reproduction... breeding/mating

Glossary

larva a young insect

cataracts medical condition that causes you to lose your sight

irreversible cannot be changed back

Effects of ultraviolet radiation

The effects of **UV radiation** include **genetic mutation**, with **subsequent** effects on health, and damage to **photosynthetic** organisms.

- Increased UV radiation causes damage to ecosystems by damaging plant tissues and **plankton**.

- UV radiation damages **marine phytoplankton**, which is one of the major primary **biological producers** of the **biosphere**.

Effects on photosynthesis

- UV radiation causes reduced rates of photosynthesis.

- In **aquatic** ecosystems, the organisms that live in the upper part of the water are most affected; these include phytoplankton, fish eggs and **larvae** (most adult fish are protected from UV radiation since they live in deep waters).

- UV radiation can cause genetic mutations in DNA.

- Recent studies of the effects of UV radiation on phytoplankton show a range of impacts; these include reduced growth and lower rates of photosynthesis.

- UV radiation also has negative impacts on **reproduction** rates.

Effects on humans

- UV radiation is damaging to human populations around the world.

- UV radiation causes eye damage and **cataracts**.

- The effects of long-term exposure to UV radiation are **irreversible** and can cause blindness.

- UV radiation can also cause sunburn and, eventually, skin cancer.

5.6.5 Describe three methods of reducing the manufacture and release of ozone-depleting substances

There are a number of ways of reducing the manufacture and release of ozone-depleting substances (ODSs).

These include:

- recycling refrigerants
- alternatives to **gas-blown plastics** and **propellants**
- alternatives to **methyl bromide**.

Method 1: Reduction of ODSs in refrigerants

The use of **CFCs** in refrigeration was one of the most important uses for CFCs. Now a combination of **HFCs** and **hydrocarbon** refrigerants has largely replaced CFCs in fridges. Fridges with ODS refrigeration can be replaced with 'greenfreeze' technology that uses **propane** and/or **butane**. Old CFC coolants in fridges and air conditioning units can be recycled.

Method 2: Alternatives to gas-blown plastics and propellants

Huge quantities of CFCs were used as propellants in aerosol sprays. Alternatives to **aerosol sprays** can be used. A good example is using soap instead of shaving foam. Pump-action sprays and trigger sprays can be used instead of aerosols.

Method 3: Phase out of methyl bromide

Methyl bromide gas is an ODS that has been used to control pests. Its production and import in the USA and Europe was **phased out** in 2005. There are some exceptions. It can be used to **eliminate** quarantine **pests** and it can be used in farming where there are no alternatives.

There are alternative chemicals to methyl bromide. Some of these react in ultraviolet radiation to have an impact on germs. Other non-chemical alternatives include **biofumigation** and **crop rotation**. These are examples of **organic farming**. Cultivation of plants in water (**hydroponics**) can also reduce the risk of pests.

5.6.6 Describe and evaluate the role of national and international organizations in reducing the emissions of ozone-depleting substances

Model sentence: The 1987 Montreal Protocol on Substances that Deplete the Ozone Layer is the most significant and successful international agreement relating to an environmental issue.

By 2012, the world had **phased out** 98 per cent of **emissions** of ozone-depleting substances (ODSs) contained in nearly 100 **hazardous** chemicals worldwide.

Successes of the Montreal Protocol

Nearly 200 governments have signed up and implemented the agreed changes according to the Montreal Protocol; as a result it is believed that ozone could recover by 2050. It has been revised seven times since it was first introduced in 1987. **Subsequent** revisions have reduced the phasing-out timescale because of success – phase-out in Europe was achieved by 2000. Total global phase-out is expected by 2030. The Protocol provided an incentive for countries to find alternatives. It also raised public awareness of the use of **CFCs**. Technology has been transferred to low-income countries to allow them to replace ozone-depleting substances.

Problems related to the reduction of ODSs

Some substances that replaced CFCs are powerful **greenhouse gases**, such as HFCs (hydrofluorocarbons). The long life of the chemicals in the atmosphere means that damage will continue for some time – some argue until 2100. It is harder for **LEDCs** to make changes. The **second-hand appliance market** means old fridges are still in circulation. The Protocol depends on national governments and **international organizations** being willing to co-operate.

Attempts at a national level

Some countries have **adopted** other measures. There has been investment in **alternative energy sources** to reduce NO_x and ozone depletion from **fossil fuels**. Some countries found this an easy policy to implement, as few changes were needed and substitutes were available. Low-income countries cannot always meet the cost of alternative energy technology. In Australia there was a national education campaign. People were advised to use sunblock, avoid being outside during the hottest part of the day, and to wear T-shirts and sunglasses.

Hints for success: Some candidates confuse global warming and ozone depletion. However, some ODSs – such as ozone – have global warming potential.

5.7.1 State the source of and outline the effect of tropospheric ozone

Tropospheric ozone – or ground-level ozone – is a pollutant. It is a secondary pollutant because it is formed by reactions involving oxides of nitrogen (NO_x).

The main cause of ground-level **ozone** is the volume of road transport concentrated in cities. Two important pollutants are released when fossil fuels are burnt. These are hydrocarbons (from unburnt fuel) and nitrogen monoxide (also called nitric oxide or NO). Nitrogen monoxide reacts with oxygen to form nitrogen dioxide (NO_2). This is a brown gas that contributes to **urban haze**. It can also absorb sunlight and break up to release oxygen atoms that combine with oxygen in the air to form ozone.

The effects of tropospheric ozone

Ozone is a **toxic** gas and an **oxidizing agent**. It **irritates** eyes and can cause breathing difficulties in humans. It may also increase **susceptibility** to infection. Ground-level ozone reduces plant **photosynthesis** and can reduce crop **yields** significantly. It damages crops and forests. Ozone pollution has been suggested as a possible cause of the **die-back** of German forests (previously it was believed these had died as a result of **acid rain**). Ozone is highly reactive and can attack fabrics and rubber materials.

Figure 5.16 *Smog in Beijing*

Subject vocabulary

tropospheric ozone ozone found at ground level, i.e. in the troposphere

ozone a molecule made up of three atoms of oxygen

oxidizing agent a substance that removes electrons from another substance in a chemical reaction

photosynthesis a process in plants that changes light energy into chemical energy

die-back the early death of large parts of vegetation

acid rain (acidification) rain that contains acid, which can harm the environment, and can be caused by chemicals in the air, e.g. from cars and factories

Glossary

urban belonging to a town or city

haze smoke/dust/mist in the air which makes it difficult to see

irritates makes painful and sore

susceptibility how easily affected you are by something

Synonyms

toxic .... poisonous/harmful

yield .... production/output

Photochemical smog

Photochemical smog is a mixture of about 100 **primary** and **secondary pollutants** formed under the influence of sunlight.

Fossil fuels are burnt and nitrogen oxides are released in vehicle emissions. Nitrogen oxides interact with other pollutants in the presence of sunlight to produce **tropospheric ozone**. Ozone formation can take a number of hours, so the polluted air may have drifted into **suburban** and surrounding areas. **Smog** is more likely under **high-pressure** (calm) conditions. Rain cleans the air and winds **disperse** the smog – these are associated with **low-pressure** conditions.

Local conditions

The **frequency** and severity of photochemical smogs depend on local factors. These factors include **topography** and climate, as well as population density and use of fossil fuels. **Temperature inversions** may trap smog in valleys. The following diagram shows how temperature inversions occur.

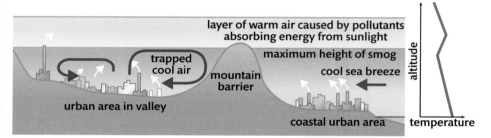

Figure 5.17 *Temperature inversions.*

Temperature inversions

Temperature inversions happen regularly in Los Angeles and Mexico City. The air is unable to disperse since cold dense air sinks in from surrounding hills. Cold air is denser than warm air and so remains near the surface. Warmer air is found above the cold air. As a result of this temperature inversion, concentrations of air pollutants can build up to harmful levels.

Urban microclimates

Urban microclimates also affect the production of ground-level ozone. Urban areas generally have less vegetation than surrounding **rural** areas. Urban areas also have a greater concentration of buildings and industries that **generate** heat.

5.7.3 Describe and evaluate pollution-management strategies for urban air pollution

Reducing urban air pollution

There are many **strategies** for managing **urban** air pollution:

- Some measures may lead to a reduction in the use of fossil fuels, such as reducing demand for electricity and switching to renewable energy.

- Increased use of public transport and 'park and rides' reduces individual car use, hence reduces **emissions** of fossil fuels.

- The promotion of clean technology/hybrid cars also reduces the use of fossil fuels.

- Preventing cars from entering parts of a city can result in improved air quality (in Mexico City, cars with an odd-numbered number plate are allowed into the city centre on certain days, whereas cars with an even-numbered number plate are allowed in on other days).

- By providing more bus lanes and cycle lanes, more people are encouraged to cycle or travel by bus.

- **Tolls** for private cars to enter a city centre, such as the London Congestion Charge, can reduce the number of vehicles entering.

- Other strategies include the development of catalytic converters in cars to reduce emissions of NO_x.

Urban design

Reducing the **consumption** of fossil fuels through urban design (e.g. south-facing windows and triple-glazed windows) can lead to an improvement in air quality. Reducing fossil fuel **combustion** by switching to renewable energy methods also improves air quality. The relocation of industries and power stations away from centres of population leads to an improvement in air quality for people living in cities.

The chimneys used in industries and power stations should be tall chimneys to help **disperse** pollutants. It is possible to filter and trap pollutants at the point of emission. Urban design can be made more **sustainable**. Open space and water courses help reduce the temperature and allow evaporative cooling.

Weaknesses of pollution-management strategies

Most urban pollution comes from cars. Old cars tend to be more polluting than new cars. Vehicles using diesel fuel produce emissions of particulate matter. The use of catalytic convertors reduces fuel efficiency and increases CO_2 emissions. Public transport can be expensive and may be inconvenient. Sustainable urban design is expensive.

Synonyms

strategies........ methods/approaches

consumption... use

combustion .... burning

disperse .... spread/scatter

Glossary

urban built-up areas such as towns or cities

emissions gas/other substances sent into the air

tolls payment for the use of certain roads/bridges

sustainable able to continue without harming the environment

Subject vocabulary

fossil fuels energy sources from the remains of plants and animals, such as oil, natural gas, and coal

renewable energy energy sources that can be used indefinitely, such as solar and hydroelectric power

hybrid car a car that can run on an alternative energy source, such as electricity, as well as fossil fuels

catalytic converter a vehicle emissions control that changes toxic substances into non-toxic substances

particulate matter tiny pieces of solid or liquid matter held in the atmosphere having a diameter of less than 10 μm

5.8.1 Outline the chemistry leading to the formation of acidified precipitations

Acid precipitation

Acid deposition includes acid precipitation (rainfall) and dry deposition.

Acid precipitation is the increased acidity of rainfall. This is largely as a result of human activity. Rain and snow are naturally acidic. This is caused by carbon dioxide in the atmosphere combining with moisture in the atmosphere to produce a weak carbonic acid. Rainfall has a pH of about 5.5. **Dry deposition** is the fallout of particulates of SO_x and NO_x close to their sources.

The causes of acidification

The major causes of **acidification** are the sulfur dioxide and nitrogen oxides produced when **fossil fuels** are burnt.

Sulfur dioxide and nitrogen oxides are released into the atmosphere. There they are absorbed by moisture and become sulfuric and nitric acids. The pH of this rain can be as low as 3.

Dry deposition typically occurs close to the source of **emission**.

Wet deposition occurs when the acids are dissolved in water vapour and travel in clouds to fall at great distances from the sources.

Wet deposition has been called **trans-frontier pollution**, as it crosses international boundaries. Figure 5.18 shows the formation and impacts of acid rain.

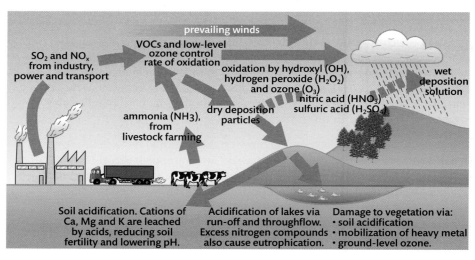

Figure 5.18 *The formation of acid rain.*

Hints for success: Knowledge of chemical equations is not required.

5.8.2 Describe three possible effects of acid deposition on soil, water, and living organisms

The impacts of acid deposition on soils

The following diagram shows the effect of soil **pH** on plant nutrient availability. The thickness of the band indicates the relative availability of each plant nutrient at various pH levels in a soil.

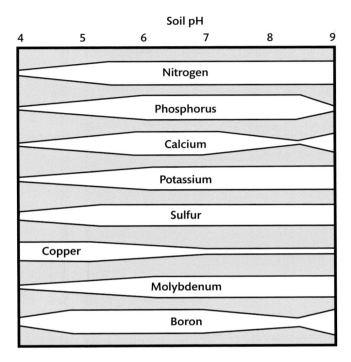

Figure 5.19 *The effect of soil pH on nutrient availability.*

With increasing levels of acidity caused by **acid deposition**, many nutrients become unavailable to plants. These include nitrogen and phosphorus. Calcium and magnesium can be **leached** from soil as it becomes more acidic. Some nutrients become more common. Copper becomes more available in acidic soils.

Iron and aluminium may be **mobilized** when soil pH becomes lower than 4.5. Aluminium leaches more easily under acidic conditions, and hence runs off. However, it may also be released from plant roots under acidified conditions, damaging plant cells.

The impact of acidification on coniferous trees

Acid rain has many impacts on **coniferous** trees. These are shown in the following diagram.

Subject vocabulary

pH the unit of measurement of acidity

acid deposition the increased amount of acid in rainfall and the placing/leaving of acid on rocks and in soil, largely as a result of human activity

leached taken down through the soil by acidic water

coniferous trees that keep their leaves during winter

Synonyms

mobilized ..... moved

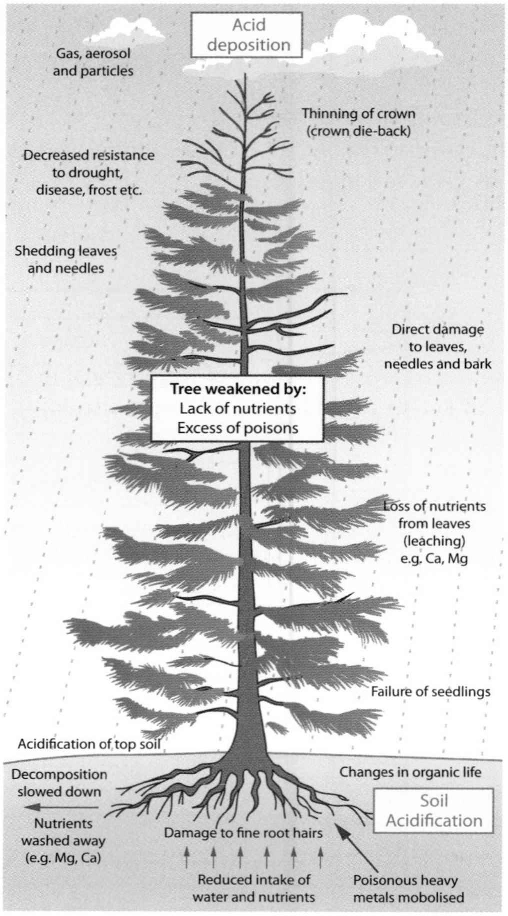

Figure 5.20 *The impact of acid rain on coniferous trees (Source Nagle, G., 1999,* Thinking Geography, *Hodder).*

Coniferous trees are more at risk than **deciduous** trees. This is because coniferous trees do not drop their leaves at the end of the year. The trees may also take up aluminium ions from the soil. This may be **toxic** to coniferous trees. The trees fail to grow because of a lack of nutrients and the presence of too many aluminium ions. Root hairs may be damaged and so there is less uptake of water from the soil. Needles are lost and there may be **die-back** of the **crown**.

The impact of acidification on living organisms

Increasing acidity leads to falling numbers of fungi, bacteria, and earthworms. Increased aluminium and mercury concentrations decrease the number of soil microorganisms. Earthworms cannot tolerate soils with a pH below 4.5. Aluminium ions increase in concentration in water bodies such as lakes, leading to damage to fish **gills** by causing **mucus** to build up. This makes it difficult for fish to breathe and may cause them to die.

The impact of acidification on water

Iron and aluminium are washed from the soils into streams and lakes. The water may become too acidic to support fish. In Canada and the eastern USA, there are over 48,000 lakes that are too acidic to support fish.

Subject vocabulary

deciduous trees that drop their leaves during winter

die-back the early death of large parts of vegetation

gills the organs that allow fish to breathe underwater

Synonyms

toxic .... harmful/poisonous

Glossary

crown the top level of the trees

mucus a thick liquid

5.8.3 Explain why the effect of acid deposition is regional rather than global

> ## Opening sentence:

In this answer I will explain why the effect of **acid deposition** is regional rather than global.

Acid deposition – a regional problem

Model sentence: The areas affected by acid deposition are closely linked to areas of sulfur dioxide and nitrogen dioxide emissions.

Acid deposition is called **trans-frontier pollution** because it crosses international boundaries. The area producing the acid deposition is not the same as the regions receiving it. Areas experiencing acid deposition are **downwind** from the main sources of sulfur dioxide and nitrogen dioxide. **Coal-fired power stations** and **heavy concentrations** of vehicles emit large quantities of sulfur dioxide and nitrogen dioxide.

Areas are affected by acidification

The main areas experiencing acid rain are those areas downwind of major industrial regions, such as Scandinavia. Scandinavia is downwind from major industrial belts in Western Europe. There is also much acid deposition in the northeast of the USA and eastern Canada. These areas are downwind from the US industrial belt. There is less **acidification** in Scandinavia now compared with the 1980s, as there is less **heavy industry** in Western Europe. Areas that are causing acidification now include China and India. This is because both countries are now burning large amounts of coal.

Areas experiencing acidification usually have high rainfall and thin soils. Many of them have forests and lakes.

Areas not affected by acidification

Some soil and water systems are able to neutralize the effects of acid rain. This is called the **buffering capacity**. **Chalk** and **limestone** areas are very alkaline and can neutralize acids effectively. The underlying rocks over much of Scandinavia and northern Canada are **granite**. They are naturally acidic and have a very low buffering capacity. These areas have had the worst damage from acid rain.

Subject vocabulary

acid deposition settling of substances with a pH of less than 5.5, due to the addition of SO_2 and NO_2, the increased amount of acid in rainfall, and the placing/leaving of acid on rocks and in soil, largely as a result of human activity

trans-frontier pollution a type of pollution that crosses international boundaries

downwind being in the direction that the wind is blowing towards

coal-fired power stations power stations that burn coal as their main source of energy

acidification an increase in the acidity of precipitation (rain and snow), in fresh water (lakes and streams), in soil, in oceans, and dry deposition on buildings

heavy industry large-scale polluting industries such as ship-building, iron and steel, and engineering

buffering capacity the ability to offset the effects of acid deposition

Glossary

emissions gas/other substances sent into the air

heavy concentrations large numbers in one place

chalk soft white-grey rock made of small sea animal shells

limestone type of rock containing calcium

granite very hard, grey rock

5.8.4 Describe and evaluate pollution-management strategies for acid deposition

Subject vocabulary

acid deposition the increased amount of acid in rainfall and the placing/leaving of acid on rocks and in soil, largely as a result of human activity

limestone scrubbers pollution control mechanisms to remove particulates or gases from the point of emission

transboundary air pollution a form of pollution that originates in one country and affects another country

catalytic converters a vehicle emissions control that converts toxic substances into non-toxic substances

Glossary

limestone a hard rock that has a pH of about 7

emissions gas/other substances sent into the air

neutralize to reduce the acidic content of a substance

smog polluted fog at ground level

sole the only one

pinpoint locate accurately

variable a factor that can change

culprits those who have caused a problem or committed a crime

Strategy 1: Powdered limestone

One way to reduce the damaging effects of **acid deposition** is to add powdered **limestone** to lakes to increase their pH values. This was used in Norwegian lakes in the 2010s and was very cost-effective.

Strategy 2: Reducing emissions of SO_x and NO_x

The most effective long-term treatment is to reduce the **emissions** of SO_x and NO_x. This can be achieved in a variety of ways:

- by reducing the demand for electricity
- by increasing the use of public transport and reducing the use of private cars
- by using alternative energy sources that do not produce nitrate or sulphate gases
- by using **limestone scrubbers** in power station chimneys to **neutralize** acid
- by removing pollutants before they reach the atmosphere, for example with filters in chimneys.

Strategy 3: The role of international agreements in reducing acidification

There are a number of international agreements concerning acidification. The first was the 1979 Convention on Long-Range **Transboundary Air Pollution**. This was important for the clean up of acid rain in Europe. The 1999 Gothenburg Protocol commits countries to reduce emissions of sulfur dioxide and oxides of nitrogen in an attempt to reduce acidification and other forms of pollution. In North America, the 1991 Air Quality Agreement between USA and Canada focused on reducing the impacts of acid rain and **smog**.

Uncertainties regarding acidification

Increased SO_2 and NO_x are not the only causes of acidification. Rainfall is naturally acidic and could cause some of the damage. No single industry/country is the **sole** emitter of SO_2/NO_x – so it is impossible to **pinpoint** the polluter. Car owners with **catalytic converters** have reduced emissions of NO_x. Different types of coal have **variable** sulfur content – some coal is 'cleaner' than others.

Conclusion

There are many ways to reduce acidification. Some tackle the impacts of acidification, whereas others try to reduce emissions. However, some people believe that it is impossible to identify the causes and **culprits** of acidification.

6.1.1 Describe the role of greenhouse gases in maintaining global temperatures

Greenhouse gases and the greenhouse effect

Model sentence: **The greenhouse effect is a normal and necessary condition for maintaining life on Earth.**

The following diagram shows how the greenhouse effect works.

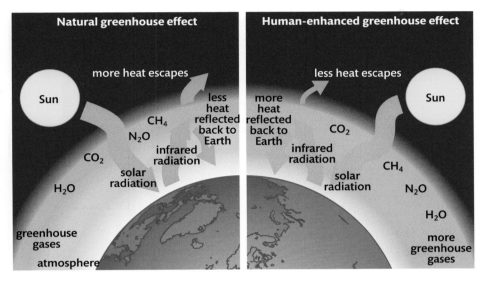

Figure 6.1 *The greenhouse effect.*

Model sentence: **Greenhouse gases cause the greenhouse effect. Increased concentrations of them can lead to global warming.**

Greenhouse gases let through short-wave ultraviolet radiation but trap longer wavelength infrared radiation. This is known as the greenhouse effect. The long-wave radiation warms the planet. Glass in greenhouses performs the same function, keeping the inside of the greenhouse warm.

The greenhouse effect is a normal and necessary condition for life on Earth. Greenhouse gases have raised the Earth's temperature by about 33°C and make life on Earth possible.

Variations of carbon dioxide levels in geological times

There have been considerable changes in the levels of carbon dioxide in geological times. Generally, higher levels of carbon dioxide are associated with higher temperatures. Lower levels of carbon dioxide are associated with lower temperatures and with glacial periods. The following two diagrams show changes in carbon dioxide levels and associated temperatures during the geological past.

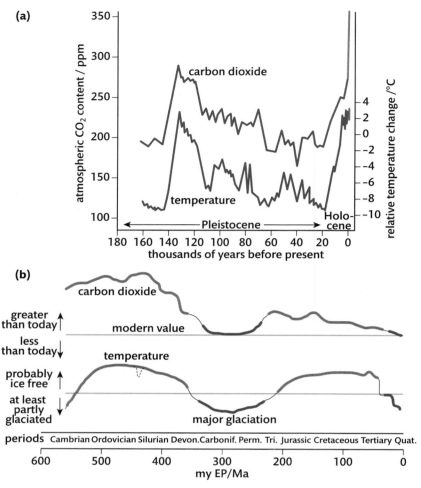

Figure 6.2 *Carbon dioxide levels and temperature changes during the geological past.*

Subject vocabulary

ppm concentrations of atmospheric gases in parts per million

Glossary

correlate a relationship between two variables

Atmospheric concentrations of carbon dioxide in the Early Carboniferous Period (350 million years ago) were very high at around 1500 **ppm**. By the Middle Carboniferous (300 million years ago), carbon dioxide had fallen to about 350 ppm – comparable to today's figure. Average global temperatures in the Early Carboniferous Period were approximately 20°C. Thus high temperatures **correlate** with high carbon dioxide levels. Cooling during the Middle Carboniferous Period reduced average global temperatures to about 12°C. This is similar to today's levels.

In the last 600 million years of the Earth's history, carbon dioxide levels have generally been higher than 400 ppm. It is only during the Carboniferous Period and our present age (the Quaternary Period) that carbon dioxide levels have been less than 400 ppm.

Current changes in carbon dioxide levels

Levels of carbon dioxide are currently rising and the increase is thought to be mainly due to human activities. Carbon dioxide levels have risen from 280 ppm in 1850 to over 400 ppm today. This is a significant rise in 160 years. Atmospheric temperatures have been rising over this same period.

6.1.2 Describe how human activities add to greenhouse gases

Model sentence: There are many human activities that release greenhouse **gases.**

The main greenhouse gases include water vapour, carbon dioxide (CO_2), methane and chlorofluorocarbons (CFCs). Human activities are increasing levels of CO_2 and methane in the atmosphere.

Human activity 1: Carbon dioxide production

The increase in carbon dioxide levels is due to human activities – burning **fossil fuels** (coal, oil, and natural gas) and **deforestation**. Deforestation of the tropical rainforest is a double blow – not only does it increase atmospheric CO_2 levels, it removes the trees that convert CO_2 into oxygen.

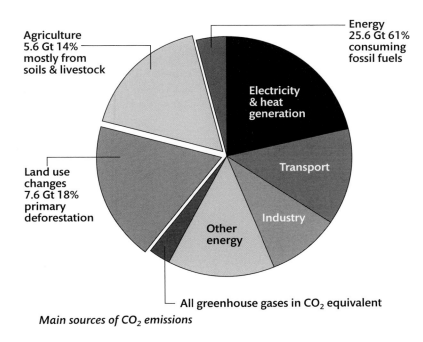

Agriculture
5.6 Gt 14%
mostly from
soils & livestock

Energy
25.6 Gt 61%
consuming
fossil fuels

**Electricity
& heat
generation**

**Land use
changes
7.6 Gt 18%
primary
deforestation**

Transport

**Other
energy**

Industry

All greenhouse gases in CO_2 equivalent

Main sources of CO_2 emissions

Figure 6.3 *Global emissions of greenhouse gases come from a wide range of sources. The increase in greenhouse gases in the atmosphere due to human activity may be causing global warming.*

Human activity 2: Methane production

Methane is the second largest contributor to global warming, and is increasing at a rate of 1 per cent per annum. It is estimated that cattle convert up to 10 per cent of the food they eat into methane, and emit 100 million tonnes of methane into the atmosphere each year. Natural wetland and paddy fields are another important source – paddy fields emit up to 150 million tonnes of methane annually. As global warming increases, bogs trapped in permafrost will melt and release vast quantities of methane.

Recent trends in global warming

Figure 6.4 shows how temperatures varied between 1850 and 1990.

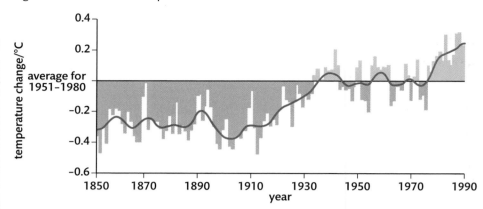

Figure 6.4 *Mean global climate change from 1850 to 1990.*

The graph shows a smoothed curve of annual average temperature. There is an overall upward trend. This upward trend **accelerated** in the last quarter of the graph. Temperatures before the 1930s were all below the average for 1951–1980. Temperatures since the 1980s have all been above the 1951–1980 average.

Reasons for the changes in levels of carbon dioxide in the atmosphere

There are various explanations for the trend of temperature increase seen in the graph in Figure 6.4:

- **industrialization** and the pollution from fossil fuels that release, among other gases, carbon dioxide

- deforestation of rainforest areas

- **volcanic activity**

- **sunspot activity**.

The first two bullet points above assume a link between carbon dioxide **emissions** and temperature increase. The last two suggest possible natural **phenomena** that may have increased temperatures. Most scientists make the assumption that the increase in temperature is caused by human activities. This is due to the large increase in carbon dioxide concentrations since the **Industrial Revolution**.

6.1.3 Discuss qualitatively the potential effects of increased mean global temperature

Opening sentence:

In this answer I will discuss **qualitatively**, that is in subjective terms – both positive and negative, the potential effects of increased **mean** global temperature.

There are many potential impacts of increased mean global temperature.

These include some impacts on the natural environment and some impacts on the human environment. Potential effects on the natural environment include the distribution of biomes and changes to weather patterns. Potential effects on the human environment include changes to global agriculture and the spread of tropical diseases.

Changes in biotic components of ecosystems

One impact of increased mean global temperatures is **biome** shifting. This means that biomes could shift by **latitude** or by **altitude**. The following diagram shows altitudinal shifts in biomes.

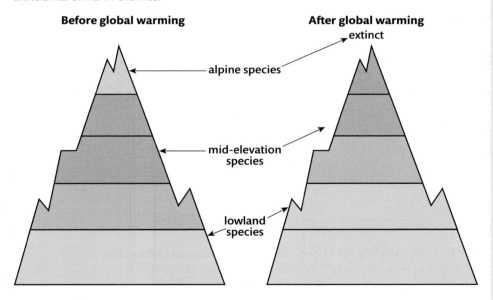

Figure 6.5 *Altitudinal shift of biomes as a result of global warming.*

Alpine (mountain) species are particularly at risk, because altitude boundaries of various zones may move up the mountain. There may be some loss of **species diversity** as species unable to adapt or with limited scope for shifting may become extinct. Animals can migrate but plants shift their range more slowly.

Changes in location of crop-growing areas

There may be an increase in **primary productivity** in some areas as a result of global warming. Shifting biomes mean crop-growing areas will shift. Scientists project a northward shift of wheat-growing areas in North America. This is shown in Figure 6.6 below.

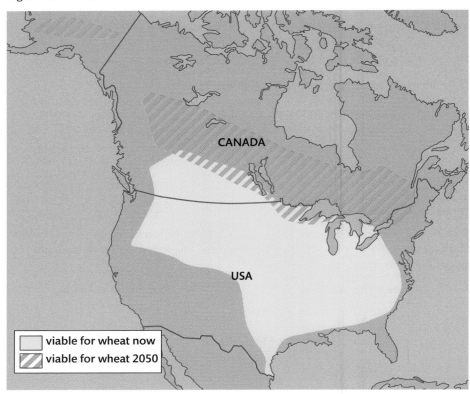

Figure 6.6 *The predicted change in wheat-growing areas in North America (map is simplified because existing boundaries are highly complex).*

As some areas become warmer and drier, the increased temperature could affect crop production, hence affecting food supply, leading to increased conflict over water or food.

Coastal flooding

Coastal flooding will occur as global warming leads to **thermal expansion** of water and melting of **glacier** and **ice cap sheets**. These effects contribute to a rise in sea level. This rise could have many impacts, such as increased coastal **erosion**. The harmful presence of rising amounts of salt water could cause the **contamination** of soils and the fall of **agricultural** production. **Ecosystems** could also be affected. Coastal flooding could cause a reduction in the area of **mangrove forests**. It could also prevent coral reefs from obtaining enough light.

The impact on human health

Global warming can have different impacts on human health. More mosquitoes may cause diseases due to an increase in temperature allowing the mosquitoes' range to increase. Changes in **distribution** of organisms may cause new diseases to occur in an area. The risk of heat stroke will increase in a warmer world. The harmful presence of rising amounts of salt water and a fall in food production could lead to hunger and **malnutrition**.

Changes in weather patterns

Researchers have considered the effect of a doubling of CO_2 from the 270 ppm in **pre-industrial times** to 540 ppm. They believe this will lead to an increase of temperatures by about 2°C. Increased warming is likely to be greater at the poles rather than at the Equator. There are also likely to be changes to **prevailing winds** and to **precipitation patterns**. Continental areas will become drier.

The impact of changing temperatures depends on how great the temperature changes are. Figure 6.7 shows some impacts at different levels of temperature change.

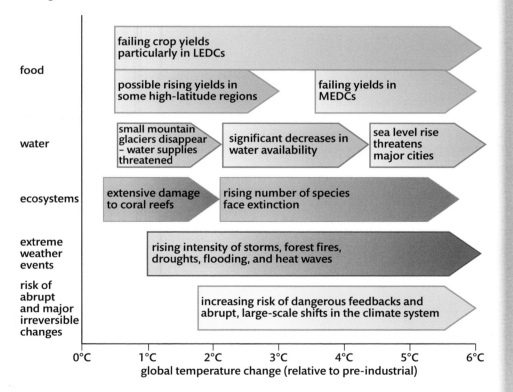

Figure 6.7 *The projected impacts of climate change.*

6.1.4 Discuss the feedback mechanisms that would be associated with an increase in mean global temperature

There are many feedback mechanisms that are **associated** with an increase in **mean** global temperatures.

Some of these involve negative feedback and some involve positive feedback.

Negative feedback

Negative feedback may involve increased **evaporation** in tropical latitudes leading to increased snowfall on the **polar ice caps**. The surface of snow and ice is very **reflective**, so the albedo is increased. Increased reflectivity reduces the amount of **solar** radiation received and so lowers temperatures. This is shown in the diagram below.

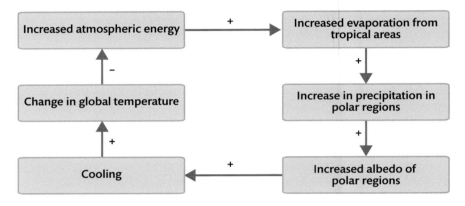

Figure 6.8 *Negative feedback and global climate change.*

Positive feedback

In contrast, positive feedback may involve increased **thawing** of **permafrost**, leading to an increase in methane gas levels, which increases the mean global temperature. As methane is a **greenhouse gas**, it has the potential to increase temperatures, thereby reinforcing the rise in temperature. This is shown in Figure 6.9.

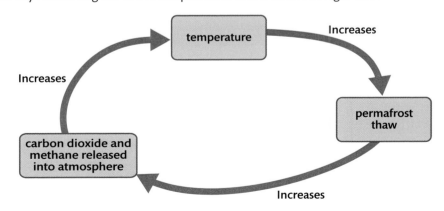

Figure 6.9 *Positive feedback and global climate change.*

Any feedback mechanisms associated with global warming may involve very long time-lags.

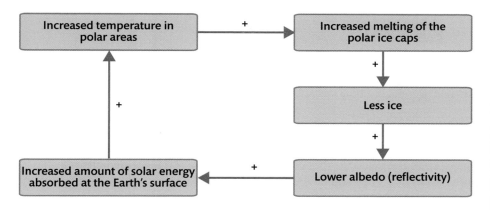

Figure 6.10 *Positive feedback in polar areas.*

6.1.5 Describe and evaluate pollution-management strategies to address the issue of global warming

There are many ways in which it is possible to address the issue of global warming.

These range from the global to the local scale, and include **preventive** as well as **reactive** measures.

Strategy 1: The Kyoto Protocol

The Kyoto Protocol (1997) encouraged most **MEDCs** to take on **legally binding** targets for cuts in greenhouse gas **emissions** from the 1990 level by 2012. The EU agreed to cut emissions by 8 per cent and the USA by 6 per cent. Not all MEDCs signed up to the Kyoto Protocol. The USA and Australia did not sign up for a number of years. They argued that to sign up would damage their economy and make them less competitive against many **emerging economies**.

Even if **greenhouse gas** production is cut by between 60 per cent and 80 per cent, there is still enough greenhouse gas in the atmosphere to raise temperatures by 5°C. The Kyoto agreement was only meant to be the beginning of a long-term process. The Kyoto Protocol ran out at the end of 2012, although it has been extended to 2015. At the 2011 Durban (South Africa) conference, the debate about a legally binding global agreement was reopened. Countries now have until 2015 to decide how far and how fast they can cut their carbon emissions. The Durban Agreement differs from the Kyoto Protocol in that it includes MEDCs and **LEDCs**, rather than just MEDCs.

Strategy 2: Carbon taxes

Some countries have introduced **carbon taxes** to encourage producers to reduce emissions of carbon dioxide. These tax the burning of **fossil fuels** in proportion to how much carbon they contain. Britain has a tax on emissions. It is one of the few EU countries where carbon emissions have fallen and the country should meet its target of a 20 per cent cut in emissions.

Strategy 3: Carbon trading

Carbon trading is an attempt to create a market in which **permits** issued by governments to emit carbon dioxide can be **traded**. Governments set targets for the amount of carbon dioxide that can be emitted by industries. Companies that go over the limit are forced to buy permits from others that do not. It is working, but not very well. **Critics** argue that the targets are too generous.

Strategy 4: Carbon offset schemes

Carbon offset schemes are designed to reduce the effects of increased carbon dioxide by investing in projects that cut emissions elsewhere or trap carbon dioxide. Offset companies typically buy carbon credits from projects that plant trees or encourage a switch from fossil fuels to renewable energy. They offset their emissions of carbon against the carbon they help grow. For example, the Dutch company

FACE Foundation has an offset project in Ecuador – they have planted 220 km of eucalyptus and pine plantations. They sell credits to individuals and companies who want to go 'carbon neutral', i.e. on balance they lock up as much carbon as they use. Some climate experts say offsets are dangerous because they do not encourage people to change their behaviour.

Strategy 5: Alternative energy sources

The use of **alternative energy sources** would reduce emissions of carbon dioxide. These sources include **hydroelectric** power and **solar** power. They do not produce carbon dioxide when they are operating, although carbon dioxide is released when building the facilities. **Alternative** energy sources cannot be built everywhere, but require the right climate and topography.

Strategy 6: Individuals' reductions in greenhouse gases

There are ways in which individuals can help to reduce greenhouse gas emissions:

- grow their own food and/or eat locally produced foods
- choose energy-efficient products (for example, energy-saving light bulbs)
- reduce their heating – weather-proof their homes
- unplug appliances when not in use
- turn off lights where electricity is generated by fossil-fuel combustion
- reduce the use of air conditioning and refrigerants
- use a manual lawnmower rather than an electric or diesel one
- walk or ride a bike
- use public transport
- use biofuels (made from animal/plant waste)
- eat lower down the food chain (vegetables rather than meat)
- buy organic food (not produced using harmful chemicals).

There are many ways in which global warming can be managed. However, many LEDCs and MEDCs believe that cutting carbon dioxide emissions may harm their economy. Alternative energy sources that do not emit carbon dioxide can be expensive and cannot be installed everywhere. There are many ways in which individuals can reduce their personal carbon dioxide emissions. This may involve lifestyle changes. However, emissions of carbon dioxide continue to rise.

Subject vocabulary

alternative energy sources forms of renewable energy, such as hydroelectricity and wind power, that do not release greenhouse gases once they have been built

Glossary

hydroelectric using water power to make electricity

solar relating to the Sun

Synonyms

alternative .... different

6.1.6 Outline the arguments surrounding global warming

Subject vocabulary

greenhouse gas gases, such as carbon dioxide and methane, that allow incoming solar radiation to pass through the atmosphere but block some of the out-going radiation from leaving the atmosphere; they can lead to global warming

Milankovitch cycles changes in the Earth's orbit around the Sun, in the length of seasons, and the direction the poles are facing (either towards or away from the Sun), leading to glacial periods

global dimming a reduction in global temperatures as a result of pollution

aerosols a gas containing fine solid particles or liquid droplets

pollution the addition to an environment of a substance/ agent (such as heat) by human activity, faster than it can be made harmless by the environment, and which has a significant effect on the organisms within it

Synonyms

stress .... emphasize

combustion .. burning

rapid .... fast

fluctuations... changes

Glossary

fossil fuel natural fuels, such as coal or gas, formed from the remains of organisms

industrialization when a country/ place develops a lot of industry

sceptical in disagreement/disbelief

verifiable can be proved true/ correct

conclusive showing that something is really true

reflective sends/bounces back light

solar relating to the Sun

There are natural causes of climate change as well as those caused by humans.

Just because the natural ones exist does not mean that there is no human impact on climate change.

Global warming

Many people believe that scientific data proves that the climate is warming. They state that scientific data shows that carbon dioxide levels and greenhouse gas levels are increasing. Moreover, data from a wide variety of sources and times indicates warming. They **stress** that human activities and/or **fossil fuel combustion** are known to increase carbon dioxide levels. The **rapid** rate of increase in carbon dioxide since **industrialization** implies a human link. They also argue that carbon dioxide and other greenhouse gases are known to impact global temperatures. Therefore it is likely that human activities are resulting in global climate change.

Global warming sceptics

Some people **sceptically** claim that natural **fluctuations** occur so that the current increase in temperature could be due to short-term changes. They claim that the only technologically **verifiable** data we have has been collected over a short period of time. Moreover, they also state that other aspects of climate change are not all fully understood. Climate has changed in the past due to due to natural fluctuations, such as Milankovitch cycles. Current carbon dioxide levels and global temperature fluctuations are moderate compared to geologic history. Therefore it is not **conclusive** that humans are causing global climate change.

Global dimming

Global dimming refers to a reduction in global temperatures as a result of pollution. Aerosols are highly **reflective** and reflect **solar** energy. This blocks some of the solar energy from entering the lower atmosphere, which has a cooling effect. Air pollution has a similar impact. It is possible that global dimming has slowed down global warming. Scientists showed that from the 1950s to the early 1990s, the level of solar energy reaching the Earth's surface had dropped due to high levels of pollution at that time.

Natural particles in clean air provide points of attachment for water. Polluted air contains far more particles than clean air (for example, ash, soot, and sulfur dioxide) and therefore provides many **sites** for water to **bind** to. These tend to be smaller than natural droplets. Many small water droplets reflect more sunlight than a few larger ones. Thus polluted clouds reflect far more light back into space. This reduces the power of the Sun's rays getting through. By cleaning up air pollution, global warming may be **accelerated**.

Subject vocabulary

points of attachment places for water to stick to

Synonyms

sites.............places

bind ....stick

accelerated...speeded up

Figure 6.11 *Deck chairs on glaciers (here at Seefeld, Austria) may soon be a thing of the past!*

6.1.7 Evaluate contrasting human perceptions of the issue of global warming

Perceptions of global warming issues

Your response to climate change and global warming depends on your personal viewpoint. One person may focus on the positive benefits **associated** with the predicted changes in world climate. Some parts of the world will experience more rainfall, which will improve farming. Trade may benefit from new routes opening up as ice sheets melt, for example the north-west passage between the Atlantic and Pacific Oceans. Tourist revenue from warmer locations may increase.

Most scientists are now convinced that there is a **causal link** between carbon dioxide levels and global temperature change. Some still argue that relationships are more **complex** and that the effects of global warming remain unclear. Some claim that current changes are part of wider patterns of natural **fluctuation**.

Contrasting perceptions of global warming

1 Al Gore, *An Inconvenient Truth*

The former US Vice President Al Gore won the 2007 Nobel Peace Prize 'for efforts to build up and **disseminate** greater knowledge about man-made climate change'. In his book, *An Inconvenient Truth*, he states:

> Our climate crisis may at times appear to be happening slowly, but in fact it is happening very quickly – and has become a true planetary emergency. The Chinese expression for crisis consists of two characters. The first is a symbol for danger; the second is a symbol for opportunity. In order to face down the danger that is stalking us and move through it, we first have to recognize that we are facing a crisis.

2 Bjørn Lomborg, *The Skeptical Environmentalist*

The Skeptical Environmentalist: Measuring the Real State of the World was written by Danish environmentalist Bjørn Lomborg. He argues that many global problems, such as aspects of global warming and water shortages, are unsupported by statistical analysis. He argues that many of the problems are localized and related to poverty rather than being of global proportions. He accepts that human activity has added to global temperature increases. He outlines a number of uncertainties and some weaknesses in the collection of data worldwide. He also believes that the Kyoto Protocol and various carbon taxes are among the least efficient ways of dealing with global warming. Instead, he argues that a global cost–benefit analysis should be carried out before deciding on how to deal with global warming.

3 The Stern Report

The report by Sir Nicholas Stern analysing the **financial implications** of climate change has a simple message:

- climate change is changing the planet

- the risks that exist from not taking any action are high

- time is running out.

Subject vocabulary

global warming an increase in average temperature of the Earth's atmosphere

Kyoto Protocol an international treaty that sets binding obligations on MEDCs to reduce their emissions of greenhouse gases

Synonyms

contrasting ... different

perceptions .. ideas/thoughts

associated .... linked

complex .... complicated

fluctuations... changes

Glossary

causal link the connection between two things; how one thing makes the other happen/exist

disseminate spread to as many people as possible

financial implications possible future effects on money/cost

The report states that climate change is a threat to the world economy and it will be cheaper to address the problem than to deal with the consequences. The global warming argument had seemed to be a straight disagreement between the scientific case to act and the economic case not to. Now economists are encouraging action.

The Stern Report says that doing nothing about climate change – the **business-as-usual approach** – would lead to a reduction of between 5 per cent and 20 per cent of **GDP** to world economies. This would be due to natural disasters and the creation of hundreds of millions of climate refugees displaced by sea-level rise. Dealing with the problem could cost just 1 per cent of global GDP.

The main points of the Stern Report

- Carbon emissions have already increased global temperatures by more than 0.5°C

- With no action to cut greenhouse gases, the world will warm by 2–3°C within 50 years

- Temperature rise will change the physical geography of the planet and the way humans live

- Natural hazards and water shortages will become more frequent

- The poorest countries will suffer earliest and most.

Personal factors

Opinions of ordinary citizens depend on what scientific evidence they find most convincing. This depends on their level of education and specialized knowledge of the issues. The growth of the **environmental movement** has played a large role in raising awareness of the issue.

Your cultural or religious group may play a role in your views on climate change, and where you live may affect your views. People who live close to the sea are more at risk from coastal flooding. **Socio-economic status** plays a role. **Extreme poverty** leads to short-term views and wealth leads to faith that money will solve the problem. Age may also be important. Young people tend to be more concerned than the old. Some citizens feel they have a responsibility to change the way in which they live to reduce their **emissions** of greenhouse gases.

Subject vocabulary

business-as-usual approach the practice of not changing an activity when it is known to be causing damage

climate refugees people forced to leave an area due to climatic factors

greenhouse gases gases, such as carbon dioxide and methane, that allow incoming solar radiation to pass through the atmosphere but block some of the out-going radiation from leaving the atmosphere; this can lead to global warming

Glossary

GDP (gross domestic product) total values of goods/services produced in one country in one year

displaced made to leave where they usually live

environmental movement all the groups worried about the environment

socio-economic status relating to social and economic position

extreme poverty being very poor

emissions gas/substances sent/released into the air

7.1.1 State what is meant by an *environmental value system*

Subject vocabulary

environmental value system (EVS) a particular world view that influences the way an individual or group of people recognize and evaluate environmental issues

society a group of individuals who share some common characteristics, such as geographical location, cultural background, historical timeframe, religious perspective, or value system

input the movement into something

output the movement out from something

system a collection of parts and the relationships between them, which together make a whole

transfer a process involving a change in location within the system but no change in state

transformation a process that leads to the formation of new products or involves a change in state

flow movement from one place to another

social system the people in a society viewed as a system and organized by a characteristic pattern of relationships

Glossary

socio-political relating to society and politics

context situation in which something exists

democracy system of government in which all adults can vote to choose a government

authoritarian system of government where people have to obey the government instead of having individual freedom

doctrine a set of important beliefs

Synonyms

perspectives .. viewpoints

Model sentence: An environmental value system can be defined as a particular world view that influences the way an individual or group of people recognize and evaluate environmental issues.

An environmental value system (EVS) is influenced by cultural factors. An EVS is also influenced by economic and **socio-political context**, such as whether the **society** is more economically developed or less economically developed, or from a **democratic** or **authoritarian** society.

Model sentence: An environmental value system is like other systems and has inputs and outputs.

EVS inputs are:

- education
- cultural influences
- religious texts and **doctrine**
- the media.

EVS outputs are:

- **perspectives**
- decisions on how to act regarding environmental issues
- courses of action.

Model sentence: An environmental value system has transfers and transformations.

Flows of information into individuals within societies can undergo transformations into changed awareness of the environment and changed decisions about how best to act on environmental issues. At their strongest, such flows of information cause people to take direct action to address environmental concerns. It is possible that inputs will transfer through the individual or group without having any effect, although it is unlikely that the input will have no effect at all.

EVSs act within **social systems**.

Model sentence: Social systems can be compared with ecosystems.

Rather than the flows of energy and **matter** we see in ecosystems, social systems have flows of information, ideas, and people. Both ecosystems and social systems exist at different **scales**. Both ecosystems and social systems have common features, such as **feedback** and **equilibrium**. **Trophic levels** exist in ecosystems, and in social systems there are social levels within society. Both ecosystems and social systems contain **consumers** and **producers**. Producers in social systems are responsible for new input, such as ideas, films, books, and documentaries. Consumers in social systems **absorb** and process this information.

The following table summarizes the differences between ecosystems and social systems:

	Ecosystem	Social system
Flows	Energy and matter	Information, ideas, and people
Storage	Biomass, the atmosphere, soils, lakes, rivers, sea	Environmental value systems
Levels	Trophic levels	Social levels
Producers	Plants, algae, and some bacteria	People responsible for new input such as ideas, books, films
Consumers	Consume other organisms	Absorb and process new input such as ideas, food, material possessions

Environmental value systems are like all other systems, with inputs, outputs, transfers, and transformations.

Inputs in environmental value systems include education, cultural influences, religious texts and doctrine, and the media.

Inputs can be transforrmed into changed outputs, such as environmental awareness, perspectives, decisions, and actions.

Subject vocabulary

ecosystem a community of organisms that depend on each other and the environment they live in

feedback where the results of a process affect the input of the process

equilibrium a state of balance among the parts of a system

trophic level the position that an organism, or group of organisms, occupies in a food chain

consumer an organism that eats other organisms to obtain their food

producer an organism that makes its own food, for example a green plant that can photosynthesize

Synonyms

matter ....substance/material

scales...........levels

absorb ....take in

7.1.2 Outline the range of environmental philosophies with reference to Figure 7.1

Model sentence: Environmental value systems can be applied to a range of environmental philosophies.

An environmental philosophy determines the global **perspective** of an individual or group of individuals, the decisions they make, and the course of action they take regarding environmental issues.

Environmental philosophies can broadly be divided into technocentrist and ecocentrist, with anthropocentrists in the middle between the two. Anthropocentrism is a human-centred worldview that spans the range of the environmental value system that includes both ecocentrists and technocentrists.

Technocentrists

Model sentence: Technocentrists believe that technology will keep pace with, and provide solutions to, environmental problems.

Technocentrists state that technology will provide solutions to environmental problems even when human effects are pushing natural systems beyond their normal boundaries.

At one end of the technocentric **spectrum** are the cornucopians. A cornucopian view is a belief in the never-ending **resourcefulness** of humans and their ability to control their environment. A cornucopian view leads to an optimistic view about the state of the world. A more anthropocentric world view is shown by environmental managers. Environmental managers see progress happening within closely defined frameworks to prevent **overexploitation** of the Earth's resources.

Ecocentrists

Model sentence: An ecocentrist worldview sees nature as having an inherent value.

This means that the natural world has **integral** worth independent of its value to anyone or anything else. The ecocentric worldview is nature-centred and does not trust modern, large-scale technology. Ecocentrists prefer to work with natural environmental systems to solve problems, and to do this before problems get out of control. Ecocentrists see themselves as subject to nature rather than in control of it. Ecocentrists see a world with limited resources where growth needs to be to be controlled so that only **beneficial forms** occur (for example, not leading to habitat destruction or overuse of natural resources).

At one end of the ecocentrist worldview are the self-reliance soft ecologists, who reject **materialism** and tend to a **conservative** view on environmental problem-solving. Self-reliance soft ecologists hold a people-centred (anthropocentric) view that is essentially ecocentric in nature. These environmentalists see humans as having a key role in managing sustainable global systems. At the other end of the ecocentrist spectrum are deep ecologists. The deep ecology movement believes that all species have an **intrinsic** value and that humans are no more important than other species. Deep ecologists put more value on nature than humanity. This philosophy rejects the concept of natural resources because it implies that organisms and ecosystems are only important as economic **commodities** for humans. Deep ecologists argue that an anthropocentrist viewpoint (where nature is seen to exist for, and be used by, humans for human benefit), is at the root of our environmental crisis.

Figure 7.1 shows the range of environmental philosophies:

Environmental philosophy

Ecocentrism (nature centred)

Holistic world view. Minimum disturbance of natural processes. Integration of spiritual, social, and environmental dimensions. Sustainability for the whole earth. Self-reliant communities within a framework of global citizenship. Self-imposed restraint on resource use.

Anthropocentrism (people centred)

People as environmental managers of sustainable global systems. Population control given equal weight to resource use. Strong regulation by independent authorities required.

Technocentrism (technology centred)

Technology can keep pace with and provide solutions to environmental problems. Resource replacement saves resource depletion. Need to understand natural processes in order to control them. Strong emphasis on scientific analysis and prediction prior to policy-making. Importance of market and economic growth.

Deep ecologists

1 Intrinsic importance of nature for the humanity of man.

2 Ecological (and other natural) laws dictate human morality.

3 Biorights – the right of endangered species or unique landscapes to remain unmolested.

Self-reliance soft ecologists

1 Emphasis on smallness of scale and hence community identity in settlement, work, and leisure.

2 Integration of concepts of work and leisure through a process of personal and communal improvement.

3 Importance of participation in community affairs, and of guarantees of the rights of minority interests. Participation seen as both a continuing education and a political function.

4 Lack of faith in modern large-scale technology and its associated demands on elitist expertise, central state authority, and inherently anti-democratic institutions.

5 Implication that materalism for its own sake is wrong and that economic growth can be geared to providing for the basic needs of those below subsistence levels.

Environmental managers

1 Belief that economic growth and resource exploitation can continue assuming:
a suitable economic adjustments to taxes, fees, etc.
b improvements in the legal rights to a minimum level of environmental quality
c compensation arrangements satisfactory to those who experience adverse environmental and/or social effects.

2 Acceptance of new project appraisal techniques and decision review arrangements to allow for wider discussion or genuine search for consensus among representative groups of interested parties.

Cornucopians

1 Belief that people can always find a way out of any difficulties, whether political, scientific, or technological.

2 Acceptance that pro-growth goals define the rationality of project appraisal and policy formulation.

3 Optimism about the ability of humans to improve the lot of the world's people.

4 Faith that scientific and technological expertise provides the basic foundation for advice on matters pertaining to economic growth, public health and safety.

5 Suspicion of attempts to widen basis for participation and lengthy discussion in project appraisal and policy review.

6 Belief that all impediments can be overcome given a will, ingenuity, and sufficient resources arising out of growth.

Adapted from Figure 10.1: The evolution of environmentalist objectives and strategies in the seventies, page 372. First published in O'Riordan, T. 1981. *Environmentalism* London, UK. Pion Limited.

Figure 7.1 *The range of environmental philosophies.*

Glossary

materialism attitude where someone gives more value to things they own than to spiritual values

conservative holding traditional attitudes and cautious about change

Subject vocabulary

sustainable able to carry on without damaging the environment

deep ecologist an ecocentrist who sees humans as subject to nature not in control of it

Synonyms

intrinsic........ natural/real

Glossary

commodities things that can be bought and sold

Model sentence: A technocentrist is a person who has a technology-centred environmental philosophy, while a person who is nature-centred is called an ecocentrist.

Model sentence: I will discuss the issues using two different examples: fossil fuel use and demand for water resources.

Use of fossil fuels

Model sentence: There are problems associated with the use of fossil fuels, such as global warming. A technocentrist would:

- use science to find a useful alternative, such as hydrogen fuel cells; technocentrists see this as a good example of resource replacement, where an environmentally damaging industry can be replaced by an alternative one

- develop technology to reduce the output of carbon dioxide from fuel use rather than change lifestyles to reduce the use of fuel

- say that economic systems have a vested interest in being efficient so the existing problems will self-correct given enough time

- believe that new technological developments would increase standards of living thereby increasing demands for a healthy environment

- believe that scientific efforts should be focused on removing carbon dioxide from the atmosphere rather than slowing economic growth

- believe that a technology-centred environmental philosophy would predict that market pressure would eventually result in lowering of carbon dioxide emission levels.

An ecocentrist's approach to the same problem would:

- call for the reduction of greenhouse gases through limiting existing gas-emitting industry, even if this restricts economic growth

- say that people should change their lifestyle to reduce fossil fuel use; reduction in energy consumption and lower consumption overall would reduce fossil fuel use.

Demand for water resources

Model sentence: Next, I will discuss how environmental philosophies influence the decision-making process with respect to the increasing demand for water resources.

A technocentrist manager would:

- suggest that future needs can be met by technological innovation and the ability to use reserves that have yet to be used

- support desalination activities where fresh water is extracted from sea water

- would support iceberg capture and transport, where icebergs from colder areas are used as a source of fresh water

- encourage waste-water **purification**

- support synthetic water production, where water is made through chemical reactions. Cloud seeding could be used. The following figure shows cloud seeding:

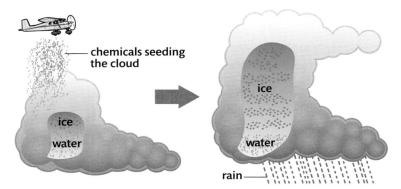

Figure 7.2 *Chemicals, such as silver iodide or frozen carbon dioxide, are scattered into clouds. They provide surfaces around which ice crystals form. When these crystal are large enough, they fall out of the cloud and become rain.*

An ecocentrist manager would:

- highlight the overuse and misuse of water

- encourage the conservation of water and greater recycling

- say that water use should be within **sustainable** levels

- recommend monitoring to ensure that water use remained within sustainable limits

- encourage water use that had few harmful impacts on habitat, wildlife, and the environment.

7.1.4 Outline key historical influences on the development of the modern environmental movement

Model sentence: I will select important historical events to show the development of the environmental movement and outline these in chronological order.

Minamata

In 1956, a new disease was discovered in Minamata City in Japan. It was named Minamata disease and was found to be linked to the release of methyl mercury into the waste-water produced by the Chisso Corporation's chemical factory. The mercury accumulated in shellfish and fish along the coast. The contaminated fish and shellfish were eaten by the local population and caused mercury poisoning. The symptoms were numbness of the hands; damage to hearing, speech, and vision; and muscle weakness. In extreme cases, Minamata disease led to insanity, paralysis, and death.

Rachel Carson's *Silent Spring*

In 1962 American biologist Rachel Carson's influential book *Silent Spring* was published. Carson wrote about the harmful effects of pesticides and made a case against the chemical pollution of natural systems. The book led to widespread concerns about the use of pesticides in crop production and the consequent pollution of the natural environment (mainly terrestrial systems).

The Club of Rome

In 1972 a global think-tank called the Club of Rome published *The Limits to Growth*. The group contained academics, civil servants, diplomats, and industrialists and first met in Rome. The report examined the consequences of a rapidly growing world population on finite natural resources. It has sold 30 million copies in more than 30 translations and has become the best-selling environmental book in history.

'Save the Whale' campaign

The environmental movement Greenpeace became well known in 1975 by starting an anti-whaling campaign. Greenpeace is a non-governmental organization. Greenpeace found Soviet whalers in the Pacific Ocean off the Californian coast, which led the organization to launch its first anti-whaling campaign. The confrontation between Greenpeace and the North Pacific whaling fleets eventually developed into the 'Save the Whale' campaign, which set the blueprint for future environmental campaigns. In the 1980s, Greenpeace made even bigger headlines with its anti-nuclear testing campaign. Campaigns by Greenpeace have resulted in increased media coverage that has raised public awareness about these issues.

James Lovelock's *Gaia*

James Lovelock's book *Gaia*, published in 1979, proposed the Gaia hypothesis – that the Earth is a living organism with self-regulatory mechanisms that maintain its climatic and biological conditions. He saw the actions of humanity upsetting this balance with potentially disastrous outcomes. Later books, up to the present day, have developed these ideas.

Bhopal

On 3 December 1984, the Union Carbide pesticide plant in the Indian city of Bhopal released 42 tonnes of toxic methyl isocyanate gas. The release was caused by one of the tanks involved with processing the gas overheating and bursting. Some 500 000 people were exposed to the gas. It has been estimated that between 8000 and 10 000 people died within the first 72 hours following the exposure, and that up to 25 000 have died since from gas-related disease.

Chernobyl

On 26 April 1986, a nuclear reactor at the Chernobyl plant in the Ukraine exploded. A cloud of highly radioactive dust was sent into the atmosphere and fell over an extensive area. Large areas of the Ukraine, Belarus, and Russia were badly **contaminated**. The disaster resulted in the **evacuation** and **resettlement** of over 336 000 people. The **fallout** caused increased incidence of cancers in the most exposed areas. An area around the plant still remains a no-entry area due to radiation. The incident raised issues concerning the safety of nuclear power stations.

Our Common Future

In 1987, a report by the UN World Commission on Environment and Development (WCED) was published. The report was called *Our Common Future*. It linked environmental concerns to development and aimed to promote sustainable development through international **collaboration**. It also placed environmental issues firmly on the **political agenda**.

UN's Earth Summit

The publication of *Our Common Future* and the work of the WCED provided the groundwork for the UN's Earth Summit at Rio in 1992. The summit's message was that nothing less than a change in our attitudes and behaviour towards environmental issues would bring about the necessary changes. The conference led to the **adoption** of Agenda 21, which is a **blueprint** for action to achieve sustainable development worldwide.

> **Hints for success:** You do not have to include every event listed here if you are asked to outline key historical influences on the development of the modern environmental movement. Select a few to learn and make sure you know the details of each event.

7.1.5 Compare and contrast the environmental value systems of two named societies

Judaeo-Christian and Buddhist societies

Model sentence: In this answer I will compare and contrast the environmental value systems of Judaeo-Christian and Buddhist societies.

The view of the environment in Judaeo-Christian religions is one of **stewardship**. Stewardship is a concept where humans have a role of responsibility towards the Earth. The Genesis story suggests that God put humans in charge of the planet. Other biblical stories indicate that humanity should make the most of this gift as **stewards**.

The Judaeo-Christian value system contrasts with the Buddhist approach to the environment. The Buddhist value system sees the human being as an **intrinsic** part of nature rather than a steward. Buddhism is sometimes seen as an ecological philosophy. This is because of its value system rather than anything that appears in Buddhist texts. Buddhism emphasizes human interrelationships with all other parts of nature. Buddhism supports the belief that it is unrealistic to think of ourselves as isolated from the rest of nature and that we are in fact a part of nature. The concept of **reincarnation** also emphasizes humanity's interconnectedness with nature. Buddhist monks are frequently active in a range of campaigns, including forest conservation in Thailand.

Indigenous Americans and European pioneers

Model sentence: In this answer I will compare and contrast the environmental value systems of indigenous American people and European pioneers.

North America was home only to indigenous Native American tribes before the colonization by Europeans in the late 16th century. Native Americans saw their environment as being shared and had a **subsistence** economy based on **barter**. Their low-impact technologies meant that they lived in harmony with the environment. Living in harmony with nature was supported by their **animistic** religion.

The incoming European pioneers operated frontier economics, which involved the exploitation of what they saw as unlimited resources. This inevitably led to environmental degradation through over-population and lack of connection with the environment. It also led to heavy and technologically advanced industry, and unchecked exploitation of natural resources.

Communist and capitalist societies

Model sentence: In this answer I will compare and contrast the environmental value systems of communist and capitalist societies.

Communist societies have been criticized for their poor environmental record. For example, between 1947 and 1991 the Buna chemical works in East Germany dumped ten times more mercury into its neighbouring river than chemical work plants in West Germany. Cars in the East emitted 100 times more carbon monoxide than those in the West, because they did not have catalytic converters

Subject vocabulary

environmental value system a particular worldview that influences the way an individual or group of people recognize and evaluate environmental issues

society a group of individuals who share some common characteristics, such as geographical location, cultural background, historical timeframe, religious perspective, and value system

Glossary

stewardship the concept of the responsible planning and management of resources

steward a person who looks after or manages something

reincarnation the belief that the human spirit is immortal and can be reborn after death in either human or animal form

indigenous people originally found in an area

subsistence providing enough for a family or small community to survive on

barter system that uses trade in goods rather than money as its economic basis

animism belief system where all things have a soul – animals, plants, rocks, mountains, rivers, and stars

communist economic system where wealth is owned and controlled by the people for the benefit of the people

capitalist economic system where wealth is mainly owned and controlled by private individuals; the system works by free market and profit motives

Synonyms

intrinsic........ natural/real

to remove this toxic gas. East German sulfur dioxide concentrations were also an environmental issue, and were the highest in the world at the time. This was due to the combustion of fossil fuels in power plants and industries across the country, and a failure to remove this gas from emissions. Some people argue that the economic principles of communism inevitably lead to environmental disaster. In communist countries it is thought that people see free natural resources as having use-value to humans alone. The communist ideal of equal distribution of resources with no profit motive means that energy, materials, and natural resources can be squandered without care.

In contrast, the capitalist model is seen by some as being environmentally friendly. People see in the capitalist model that the free market imposes checks and balances to ensure sound use of resources in order to maximize profits.

The actual story is more **complex**. Many of the criticisms of the communist environmental record stem from the period of the **Cold War**. Such criticism was used against the communist states to justify the Cold War. Capitalism itself has a mixed record with regard to the environment. In Germany, before **reunification**, the communist state (East Germany) had protected the interests of farmers, foresters, and fishermen. The state therefore unintentionally benefited certain sectors of the environment. The rise of capitalism in the former communist state led to polluters organizing into powerful **lobbies** to protect their own interests without consideration for the environment.

A state's response to environmental concerns is not just a matter of political **doctrine**. Many factors contribute, such as technology, wealth, geography, economic decision making, and **democratic** structures. In capitalist societies, **civil liberties** and the role of democracy may have played a more significant role in **combating** environmental problems than the capitalist basis of the system.

> **Hints for success:** You need to be able to compare and contrast the environmental value systems of two named societies that are significantly different from each another. This section has outlined three different pairs of societies for you to choose from.

Synonyms

complex ....complicated

combating ....fighting against

Glossary

Cold War a political battle of wills between the communist and capitalist systems lasting between 1947 and 1991

reunification the joining together of a country after a period of separation into two or more parts

lobbies groups of people trying to make the government change situations/laws

doctrine a set of important beliefs

democracy a system of government where everyone votes to choose government members

civil liberties people's freedom to do what they want while respecting others

Model sentence: There is a continuum of environmental philosophies that affect how people relate to specific environmental issues.

Environmental value systems determine a personal viewpoint and how a person responds to environmental issues. Personal viewpoints depend on many different factors. Factors include **social influences**, **personal characteristics**, **habits**, and knowledge of environmental issues.

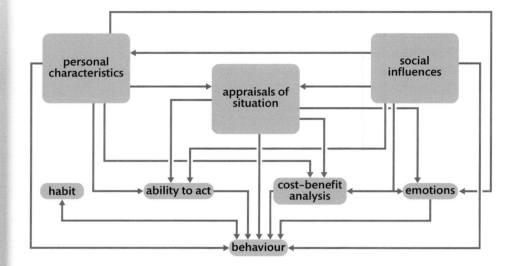

Figure 7.3 *Social influences and personal characteristics influence personal value systems.*

Personal viewpoints can be used to justify opinions about environmental issues.

Model sentence: I will now show how my personal viewpoint on an environmental issue has developed, using global warming as an example.

My personal characteristics help to determine my personal view of global warming. My social influences also help to determine my personal views on this environmental issue. I am **strong-willed**, and my parents and friends are environmentally active, so I am likely to take responsibility for solving global warming and try to make a real difference. I make efforts to reduce my energy consumption and use my bike rather than have a lift to school.

The options available to me affect my personal viewpoint. Because the city I live in provides a convenient recycling procedure, I am more likely to recycle than someone for whom recycling is inconvenient. By recycling, I reduce the need for further resources to be used in producing **commodities**, which also reduces my energy usage.

I have learnt about global warming at school and I have seen Al Gore's film *An Inconvenient Truth* about climate change. I read about the issue in newspapers and have also read books such as *Six Degrees* by Mark Lynas, which examines how temperature increase will affect the planet.

Some of my habits will be difficult to change. I am used to using air conditioning to keep my rooms at home cool. However, I believe that I can change these habits to help me make a real difference to global warming by reducing my energy consumption.

Model sentence: Finally, I will justify my personal viewpoint on an environmental issue, using the exploitation of tropical rainforests as an example.

I believe that rainforests should be conserved and not be over-exploited. Rainforests have an economic value to humans as they may contain food, medicines, and materials for human use. Ecotourism can also provide income. Rainforests are of more value to humans **intact** than being exploited for timber or cleared to produce land for **agriculture**.

Tropical rainforests also have an **intrinsic** value and the organisisms there have a right to exist free from human exploitation. Rainforests provide life-support functions such as water cycles, lock up carbon in plants that would otherwise be in the atmosphere, and provide oxygen for the planet. There are high levels of biodiversity in rainforests and many species are endemic to the area in which they are found. Rainforests provide a home to many indigenous peoples.

They also have an **aesthetic** value and give pleasure to those who visit them. Because the soil is poor and thin, the **regeneration rate** of rainforests is slow if it is cleared. Rainforests provide spiritual, cultural, and religious value to local communities. I believe it is important for humans to act as **stewards** for rainforests so that they can be enjoyed by future generations.

Hints for success: Make sure you can justify your personal viewpoint concerning at least one of the environmental issues covered in the course.

Personal viewpoints are influenced by society, personal characteristics, habits and knowledge of environmental issues.

Emotions, personal benefits and costs, and the ability to act will also determine how a person responds to environmental issues.

Glossary

exploitation making use of something to gain maximum profit from it

indigenous people originally found in an area

aesthetic concerned with how beautiful something is

regeneration rate how long it takes for something to develop/grow again

stewards people who look after or manage something

Subject vocabulary

ecotourism travel to undisturbed natural areas to observe wildlife; ecotourism usually supports conservation efforts, helps to protect the wildlife, and supports local people

endemic a species only found in one particular area

Synonyms

intact...........not damaged/spoiled

agriculture....farming

intrinsic........natural/real

Internal Assessment

Internal Assessment in ESS includes a series of practical and fieldwork activities. Your written reports are marked by your teacher using the IB assessment criteria. Internal Assessment enables you to demonstrate the application of the skills and knowledge that you have gained during the course.

An Internal Assessment report should contain the following sections:

1. **Planning**
   - Research question
   - Variables
2. **Method** (including materials used)
3. **Results**
   - Data collection
   - Data processing and presentation
4. **Discussion**
5. **Evaluation**
6. **Conclusions**

Advice on each section

1. Planning

a. **Research question** – this is a short statement about the intention of the investigation. It may include a prediction of the expected relationship that will be seen to be either supported or not supported by the results.

b. **Variables**

   i. **Independent variable** – this is the variable that you are changing in the investigations. State what this is and include units.

   ii. **Dependent variable** – this is the variable that you are measuring. State what this is and include units.

   iii. **Control variables** – these are variables that you will be keeping the same to ensure a **fair test**. List at least three and say how you will be keeping them the same. In an ecological study, it may not be possible to keep other variables constant (e.g. weather), so in such instances you should say that you will monitor and record these variables.

2. Method

   - Materials can be given as a list. Include sizes, volumes, and other appropriate information.
   - The method should be written in the **passive voice** and with **sufficient** detail and clarity so that someone else can follow the instructions.

3. Results

c. **Data collection** – present your raw data in an appropriate format, normally as a table of results. Make sure that any tables of data include:

   i. *Title* – this should be full and descriptive.

ii. *Column headings* – should include the variable, with units. Units should only be included in the column headings and not in the body of the table. Include the **precision** of the equipment if recorded, e.g. temperature (°C ± 1°C).

d. **Data processing** – show how you have processed the data in appropriate detail. Processing can include statistical tests or other calculations. The method of processing will depend on the nature of the investigation. State any formulae you have used. Where appropriate, show key steps in any calculation so that they can be checked.

e. Present the processed data in a way that displays the results to best effect and helps interpretation. You must not present raw data but data that has been manipulated. Presentation of data may take many forms, including graphs, sketch maps, charts, flow diagrams, or **annotated** drawings. In a graph, the **x-axis** shows the independent variable and the **y-axis** shows the dependent variable.

4. Discussion

- This section should analyse, discuss, and review your results. Consider your results in relation to the relevant part of the ESS syllabus and in the **context** of relevant literature and accepted scientific understanding and **models**.
- It is good to reference source material. For example, a website you consulted: list the URL and date you visited the site.
- The review and analysis can include the identification of trends, patterns, or **anomalies** that may or may not agree with established **theoretical principles**.
- The review and analysis should also say whether your results fit the prediction you made in the Introduction.

5. Evaluation

- This section needs to evaluate the investigation and suggest improvements to the method. These suggestions must be realistic – that you could actually carry out, were you to repeat the study. Describe the strengths and limitations of the study. When commenting on limitations, you need to consider the procedures, the equipment, the use of equipment, the quality of the data (e.g. its **accuracy** and precision) and the relevance of the data.
- Consider the extent to which the limitations may actually have affected the results. Suggest realistic improvements to the investigation that address the limitations. Improvements should refer to specific aspects of the investigation.

6. Conclusions

- These should be **concise**, reasonable, and be supported by the data and discussion.
- The conclusion should be your response to the research question set at the start.

Five examples of possible IAs are given in this book, with suggestions about how they may be carried out and written up.

IA Investigation – The effect of light intensity on the rate of photosynthesis

Synonyms

aquatic.........water/marine

Subject vocabulary

hypothesis an untested proposal that can be investigated using the experimental method

photosynthesis a process that captures sunlight energy and transforms it into the chemical bonds of the glucose molecule. Carbon dioxide, water, and light are transformed into glucose and oxygen in the process

light intensity the amount of light that falls on a particular area from a specific direction

variable a factor that is being changed, investigated, or kept the same in an investigation

independent variable the variable that is being changed

dependent variable the dependent variable 'depends' on the independent variable

control variable the variable that is being kept the same to ensure a fair test

controlled method that uses control variables

In this investigation, the effect of light intensity on the rate of photosynthesis is investigated. A lab-based experiment can be carried out that changes the distance, and therefore light intensity, from a lamp to an **aquatic** plant (pondweed).

Divide your write-up into sections as shown below.

1. Planning

- State clearly the research question to be investigated. For example, *What is the relationship between the distance of pondweed from a lamp and rate of photosynthesis?* Alternatives could include: *How does the rate of photosynthesis vary with distance/light intensity?*
- State clearly the prediction for the investigation. For example, *The rate of photosynthesis of pondweed (Elodea), as measured by the number of bubbles produced per minute, will be higher the closer the pondweed is to the lamp.* Alternatively, the light intensity could be used as the dependent variable, and so the hypothesis would be: *The rate of photosynthesis of pondweed (Elodea), as measured by the number of bubbles produced per minute, will increase as light intensity increases.*
- The number of bubbles represents the rate at which oxygen, a product of photosynthesis, is released.
- Define the key terms, in this case photosynthesis and light intensity.
- Briefly explain the theoretical relationship between the two variables.
- Identify the independent, dependent, and control variables. In this example, the distance of the lamp from the pondweed/light intensity is the independent variable and the number of bubbles produced per minute (as a measure of the rate of photosynthesis) is the dependent variable. This is because the rate of photosynthesis is influenced by the distance of the pondweed from the plant/light intensity. Control variables include the temperature of water the pondweed is in, the amount of carbon dioxide in the water, the surface area of the pondweed (i.e. size of plant), light from elsewhere in the room (ambient light), the direction of the plant from the light source – these could affect the results and so the only factor that varies in the samples should be the distance of the pondweed from the lamp.

2. Method

- Cut a length of pondweed that will fit into a test tube, with space remaining at the top for bubbles to be counted.
- Carbon dioxide (CO_2) can be **controlled** by adding a small amount (one spatula) of sodium bicarbonate powder to the water.
- Make sure that the stem of the pondweed is cut at an angle – this ensures that bubbles of oxygen are easily released. The pondweed should be placed with the cut end towards the top of the test tube.
- Hold the test tube in a clamp-stand and place a set distance from a lamp.
- Measure the number of bubbles released by the pondweed each minute. Repeat this five times at each distance. Make sure that all other factors (control variables such as the amount of CO_2 in the water, the plant, amount of ambient light in the room) are the same.

- Five samples at each distance are needed to ensure the readings are **reliable**. By repeating the measurements, **valid** **quantitative** **data** are collected.

3. Results

Data collection

- Include all relevant tables (including units) – this must be able to **stand alone**.

Processing of data

Data must be processed, e.g. **mean** values calculated, statistical tests carried out.

- If your hypothesis includes light intensity, work out light intensity by dividing 1 by the distance squared. For example, if the distance is 5 cm then the light intensity is $1 / 25 = 0.04$ lux.

- Spearman's Rank can be used to test whether the **correlation** between distance from the lamp/light intensity and the number of bubbles produced per minute is statistically significant.

For example, raw and processed data could be presented as follows:

Distance (d) (cm)	Light intensity ($1/d^2$) (lux)	Number of bubbles per minute					Mean	Standard deviation
		Repeat 1	Repeat 2	Repeat 3	Repeat 4	Repeat 5		
5	0.0400	86	90	93	86	80	87	4.90
10	0.0100	75	72	79	70	75	74	3.42
15	0.0040	49	43	45	43	45	45	2.45
20	0.0025	25	29	23	21	25	25	2.97
25	0.0016	10	15	13	12	11	12	1.92
30	0.0011	6	8	5	9	6	7	1.64
35	0.0008	2	5	4	3	5	4	1.30

Calculation to work out Spearman's Rank for the above data would be done as follows:

n	Light intensity (lux)	Rank	Bubble average	Rank	Difference (d)	d^2
1	0.0400	1	17	1	0	0
2	0.0100	2	13	2	0	0
3	0.0040	3	8	3	0	0
4	0.0025	4	4	4	0	0
5	0.0016	5	3	5	0	0
6	0.0011	6	2	6	0	0
7	0.0008	7	1	7	0	0

Subject vocabulary

reliable/reliability results are repeated so that any results that do not fit the overall pattern of data can be identified and mean results calculated

validity when an experiment is controlled and repeated

data results collected together for analysis

Glossary

quantitative relating to the amount/number of something

stand alone can be looked at on its own and it makes sense

Synonyms

mean .... average

correlation .... link/connection

Spearman's Rank $(r_s) = 1 - \dfrac{6\Sigma d^2}{n(n^2 - 1)}$

Where $\quad 6\Sigma d^2 = 6 \times 0 = 0$

and $\quad n(n^2 - 1) = 7(49 - 1) = 336$

Therefore, $\quad r_s = 1 - (0 / 336) = 1 - 0 = 1$

When $n = 7$, the critical value for Spearman's Rank, at 5 per cent probability level = 0.7143.

As the r_s value of 1 is higher than the critical value of 0.7143, the result is significant at the 5 per cent probability level.

An r_s value of 1 indicates a perfect **correlation** between the two **variables** (see ESS student textbook page 341).

Presentation of data

Graphs must show processed **data**, not raw data.

A scatter graph can be plotted to show the correlation between the **mean** number of bubbles produced per minute and the distance from the light/**light intensity**. **Standard deviation** is calculated for each mean value and plotted on the graph as **error bars** – processed data is therefore presented.

NB: The **independent variables** are shown on the **x-axis** (horizontal axis) and the **dependent variables** are shown on the **y-axis** (vertical axis).

For example, for the data presented above, the graph would be drawn as follows:

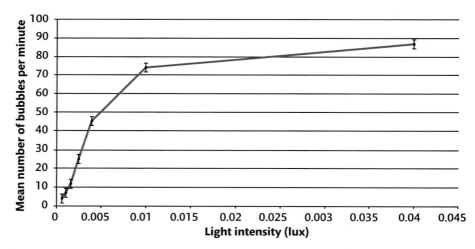

Figure 1 *Graph showing the relationship between light intensity and the number of bubbles of oxygen produced by* Elodea.

4. Discussion

- Fully describe the graph – try to refer to specific data, *in this case the number of bubbles produced per minute*. A useful method is to identify the trend and any exceptions to the pattern. *In the above graph, there is a steep increase in the number of bubbles per minute as light intensity increases, and then the rate begins to level off at higher light intensities.*

Synonyms

correlation....link/connection

mean...........average

Subject vocabulary

variable a factor that is being changed, investigated, or kept the same in an investigation

data results collected together for analysis

light intensity the amount of light that falls on a particular area from a specific direction

independent variable the variable that is being changed

x-axis the horizontal axis of a graph; this axis contains information about the independent variable

dependent variable the dependent variable 'depends' on the independent variable

y-axis the vertical axis of a graph; this axis contains information about the dependent variable

---

Glossary

standard deviation average variation from the mean

error bar graphical representation of the variability of data. They are used on graphs to indicate the uncertainty in a reported measurement

- Explain the results referring to appropriate concepts and theory (*in this case syllabus section 2.5 Function*). *In this investigation, you would need to explain why initially the number of bubbles increases rapidly as light intensity increases, and then begins to level off at higher light intensities.*

5. Evaluation

- Outline limitations and weaknesses of the investigation. Is the data reliable (e.g. was the sample size large enough and were enough repeat measurements taken?). Comment on the error bars; *for example, in the above graph the error bars from consecutive data points do not overlap and so the mean values are different from each other.* Overlapping or large error bars suggest that data are less reliable. Evaluate whether all variables were successfully controlled. *In this experiment you would consider, for example, the way that the bubbles were counted and limitations with this method, and whether the water surrounding the pondweed would have heated up as the lamp moved closer.* How could the data collection be improved? Try to make realistic suggestions; what you could actually do, if you were to do the investigation again.

- What are the limitations of the statistical test that you used? Why was the statistical test that you used an appropriate one? *In this case, the number of data were appropriate for the Spearman's Rank (which requires a minimum of seven pairs of data, i.e. seven different distances with corresponding bubble counts, to be reliable).*

6. Conclusions

- Summarize the main findings of the study. Quote data from your study, e.g. include the results of the statistical test.
- Did the results confirm or reject the hypothesis?
- What was the level of statistical significance of your investigation?

Subject vocabulary

reliable/reliability results are repeated so that any results that do not fit the overall pattern of data can be identified and mean results calculated

evaluation making an appraisal by weighing up the strengths and limitations of the investigation

controlled method that uses control variables

hypothesis an untested proposal that can be investigated using the experimental method

IA Investigation – Comparing soils around a school

In this investigation, **soils** around a school are compared. The location can be changed to compare any two sets of soils.

Divide your write-up into sections as shown below.

1. Planning

- State clearly the research question to be investigated. For example: *How do soils closer to a drainage channel differ from those further away from the drainage channel?* Alternatives could include: *How do soils in the middle of a footpath differ from those further away from the footpath?*
- State a prediction for the investigation. For example: *Soils close to a drainage channel will have a higher moisture content than soils away from the drainage channel.* An alternative prediction is that: *Soils in the middle of a footpath will have a lower moisture content than those at the edge of a footpath.*
- Define the key terms, in this case **drainage channel** and **moisture content**.
- Briefly explain the theoretical relationship between the two **variables**.
- Identify the **independent**, **dependent**, and **control variables**. In this example, the drainage channel is the independent variable and the moisture content the dependent variable. This is because the moisture content is influenced by a drainage channel. Control variables include depth of soil at which samples are taken, the local microclimate, vegetation cover – these could affect the results and so the only factor that varies in the samples should be proximity to the drainage channel.

2. Method

- Two areas need to be sampled: one of the areas should be close to a drainage channel, the other further away. Make sure that all other factors (control variables such as vegetation, gradient, human impact, weather) are the same.
- Five sample sites need to be randomly chosen in each sample area, with five soil samples taken at random from each sample site. This makes a total of 25 soil samples taken from each area.
- In each area, five sample sites and five soil samples from each site are needed to ensure the readings are **reliable**.
- Repeats ensure that **valid quantitative data** are collected.
- Collect the samples from a depth of 5 cm below the surface to ensure that the soils have not been affected by surface processes.
- Place the soil sample in an air-tight food bag, close the bag and give it a label.
- Weigh each individual soil sample (S1).
- Place it in an oven and heat it at 100°C for 24 hours.
- Reweigh each individual sample (S2).
- Work out the moisture content of each individual sample using the formula: Moisture content = $((S1 - S2) \div S1) \times 100\%$

3. Results

Data collection

- Include all relevant tables (including units) – this must be able to **stand alone**.

Processing of data

Work out the **mean** for the moisture content by adding up the 25 individual samples and dividing by 25. The range shows the difference between the largest and smallest reading.

Presentation of data

Graphs must show processed data, not raw data. A box and whiskers graph is used to show differences in the mean and range (i.e. the difference between the maximum value and the minimum value) of the moisture content for the two soils.

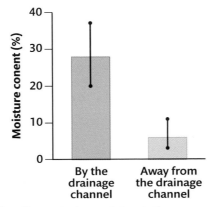

Figure 2 *Box and whiskers diagram to show variations in the mean and range of moisture content at the drainage channel site and away from the drainage channel.*

4. Discussion

- Fully describe the graph – try to refer to specific data, in this case the moisture content of the soils. A useful method is to identify the maximum, the minimum, the trend, and exceptions to the pattern. Note that the ranges – the 'whiskers' – do not overlap and therefore the means are different.

- Explain the results referring to appropriate concepts and theory (in this case syllabus section 3.4 *The soil system*).

5. Evaluation

- Outline limitations and weaknesses of the investigation – is the data reliable? How could the data collection be improved? Could you use more soil samples?

- What are the limitations of the statistical test that you used? Why was the statistical test that you used an appropriate one?

6. Conclusions

- Summarize the main findings of the study. Quote data from your study, e.g. include the results of the statistical test.

- Did the results confirm or reject the **hypothesis**?

- What was the level of statistical significance of your investigation?

IA Investigation – Population and development

Subject vocabulary

data results collected together for analysis

under-5 mortality rate (U5MR) the number of deaths in children under the age of five years per 1000 live births

Human Development Index (HDI) the level of development of a population taking into account life expectancy, literacy levels, and wealth

independent variable the variable that is being changed

dependent variable the dependent variable 'depends' on the independent variable

control variable the variable that is being kept the same to ensure a fair test

Glossary

bias a fundamental inaccuracy in data due to the way that was it collected, manipulated, or because of faulty sample design

stand alone can be looked at on its own and it makes sense

In this investigation, published **data** from the Human Development Report is used to investigate the relationship between a population indicator and a development indicator.

The Human Development Report can be found at http://hdr.undp.org/en/

Divide your write-up into sections as shown below.

1. Planning

- State clearly the research question to be investigated. For example: *Is there a relationship between population indicators and development indicators?*
- State clearly a prediction. For example: *There is a negative relationship between the under-5 mortality rate (U5MR) and levels of development, as measured by Human Development Index (HDI).*
- Define the key terms, in this case **under-5 mortality rate** and **Human Development Index**.
- Briefly explain the theoretical relationship between the two variables.
- Identify the independent, dependent, and control variables. In this example, the HDI is the **independent variable** and the under-5 mortality rate is the **dependent variable**. This is because the under-5 mortality rate is influenced by the level of development in a country – rich countries generally have lower under-5 mortality rates than poorer countries. **Control variables** include war and natural disasters. These could affect the results and so countries that are at war or have suffered extreme natural disasters in recent years have been removed from the data collection.

2. Method

- Collect data for eight countries in each of the four categories – very high HDI, high HDI, medium HDI and low HDI. Use a random numbers table to select the first eight countries in each category that come up in the table. The use of a random numbers table avoids **bias** and gives every country an equal chance of being used. For each country record its HDI (Statistical Table 1 in the Report) and under-5 mortality rate (Table 9).
- 32 countries are used here because 30 represents a 'large' sample in statistical terms and so should avoid bias.

3. Results

Data collection

- Include all relevant tables (including units) – this must be able to **stand alone**.

Sample of raw data:

	HDI	U5MR/1000
Very high		
Norway	0.94	3.0
Ireland	0.91	4.0
Japan	0.90	3.0
High		
Saudi Arabia	0.77	21.0
Russia	0.76	12.0
Brazil	0.72	21.0
Medium		
Jordan	0.70	25.0
El Salvador	0.67	17.0
South Africa	0.62	62.0
Low		
Pakistan	0.50	87.0
Bangladesh	0.50	52.0
Ethiopia	0.36	104.0

Processing of data

- Work out the **mean** for the HDI and under-5 mortality rate for each of the four groups, by adding up the eight individual readings and then divide by eight.
- You can use the Spearman's Rank equation to see if the **correlation** is positive or negative and to see how significant it is. You must show all the workings and state the level of statistical significance at the end of your workings.

Presentation of data

Graphs must show processed data, not raw data.

A box and whiskers graph is used to show differences in the mean and range (i.e. the difference between the maximum value and the minimum value) of the under-5 mortality rates for different HDI categories.

Synonyms

mean............average
correlation.....link/connection

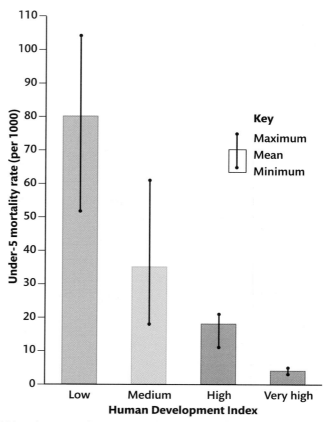

Figure 3 *Box and whiskers diagram to show variations in the mean and range of under-5 mortality rates for different HDI categories.*

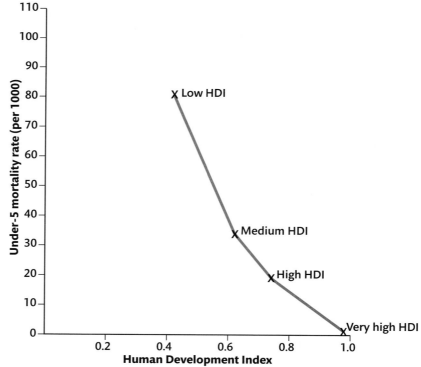

Figure 4 *Scatter graph to show levels of development, as measured by the Human Development Index (HDI) and infant mortality rate in selected countries.*

- The most useful way of showing the data here is to use a scatter graph. The axes should be clearly labelled and units identified.
- Include on the graph a line of best fit – this does not have to be a straight line but could be a curved line.

4. Discussion

- Fully describe the graph – try to refer to specific data, in this case the under-5 mortality rates and HDI of different categories. A useful method is to identify the maximum, the minimum, the trend, and exceptions to the pattern. For example, the under-5 mortality rate clearly decreases with increasing HDI.
- Explain the results referring to appropriate concepts and theory (*in this case syllabus section 3.1 Population dynamics*).

5. Evaluation

- Outline limitations and weaknesses of the investigation – are the data reliable? How could the data collection be improved? Could you use more countries? How might other indicators improve the quality of your investigation?
- What are the limitations of the statistical test that you used? Why was the statistical test that you used an appropriate one?

6. Conclusions

- Summarize the main findings of the study. Quote data from your study, e.g. include the results of the statistical test.
- Did the results confirm or reject the hypothesis?
- What was the level of statistical significance of your investigation?

Subject vocabulary

data results collected together for analysis

under-5 mortality rate the number of deaths in children under the age of five years per 1000 live births

Human Development Index (HDI) the level of development of a population taking into account life expectancy, literacy levels, and wealth

reliable/reliability results are repeated so that any results that do not fit the overall pattern of data can be identified and mean results calculated

hypothesis an untested proposal that can be investigated using the experimental method

IA Investigation – Comparing water quality using indicator species

In this investigation, water quality is compared between two sites, one above a **sewage** outlet and one just downstream from the sewage outlet, using indicator species.

Divide your write-up into sections as shown below.

1. Planning

- State clearly the research question to be investigated. For example: *How will water quality vary upstream and downstream from a sewage outlet pipe?* Alternatives could include: *How does temperature vary above and below a sewage outlet pipe?* Or, *Does dissolved oxygen vary below the outlet pipe compared to above the outlet pipe?* State clearly the prediction for the investigation; for example: *Water quality, as measured by species diversity, will be lower below the outlet pipe (the source of pollution) compared with species diversity above the outlet pipe.*

- Define the key terms, in this case **species diversity**, **water quality**, and **outlet pipe**.

- Briefly explain the theoretical relationship between the two variables: water quality and pollution.

- Identify the **independent**, **dependent**, and **control variables**. In this example, the pollution from the outlet pipe is the independent variable and the water quality/species diversity is the dependent variable. This is because water quality/species diversity is influenced by the level of the pollution from the outlet pipe. Control variables include vegetation cover, water **velocity**, the presence of a **weir**, other outlet pipes – these could affect the results and so the only factor that varies in the samples should be location relative to the outlet pipe.

2. Method

- Collect five samples from each of the two sites. One of the sites should be upstream of the outlet pipe, the other downstream. Count the number and type of indicator species in each of the samples. The downstream location should be before the weir, as the weir oxygenates the water and has an impact on species diversity. Make sure that all other factors (control variables such as vegetation, velocity, human impact, weather) are the same.

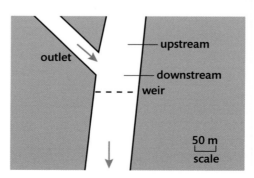

Figure 5 *Survey sites – upstream and downstream of a sewage outlet pipe.*

- Five samples are needed from each site to ensure the readings are **reliable** and give **valid quantitative** data.
- Collect the samples from the riverbed either by using a **kick sample** or by dragging a net through the water.
- Using an indicator species chart identify and record the number of *Tubifex* worms, blood worms, mayfly and stonefly nymphs.
- Repeat five times.

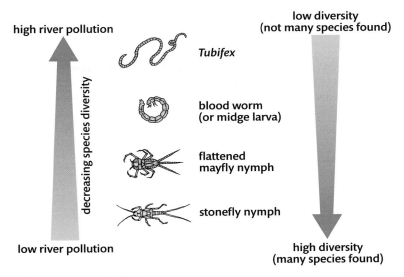

Figure 6 *Indicator species and pollution.*

Subject vocabulary

Simpson's Diversity Index one way of calculating species diversity

Glossary

stand alone can be looked at on its own and it makes sense

- Use **Simpson's Diversity Index** to compare the diversity of species upstream of the outlet with that of downstream of the outlet.

3. Results

Data collection

- Include all relevant tables (including units) – this must be able to **stand alone**.

	Individuals counted upstream of the outlet	Number (n)	n ($n-1$)	Individuals counted downstream from the outlet	Number (n)	($n-1$)
Tubifex	2, 1, 0, 0, 3	6	30	18, 13, 16, 14, 23	84	6972
Blood worms	1, 1, 2, 2, 1	7	42	15, 12, 20, 13, 22	82	6642
Mayfly	6, 4, 5, 7, 5	27	702	1, 2, 0, 2, 0	5	20
Stonefly nymph	3, 5, 2, 1, 3	14	182	0, 0, 0, 0, 0	0	0
Total (N)		54			171	

Using the **Simpson's Diversity Index**

$$D = \frac{N(N - 1)}{\Sigma n(n - 1)}$$

Where N is the total number of organisms at each site, and n is the total number of organisms of each species at each site.

Upstream of the **outlet pipe**:

$N = 54$, $N - 1 = 53$

$\Sigma n(n - 1) = 956$, hence

$D = 2862 \div 956 = 2.99$

Downstream from the outlet:

$N = 171$, $N - 1 = 170$, $\Sigma n(n - 1) = 13\,614$, hence

$D = 29\,070 \div 13\,614 = 2.14$

Processing of data

- Work out the Simpson's Diversity Index. It is expected that more polluted water will have a lower **species diversity**.

Presentation of data

Graphs must show processed **data**, not raw data.

A simple bar graph is used to show differences in the species diversity. These could be superimposed over a diagram of the study sites to highlight the importance of the outlet pipe.

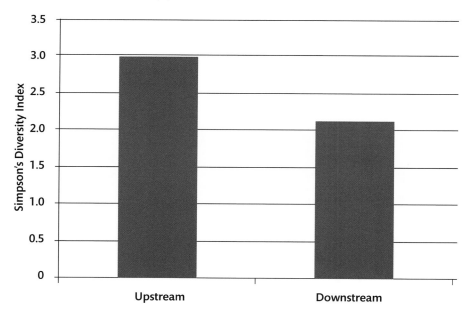

Figure 7 *Bar graph to show the Simpson's Diversity Index at sites upstream and downstream from a sewage outlet pipe.*

4. Discussion

- Fully describe the results – try to refer to specific data, in this case the presence or absence of indicator species such as *Tubifex* and mayfly nymphs. You could refer to the maximum and minimum number of each species at both sites, and refer to the trend and any exceptions to this pattern in your discussion.
- Explain the results referring to appropriate concepts and theory (*in this case syllabus section 5.2 Detection and monitoring of pollution*).

5. Evaluation

- Outline limitations and weaknesses of the investigation – are the data **reliable**? How could the data collection be improved? Could you use more samples? Were there any organisms that you could not identify? Could the weather have affected your results?
- What are the limitations of using Simpson's Diversity Index to compare water quality? Is species diversity an appropriate measurement of **water quality**?
- Could you have used another statistical test, such as a T-Test?

6. Conclusions

- Summarize the main findings of the study. Quote data from your study, e.g. include the results of the diversity index.
- Did the results confirm or reject the **hypothesis**?

IA Investigation – Investigating a shingle ridge succession

Subject vocabulary

succession the orderly process of change over time in a community

shingle ridge succession the changes in the species composition of a community over time on an area of deposited shingle/small rocks found in coastal areas

abiotic component a non-living part in an ecosystem

light intensity the amount of light that falls on a particular area from a specific direction

community group of different species living together in a common habitat

habitat the place where a species lives

soil a mixture of mineral particles and organic material that covers the land, and in which terrestrial plants grow

variable a factor that is being changed, investigated, or kept the same in an investigation

independent variable the variable that is being changed

dependent variable the dependent variable 'depends' on the independent variable

control variable the variable that is being kept the same to ensure a fair test

transect used to measure changes along an environmental gradient, ensuring all parts of the gradient are measured

controlled method that uses control variables

data results collected together for analysis

reliable/reliability results are repeated so that any results that do not fit the overall pattern of data can be identified and mean results calculated

validity when an experiment is controlled and repeated

Synonyms

velocity .... speed

In this investigation, the effect of soil depth on plant height is investigated. This is one of many investigations that can be done on the topic of succession. Field trips provide ideal opportunities to carry out ecological IAs.

Divide your write-up into sections as shown below.

1. Planning

- State clearly the research question to be investigated. For example: *Is there a relationship between soil depth and plant height on a shingle ridge succession?* Alternative investigations on a shingle ridge could include the effect of other abiotic components on plant height, such as light intensity or water content of soil, or how plant diversity changes along the succession.
- State clearly a prediction for the investigation. For example: *Plant height will increase with increased soil depth.*
- Define the key terms, in this case succession, community, habitat, and soil.
- Briefly explain the theoretical relationship between the two variables.
- Identify the independent, dependent, and control variables. In this example, the soil depth is the independent variable and plant height the dependent variable. This is because the plant height is influenced by the depth of soil. Control variables include abiotic components on the shingle ridge succession, such as soil and air temperature, wind velocity, light intensity, and amount of rainfall. Clearly, these abiotic components cannot be kept the same, and so in this investigation it needs to be clearly stated that these variables will be measured along with the independent and dependent variables.

2. Method

- Five transects 10 m in length, placed at right angles from the sea, were sampled systematically every 1 m.
- The tallest plant nearest to the transect was measured in centimetres, and the soil depth taken by pushing a metal rod into the surface until resistance was felt from underlying bedrock.
- Because other variables could not be controlled, several abiotic components were measured, including wind speed and light intensity. Wind speed was measured using an anemometer held at a standard height (5 cm) above the soil. Light intensity was measured using a light meter held at 5 cm above the ground.
- The transect was repeated to make data more reliable and to ensure valid quantitative data.
- Five repeats were made to see whether the pattern of data was roughly consistent, as this would give the researcher more confidence that the results were valid.
- Ten pairs of data, or soil depth and plant height, per transect provided sufficient data to carry out the statistical test.

3. Results

Data collection

- Include all relevant tables (including units); this must be able to **stand alone**.
- In this instance, data would be in the form of two tables: one with raw data from each transect on soil depth and plant height; the second table would contain data of other abiotic variables measured.

Processing of data

Data must be processed, e.g. **mean** values calculated, a statistical test carried out.

Spearman's Rank can be used to test whether the **correlation** between soil depth and plant height is statistically significant.

The following table contains data from a shingle ridge succession investigating the effect of soil depth on plant height. Results show the average values from five transects:

	Transect Station Number									
	1	2	3	4	5	6	7	8	9	10
Average plant height/ cm±1.0 cm	24.0	31.0	12.5	44.0	33.0	137.0	242.0	200.0	324.0	250.0
Average soil depth/ cm±1.0 cm	0.0	2.0	14.3	19.9	19.0	35.0	40.0	40.5	81.5	24.0

Station 1 is nearest the sea and 10 is furthest from it.

Data of the abiotic variables measured would also be given: this is shown in the following table (average results from all transects):

	Transect Station Number									
	1	2	3	4	5	6	7	8	9	10
Light intensity (lux)	63 380	54 800	36 900	45 500	69 600	64 584	97 900	45 040	90 400	12 180
Wind speed (km hr^{-1})	5.6	3.7	1.7	6.1	1.6	4	1.6	0.4	1.7	0.2

Spearman's Rank would be calculated in the following way:

Spearman's Rank $(r_s) = 1 - \dfrac{6\Sigma d^2}{n(n^2 - 1)}$

Where d = the difference in ranks and n = number of pairs of data.

Analysis could also be done using an Excel spreadsheet – the function provides calculations for such tests. However, you need to justify why you are using this technique even though you may use a computer to work it out.

Analysis table for Spearman's Rank:

n	Soil depth	Plant height	Rank of soil depth	Rank of plant height	Rank difference (d)	Difference² (d²)
1	0.0	24.0	1	2	1	1
2	2.0	31.0	2	3	1	1
3	14.3	12.5	3	1	2	4
4	19.9	44.0	5	5	0	0
5	19.0	33.0	4	4	0	0
6	35.0	137.0	7	6	1	1
7	40.0	242.0	8	8	0	0
8	40.5	200.0	9	7	2	4
9	81.5	324.0	10	10	0	0
10	24.0	250.0	6	9	3	9
n=10					Σd^2 =	20
					$6\Sigma d^2$ =	120
					n^3-n =	990

Spearman's Rank, $r_s = \dfrac{120}{990}$

Therefore, $r_s = 0.88$

When $n = 10$, the critical value for Spearman's Rank, at 5 per cent probability level = 0.5636.

As the r_s value of 0.88 is higher than the critical value of 0.5636, the result is significant at the 5 per cent probability level. That is, we can conclude with high (95 per cent) confidence that there is a close relationship between soil depth and plant height.

Presentation of data

Graphs must show processed data, not raw data.

A scatter graph can be plotted to show the **correlation** between the soil depth and plant height.

Subject vocabulary

data results collected together for analysis

Synonyms

correlation ... link/connection

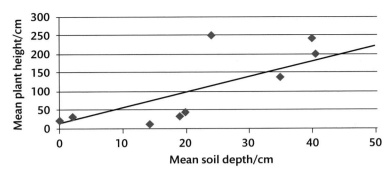

Figure 8 *Scatter graph to show the relationship between plant height and soil depth along a shingle ridge succession.*

Subject vocabulary

NB The **independent variables** are shown on the **x-axis** (horizontal axis) and the **dependent variables** are shown on the **y-axis** (vertical axis).

4. Discussion

- Fully describe the graph – try to refer to specific data, *in this case the plant height.*

- Explain the results referring to appropriate concepts and theory (*in this case syllabus sections 2.6 and 4.1 (succession); you will also need to discuss sections 2.5 photosynthesis, and 3.4 the soil system*)

5. Evaluation

- Outline limitations and weaknesses of the investigation. Is the data **reliable**? *You could point out the anomaly at station 10 on the transect, where the soil depth was an average of 24 cm and the plant height an average of 250.0 cm. Were all variables successfully controlled? In this instance you could comment on the abiotic variables you measured and how these may have affected plant growth. How could the data collection be improved?*

- What are the limitations of the statistical test that you used? Why was the statistical test that you used an appropriate one?

6. Conclusions

- Summarize the main findings of the study. Quote data from your study e.g. include the results of the statistical test.

- Did the results confirm or reject the **hypothesis**?

- What was the level of statistical significance of your investigation?

Subject vocabulary

independent variable the variable that is being changed

x-axis the horizontal axis of a graph; this axis contains information about the independent variable

dependent variable the dependent variable 'depends' on the independent variable

y-axis the vertical axis of a graph; this axis contains information about the dependent variable

photosynthesis a process that captures sunlight energy and transforms it into the chemical bonds of the glucose molecule; carbon dioxide, water, and light are transformed into glucose and oxygen in the process

reliable/reliability results are repeated so that any results that do not fit the overall pattern of data can be identified and mean results calculated

anomaly data point that does not fit the pattern of other data

variable a factor that is being changed, investigated, or kept the same in an investigation

controlled method that uses control variables

hypothesis an untested proposal that can be investigated using the experimental method

Extended Essay

Introduction

The Extended Essay is a detailed study on a particular topic. It provides the IB student with an opportunity to explore an idea or problem in one IB diploma subject. It develops research skills and provides the opportunity to produce a personalized piece of work. The essay should be no more than 4000 words in length.

Focus

Essential to a successful Extended Essay is the focus of the topic chosen. If a topic is too broad (i.e. unfocused), it can lead you into **superficial** treatment and it is unlikely you will be able to produce any fresh analysis, or **novel** and interesting conclusions of your own. So, for example, topics on the left of Table 1 are better than topics on the right.

Focused	Unfocused
The ecological recovery of worked-out bauxite quarries in Jarrahdale, Western Australia	Environmental effects of mining
A comparison of the energy efficiency of grain production in The Netherlands and Swaziland	Efficiency of world food production
The comparative significance of different sources of carbon dioxide pollution in New York and Sacramento, USA	Impacts of global warming
Managing the environmental impact of paper use at a Welsh college	Paper recycling

Table 1 *Focusing the topic of your essay.*

Topics with a sharper focus enable you to channel your research to produce your own discussions and conclusions. A short and **precise** statement outlining the overall approach of your investigation is also helpful in determining the focus of your essay, and making sure you stick to it. For example, if your topic is an examination of the **ecological footprint** of your school canteen, the research question could be: From the major **inputs** and **outputs** of the school canteen, what overall estimate of its environmental impact can be made in terms of an ecological footprint? The approach would include an analysis of the records and practical measurements that assess the inputs and outputs of the canteen, and an analysis of **data** into an environmental footprint **model** that indicates environmental impact. Writing the question in such detail is useful to you: it is clear what you need to find out, and what your conclusion will be about.

Marking criteria

The Extended Essay is marked following assessment criteria. There are 11 different criteria. The maximum total number of marks you can receive is 36. Each criterion, the details that should be covered in relation to ESS, and the number of marks allocated for each are outlined below:

Glossary

superficial not looking in detail at the deeper issues

Synonyms

novel .... new/unusual

precise .... accurate/clear

Subject vocabulary

ecological footprint the area of land and water required to support a defined human population at a given standard of living; the measure takes account of the area required to provide all the resources needed by the population, and the removal or use of all wastes

input the movement into something

output the movement out from something

data results collected together for analysis

model a simplified description that aims to show the structure or workings of a system

Criterion A: Research question (*2 marks*)

- Do you have a sharply focused research question clearly defining the purpose of the essay?

- Have you considered formulating the research question as a clearly stated **hypothesis**? This is especially appropriate in experimental investigations.

- Does the hypothesis lead to clear **critical** arguments concerning the extent to which your results will support or argue against it?

Criterion B: Introduction (*2 marks*)

- Does the introduction set the research question in **context**?

- Does the introduction give the reader a sense of why the question is worth asking?

- Does the introduction outline **theoretical principles** underlying the research question, e.g. what topics of theory does the research question explore?

- Have you outlined the history or geography of any location you will be studying that is central to the issue under discussion?

Criterion C: Investigation (*4 marks*)

- If the essay involves experimentation or practical fieldwork, have you included a detailed description of your methods, ideally including diagrams and photos?

- Have you included details of the experimental design, including **quantification**, and a description of all **variables** being considered, including **control variables**, **replication**, and **random sampling**, where appropriate?

- Have you explained the selection of techniques, and **justified** them? Have you clearly stated any **assumptions** on which they depend?

- If **secondary data** has been used, have you ensured that the sources are **reliable**? Have you referenced sources? Have you indicated how the secondary data was generated?

Criterion D: Knowledge and understanding of the topic studied (*4 marks*)

- In your essay, have you demonstrated sound understanding of the Environmental Systems and Societies course, and shown that you have read beyond the syllabus and carried out your own independent study?

- Have you shown **sufficient** knowledge of the topic, and shown that you have handled the issues and arguments effectively?

- You need to show links between your study and previous work from references you have found. You also need to use theoretical knowledge to **underpin** your essay.

Subject vocabulary

hypothesis an untested proposal that can be investigated using the experimental method

theoretical principles accepted ideas that explain observed phenomena, and that have been repeatedly tested using the scientific method

quantification applying a numerical value

variable a factor that is being changed, investigated, or kept the same in an investigation

control variables variables that are being kept the same to ensure a fair test

random sampling take a representative portion in which every part has an equal and fair chance of being measured

secondary data data that has been collected by someone else

reliable/reliability results are repeated so that any results that do not fit the overall pattern of data can be identified and mean results calculated

Glossary

critical using evaluation and judgement

context situation in which something exists

replication when results are repeated to make them more reliable

justify give valid reasons or evidence to support an answer or conclusion

Synonyms

assumptions .. models/theories

sufficient ...... enough

underpin ...... strengthen/support

Criterion E: Reasoned argument (4 marks)

- Does your essay show a clear, step-by-step, logical argument linking the raw data to the final conclusions?

- Is each step defended and supported with evidence?

Criterion F: Application of analytical and evaluative skills appropriate to the subject (4 marks)

- Have you used analytical skills to manipulate and present your data?

- Have you evaluated your data and commented on its reliability and validity?

- Have you included a model of the system studied and used the correct terminology when discussing it?

Criterion G: Use of language appropriate to the subject (4 marks)

- Have you used terminology appropriate to the subject throughout your essay? Both scientific and systems terminology should be used. A systems approach is especially important.

Criterion H: Conclusion (2 marks)

- The conclusion should be separated with its own heading within the essay – check that you have done this.

- It should contain a brief summary of the direct conclusions of your research question or hypothesis, supported by evidence and arguments already presented. It should not contain new evidence or discussion.

- You should also identify any outstanding gaps in your research or new questions that have arisen that you think would deserve further attention.

Criterion I: Formal presentation (4 marks)

- Have you checked with the assessment criteria to make sure that you have met all the formal requirements for the Extended Essay?

- Particular attention should be paid to the use of graphs, diagrams, illustrations, and tables of data. These should all be appropriately labelled with a figure or table number, a title, a citation where appropriate, and be located in the body of the essay, as close as possible to their first reference.

Criterion J: Abstract (2 marks)

- Have you included a brief summary of the essay? The abstract is judged on the clarity of the overview it presents, and not on the quality of the research, arguments, or conclusions.

Criterion K: Holistic judgement (*4 marks*)

- In your essay you should have demonstrated personal engagement, initiative, and insight in your topic.

- A major theme of this subject is the **interrelatedness** of systems and components within them. An essay that recognizes these underlying principles and the inter-relatedness of components will most clearly demonstrate an element of the 'insight and depth of understanding' referred to in this criterion.

Example essay

On the following pages there is an example essay to show how you can meet the various criteria in the **context** of a real essay.

Subject vocabulary

holistic looking at a system as a whole, rather than as individual parts

Glossary

interrelatedness how two or more things relate/link to each other

context situation in which something exists

Extended Essay: Example

A Study of the Environmental Attitudes of Pupils at St. Edmund's School, Cambridge, UK.

Criterion A: Research question

My **hypothesis** is that younger pupils will show less awareness of environmental issues than older pupils.

Criterion B: Introduction

Attitudes toward the environment are influenced by how aware people are of environmental issues.

A school has pupils of different ages and environmental attitudes can be expected to change as pupils get older.

The study was carried out at St. Edmund's School in Cambridge. This is a coeducational secondary school from ages 13 to 18.

Criterion C: Investigation

Two **questionnaires** were created to investigate the environmental attitudes of pupils and the reasons why they held these views. Both questionnaires are shown below.

Questionnaire to investigate the environmental attitudes of pupils:

Rate these statements on a scale of 1 to 6:

1   Strongly disagree

2   Disagree

3   Partly agree

4   Agree

5   Strongly agree

6   Very strongly agree

Your views	1	2	3	4	5	6
The Earth's resources are limited and finite.						
We only have one planet – we need to take good care of it.						
I believe I can make a difference through personal action.						
I would be happy to walk more and use my car less to reduce my ecological footprint.						
Environmental conditions have deteriorated over the past ten years.						
I switch off lights and electrical equipment when not needed.						
I save water.						
I do my best to reduce, reuse, and recycle.						
Environmental science should be taught in schools.						
I am concerned about the issue of global warming.						
I am aware that global warming causes a series of chain reactions.						

Questionnaire to investigate the reasons for the environmental attitudes of pupils:

	1	2	3	4	5	6
My family has had a strong influence on my views.						
I evaluate and reflect on what I am taught at school.						
I have a strong social network.						
Emotions affect my views of the world.						
I would describe myself as being a strong-willed person.						
My friends are environmentally aware.						
I am open to unconventional ways of thinking.						
I read and watch programmes about environmental issues.						

The questionnaire was given to pupils at the same time of year, at the same time of day, and with an equal number of girls and boys in each age group to ensure a **fair test**.

The questionnaire was given to 30 pupils in each age group. The age groups were 13 to 14, 15 to 16, and 17 to 18 years of age.

The **mean** value for each questionnaire was calculated for each pupil. A pupil with higher values, such as 5 and 6, demonstrated more awareness of environmental issues than a pupil with lower values, such as 1 and 2.

Subject vocabulary

fair test the experimental method involves manipulating one variable to determine if changes in this one variable cause changes in another variable; all other variables are kept the same to ensure a fair test

Synonyms

mean...........average

Subject vocabulary

T-test statistical method to compare the mean and standard deviation of two samples to see whether they are significantly different from each other or not

reliable/reliability results are repeated so that any results that do not fit the overall pattern of data can be identified and mean results calculated

normal distribution when data forms a curve that is symmetrical around a central peak; it is also known as a bell-shaped curve

environmental value system a particular world view that influences the way an individual or group of people recognize and evaluate environmental issues

input the movement into something

system a collection of parts and the relationships between them, which together make a whole

output the movement out from something

Glossary

evaluate assess and explain by weighing up the strengths and limitations

questionnaire a form containing a set of questions used as a way of gathering information for a survey

analytical using scientific analysis in order to find out about something; a logical method of thinking about something is used in order to understand it

A statistical test was carried out to compare the **means** of different age groups. The **T-test** was chosen as this statistical test shows whether mean results are statistically different or not.

Thirty pupils were included in each age group to make the sample large enough to carry out the T-test and to make the results **reliable**.

The T-test assumes a **normal distribution** of data. Given a large enough sample size, such as used in this study, a normal distribution can be assumed.

Criterion D: Knowledge and understanding of the topic studied

Environmental value systems can be defined as a particular worldview that influences the way an individual or group of people recognize and **evaluate** environmental issues.

In this essay I explore the factors that influence environmental value systems, and the effect they have on environmental attitudes.

The factors that influence environmental value systems are called the **inputs** to the **system**. The behaviour and actions that people show towards the environment are called the **outputs** of the system.

There have been few studies on the factors that affect awareness of environmental issues, and how attitudes may change with age. One study by Brewer *et al.* (2001) showed that older members of a village community in Devon, UK, showed better awareness of environmental issues than younger members of the community.

Criterion E: Reasoned argument

The mean response from the second **questionnaire**, investigating the reasons for the environmental attitudes, was 4.8 for the 17 to 18 age group, 3.8 for the 15 to 16 age group, and 2.8 for the 13 to 14 age group. These results show that older pupils were more socially aware than younger pupils, and were more emotionally mature.

Criterion F: Application of **analytical** and evaluative skills appropriate to the subject

The following graphs show the overall responses from each age group. Colours indicate the different levels of environmental awareness.

Dark green = score of 5/6 (high environmental awareness)
Medium green = score of 3/4 (medium environmental awareness)
Light green = score of 1/2 (low environmental awareness)

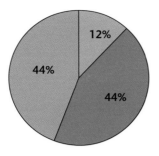

Figure 1 *Pie chart showing overall results from the 17 to 18 age group.*

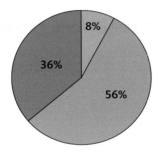

Figure 2 *Pie chart showing overall results from the 15 to 16 age group.*

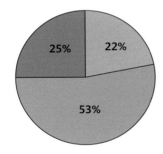

Figure 3 *Pie chart showing overall results from the 13 to 14 age group.*

A large sample was taken from each age group and so data were reliable. The sample was large enough for the T-test to be carried out.

Further repeats of each year group would have improved the reliability still further.

The **assumption** that the data had a normal distribution could be checked by plotting a **frequency distribution histogram** for questionnaire responses. The distribution should be symmetrical about the centre and fit a bell-shaped curve.

Other **variables** had been **controlled**, such as the number of boys and girls in each age group and the time that the questionnaires were carried out. Results were reliable and were linked to the variable that was being investigated and so results were **valid**.

The T-test showed a significant difference between the oldest and youngest pupils, with a T-test value of 3.25, which was higher than the critical value of 2.00. No significant difference was shown between other age groups. Results were tested at the 5% per cent significance level.

Synonyms

assumptions....... models/theories

Subject vocabulary

frequency distribution histogram a graph that shows how often a data point or a group of data points appears in a set of data; data are divided into classes of the same size and then the number of values that fall into each class is calculated

variable a factor that is being changed, investigated, or kept the same in an investigation

controlled method that uses control variables

validity when an experiment is controlled and repeated

system a collection of parts and the relationships between them, which together make a whole

input the movement into something

output the movement out from something

storage where something is kept

environmental value system a particular world view that influences the way an individual or group of people recognize and evaluate environmental issues

flow movement from one place to another

T-test statistical method to compare the mean and standard deviation of two samples to see whether they are significantly different from each other or not

The model used in this study used a **systems** approach. The **inputs** to the system were social, cultural, and educational influences on pupils. The **outputs** of the system were the attitudes and actions of pupils. The **storages** in the system were the ideas and beliefs of pupils and their **environmental value system**.

Criterion G: Use of language appropriate to the subject

The factors that influence environmental value systems are called the inputs to the system. The behaviour and actions that people show towards the environment are called the outputs of the system.

The following diagram shows the inputs, outputs, **flows**, and storage of environmental value systems.

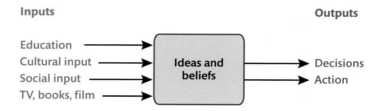

Criterion H: Conclusion

The results showed a significant difference between the oldest and youngest pupils in my survey. Differences between other combinations of age groups were not significant.

The statistical analysis between youngest and oldest pupils showed a **T-test** value of 3.25, which was higher than the critical value of 2.00. This result was significant at the 5 per cent level.

This investigation shows that **questionnaires** can be used effectively to study factors that influence environmental value systems and the effect they have on environmental attitudes, and indicates that further research would be beneficial.

Further work could focus on the differences between boys and girls and whether these play a role in determining environmental attitudes.

Criterion I: Formal presentation

Research on this topic is limited, although one study, 'Survey of Environmental Awareness and Practices,'[1] carried out in a community in Trinidad and Tobago, aimed to 'provide an understanding of the population's knowledge, behaviour and practices with respect to the environment.'[2]

1. National Institute of Higher Education, Research, Science and Technology (NIHERST), *Survey of Environmental Awareness and Practices*, May 2008. http://www.niherst.gov.tt/st-statistics/survey-highlights/survey-of-environmental-awareness-and-practices-2008.htm.

2. Ibid., Introduction

Criterion J: Abstract

This study investigated the environmental attitudes of pupils at St. Edmund's School, Cambridge, UK.

The attitudes were investigated using a questionnaire. A second questionnaire investigates the possible reasons for these attitudes. Answers were graded 1 to 6, with a grade of 1 showing low environmental awareness and 6 showing high environmental awareness. Different age groups of pupils were questioned: ages 13 to 14, 15 to 16, and 17 to 18.

The hypothesis for the study was that older pupils would be more environmentally aware than younger pupils. Thirty pupils in each age group were studied.

The T-test was carried out on mean responses so that the responses of different age groups could be tested statistically. **Mean** responses for each age group were presented as pie graphs to visually show the differences between year groups.

Results showed a significant difference between the oldest and youngest pupils, with a T-test value of 3.25, which was higher than the critical value of 2.00. No significant difference was shown between other combinations of age groups.

Results showed that the youngest pupils had lower environmental awareness than the oldest pupils, although the difference in awareness between the other combinations of age groups was not significant.

Older pupils had a higher average score on the second questionnaire, reflecting their greater maturity and emotional development.

Criterion K: Holistic judgement

I chose the topic for this essay because I am interested in the influence of social factors on people's environmental awareness.

Through studying the Environmental Systems and Societies course I have become aware of the similarities between ecological systems and social systems. Ecological systems, for example, have flows of energy and matter; social systems have flows of information, ideas, and people. Ecological systems have storages of biomass, the atmosphere, and soil; social systems have storages of ideas, beliefs, and customs.

Potential Extended Essay questions

- Is it possible to accurately reproduce an ecosystem in the laboratory?

- Would a 'Biosphere III' project be viable for establishing colonies on other planets?

- How does tourism affect succession on a shingle ridge in Slapton, Devon, UK?

- How has selective logging affected the abundance and diversity of butterflies in temperate forest in the Würzburg Forest, Bavaria, Germany?

- Does the energy input equal the energy output in an ecological system? An investigation using stick insects as a case study.

- To what extent did the Widecombe Village Committee restore the diversity of native species to the Dartmoor National Park in Devon, UK.

- Have the worked-out bauxite quarries of Jarrahdale, Western Australia, recovered ecologically?

- Has the Olympic Park development in London, UK, fulfilled the objectives of its Environmental Impact Assessment?

- Which demographic transition model is appropriate for Barra da Tijuca, Rio de Janeiro, Brazil, and how has this changed over time?

- The international use of disposable plastics: their impact on the aquatic ecosystems of the Pacific coast of Panama.

- How have invasive aquatic animals such as the lionfish affected the ecosystems of the Atlantic coast of Florida, USA?

- What are the differences in the efficiency of grain production in The Netherlands and Swaziland?

- What is the comparative significance of different sources of carbon dioxide pollution in New York and Sacramento, USA?

- Is current water consumption sustainable? A case study from the Punjab, India.

- How can the ecological footprint of St Edmund's School, Cambridge, UK, be reduced?

- What are the strengths and weaknesses of the species-based approach to conservation at Beijing Zoo, China?

- What has been the effect of a sewage outlet pipe on aquatic invertebrates in a stream in Mae Hong Son, Thailand?

- How has farming affected the aquatic ecosystems of the Gulf of Mexico, USA?

- How can eutrophication be managed in the lakes of northwestern Ontario, Canada?

- How does city planning affect albedo and the enhanced greenhouse effect?

- How is climate change affecting snowfall in Aspen, Colorado, USA, and what is being done to counter it?

- What are the environmental attitudes of students at Springfield High School, and how do these affect their response to environmental issues?

Glossary: Command terms

Analyse Break down in order to bring out the essential elements or structure.

Annotate Add brief notes to a diagram or graph.

Apply Use an idea, equation, principle, theory, or law in relation to a given problem or issue.

Calculate Obtain a numerical answer showing the relevant stages of working.

Comment Give a judgement based on a given statement or result of a calculation.

Compare and contrast Give an account of similarities and differences between two (or more) items or situations, referring to both (all) of them throughout.

Construct Display information in a diagrammatic or logical form.

Deduce Reach a conclusion from the information given.

Define Give the precise meaning of a word, phrase, concept, or physical quantity.

Derive Manipulate a mathematical relationship to give a new equation or relationship.

Describe Give a detailed account.

Design Produce a plan, simulation, or model.

Determine Obtain the only possible answer.

Discuss Offer a considered and balanced review that includes a range of arguments, factors, or hypotheses. Opinions or conclusions should be presented clearly and supported by appropriate evidence.

Distinguish Make clear the differences between two or more concepts or items.

Draw Represent by means of a labelled, accurate diagram or graph, using a pencil. A ruler (straight edge) should be used for straight lines. Diagrams should be drawn to scale. Graphs should have points correctly plotted (if appropriate) and joined in a straight line or smooth curve.

Estimate Obtain an approximate value.

Evaluate Make an appraisal by weighing up the strengths and limitations.

Explain Give a detailed account, including reasons or causes.

Identify Provide an answer from a number of possibilities.

Justify Give valid reasons or evidence to support an answer or conclusion.

Label Add labels to a diagram.

List Give a sequence of brief answers with no explanation.

Measure Obtain a value for a quantity.

Outline Give a brief account or summary.

Predict Give an expected result.

Solve Obtain the answer(s) using algebraic and/or numerical methods and/or graphical methods.

State Give a specific name, value, or other brief answer without explanation or calculation.

Suggest Propose a solution, hypothesis, or other possible answer.

Index